Dogs Love To Please ... We Teach Them How!

The SAFE & GENTLE Guide to Dog Obedience Training
through Interspecies Communication

Fourth (Revised) Edition
1994

Written & Illustrated
by
September B. Morn

Prologue by
Edi Munneke

Pawprince Press
Marblemount, Washington U.S.A.

Dedicated To

Nana
Helen L. Rooney
*Whose energy and positive outlook has been
my continuing inspiration*

With Much Thanks & Love to:
Carl Ryder
for supporting this project through laughter and tears, power failures
and forest fires, computer glitches and no dinner. Thanks, Carl!

Julie Silva. Thanks for P͞ŕoofreading!

And to Biff and Perf and Drommey and Purpose,
to Bro and Panda and Mitey and Rinnie,
and ALL the dogs who've shared their love and their puppytoys
with me... Thanks!

Dogs Love To Please... We Teach Them How!
Fourth (Revised) Edition 1994
ISBN 0-9633884-1-X
Copyright ©1992 September B. Morn
Copyright ©1994 September B. Morn
Prologue to the 1994 Edition ©Edi Munneke

Published by
Pawprince Press
815 Clark Rd.
Marblemount, WA 98267
(360) 873-4333

Recycled paper

Printed by The Lynden Tribune, Lynden, WA
Production Manager: Howard Urie   Graphics Chief: Anne Mustappa

Contents

Prologue

All healthy puppies are born with the ability to walk, to sit, to stand, to stay, to go down, to come, to fetch, etc. No dog needs to be taught how to do these things -- he just needs to be taught to do them on command. The owner must figure out how to communicate his or her wishes and it will not be exactly the same for any two dogs.

Fortunate are those puppies that start life in a home where there is a copy of DOGS LOVE TO PLEASE... WE TEACH THEM HOW! Too many puppies, like too many children, come into a family and just grow up "like Topsy." Help is not sought until delinquent behavior forces the family to consider the animal shelter or reform school.

Many mothers brought their children up on the wisdom found in Dr. Spock's book, but we have waited a long time for a September Morn to write a book that will assure all puppies a proper start in life. Her book has a wonderful message, even for people who know little about dogs but want to do the right thing. I don't know of a better book to help with home training *before, during,* and *after* obedience school.

Ms. Morn leaves no doubt that she favors gentle methods and will not tolerate roughness. She is a skilled communicator and makes it easy for the reader to understand her methods.

Not all dogs are alike, so suggestions are made to take care of the differences. Ms. Morn is also an artist who has made wonderful drawings to illustrate the lessons. Even the children can understand her philosophy of kindness and follow her directions.

You will learn how to teach your dog all the basic commands and signals. You will be prepared to train your dog to pass the A.K.C. Canine Good Citizen (C.G.C.) test or to enter basic classes to earn titles in Obedience.

This book is well indexed and interesting to read. The lessons all make sense and will do for your puppies (or any of your dogs), what Dr. Spock did for your children. DOGS LOVE TO PLEASE... now you can learn to "teach them how."

Edi Munneke
DogWorld "Obedience News"

Chapter 1

DOGS & MANKIND

Dogs have been the helpers and companions of our ancestors for thousands of years. Through good times and lean times dogs have stayed faithful, wishing only a word of kindness or the caress of their master's hand. In return for so little reward they have enthusiastically shared with us their natural talents. Dogs have herded our livestock, helped us find and catch a variety of foods, kept our laps warm and protected our homes and families. Dogs love to please... it's up to us to teach them how.

Way back in time, before there were dogs, there were wolves. Wolves lived together in family groups or packs, as they still do today

in a few wilderness areas. The pack served both social and safety needs. Wolves were (and are) cooperative creatures. They hunt together, share their food, and even help one another with the chores of raising offspring.

These characteristics of the wolf were seen as potentially useful by early humans, and eventually some wolves, most likely young cubs, were captured and tamed. The taming of wild wolves led to the intentional breeding of selected animals with desirable qualities. That was probably the beginning of the Domestic Dog (Canis familiaris)... "Man's Best Friend."

Only a few of our modern dog breeds look much like wolves, but behind most dog behaviors are the natural instincts Fido inherited from his long-ago wild ancestors.

Dogs are pack animals. Although most dog owners these days don't maintain large hunting packs, even our gentle pets will quickly form packs of their own if left to roam unattended. Even a dog who might ordinarily be quite docile could join in with a group of other dogs in destructive and violent behavior. Avoid this problem by keeping your dog home and teaching him to be a polite and respectful member of your household.

Dogs are extremely sociable animals who crave companionshipip. They also like to know who the "boss" of the group is and where they themselves rank. Dogs in a pack develop a natural command hierarchy with the most dominant and aggressive members at the top of the "pecking order." The pack follows the leadership of the dominant "Alpha" individual. He (or she) chooses the pack's activities and the others follow along.

Dog packs and human families have a similar social structure. Both are organized as multi-level hierarchies with a leader (or mated leader-couple) and followers. Dog packs and human families provide members with companionship and security. Because of these similarities, a human family is, for a dog, a satisfactory substitute for a real pack. A dog can fit easily into our family social structure and is most content when he knows his place in that pack. To be a well-adjusted member of your family, Fido must understand that you are the leader.

Dogs crave leadership. A strong and fair packleader provides the security a dog needs to feel comfortable and unafraid. A dog or wolf pack MUST have a steady leader for the social order to work properly and ensure the security and survival of the members. A weak or foolish leader compromises the safety of the group and, in a wolf or dog pack, must be deposed and replaced by a more capable leader. This instinct can present some potential problems with a family dog.

When the "master" does not give the dog secure guidance, Fido himself will attempt to take over leadership. This is NOT safe for either the dog or the humans in the "pack."

Some people put off training and discipline, avoid making decisions for the dog, give him whatever he wants... and just hope for the best. These folks have good intentions but are confused about what actually gives a dog a sense of security. Instead of placing themselves in the vital role of pack leader they may try to treat their dog as a peer. This is unwise and does nothing to increase the dog's feeling of security. He'd feel better if he knew there was a strong leader.

A dog is really not equipped to set family policies about such matters as who sits where, who eats what, who empties the garbage, or who is allowed to come into the house. Unfortunately, when Fido has no proper idea of "who's in charge here" he WILL try to make those and other important decisions.

Our dogs feel most secure when they know they can count on us as strong and wise "packleaders." A good leader is firm, but not harsh; kind, but not wishy-washy; predictable, but not inflexible. A dog appreciates knowing that his master is fair and steady. We must be good leaders for our dogs in order to gain and keep their respect. Fair and steady leadership benefits both the dog and the human in our people/pet relationships.

A DOG NEEDS A JOB

Dogs have been bred over the centuries to do specific tasks. They helped our ancestors to survive by working side by side with them. Many of the jobs dogs used to do are no longer as necessary as they once were. Hunting dogs go afield with their masters for only a few short weeks each year, now that hunting is heavily regulated and meat so easily obtained from the corner grocery. Energetic and fearless terriers, whose forebears for centuries kept the homeplace free of disease-carrying rodents, now have been replaced on the job by potent pesticides. Dogs bred to guard their masters' belongings have been forced out of that profession by "dangerous dog" ordinances and rising insurance premiums. No wonder there are so many bored dogs these days! With so few good job opportunities, what's an unemployed canine to do?

Many out-of-work dogs solve this problem by taking up "hob-bies." Spaniels and Retrievers may become avid ornithologists, watching constantly for new species of birds to chase and bark at. Terriers tend to go in for landscaping in a big way... or you might call it "moon-scaping" when you see the results. Some Collies like to herd bicycles and delivery vans for practice, just in case a real flock of sheep shows up someday. Once Fido has developed a hobby it can be very difficult to convince him to give it up. It's better to teach him something approvable to do with his spare time and energy.

An excellent substitute for a full-time job for your dog is a daily obedience practice session. Fido will feel useful and appreciated when you praise him for his quick response to your commands. Not every training session needs to be a Heeling Drill; most of the command words can be practiced in the context of everyday activities. Obedience commands are a working vocabulary your dog learns to understand. Use them in your day-to-day interactions with your dog. When Fido obeys your command he will feel smart, useful and secure.

WHO IS FIDO?

What's in a name? Why "Fido" and not "Rover"? Well, Fido's name comes from the Latin word meaning "faithful." This is obviously a positive association. Rover, as a dog's name, implies that he already has some habits that need to be changed... sort of the opposite of faithful. Names carry with them certain mental images. "Fido" represents a dog who loves to please. That is why I chose that name for the "generic dog" in this book.

The Invisible Dog

Fido is also the name of my invisible dog. Now just wait a minute... before you start wondering about my mental state, let me tell you how this invisible dog and I got together.

My invisible Fido evolved while teaching handlers how to communicate with their own (visible) dogs. I noticed that whenever I demonstrated how to teach a command using one of the dogs in the class, nobody seemed able to see what I was trying to show them. They all watched what the DOG did, but nobody really saw what was happening at the TRAINER'S end of the leash. The adorable and/or naughty dog was SO APPEALING that the trainer (myself) became functionally invisible.

I realized that something had to be done. I'd have to do without my "demonstrator dog" so the handlers would be able to focus on the TECHNIQUES being shown. That was when Fido was "born" and he's been with me ever since. Now that I demonstrate handling and training techniques with Invisible Fido at the other end of my leash, I no longer have to compete for attention with some cute *visible* pup.

Kidding aside, it's a good idea to practice each new training exercise in this book with an "invisible dog" of your own. That way you can refine your handling techniques without confusing your REAL dog, who is also new at this stuff. Practice holding and controlling your leash, saying the commands, praising, walking and turning... with an "invisible dog" at your side. Although it might seem frivolous to you at first, think about it; working with an "invisible dog" is a valuable learning exercise for handlers.

Benefits of Training

Special benefits occur when you work with your dog regularly and praise his attempts to cooperate. He will begin to pay closer attention to you because your words and gestures will have clearer meaning for him. He will understand what you say and will ENJOY doing as you command. Your dog will become so well-behaved that you'll be proud to take him with you everywhere. Your dog will be happy and secure in his noble "profession" as your Faithful Canine Companion.

Dogs LOVE to please...
It is our job to teach them HOW!

Chapter 2

CHOOSING A DOG

Each dog is an individual. Every puppy in a litter has certain unique qualities. The dog one person selects might be perfect for him, but not for his next-door neighbor. The next dog you adopt will NOT be just like the last dog you had. He will be special in his own ways.

WHERE TO LOOK?

There are a number of sources you might consider in your search for a new dog. You could ask around at dog shows or call the local kennel club for a directory of breeders, visit animal shelters, enquire of your veterinarian, search through classified ad columns, ask your neighbors and friends, check bulletin boards at pet supply stores, or even decide to take in a foundling puppy. You will certainly find many willing-to-be-adopted pets wherever you go in your quest, and you'll probably soon find "the perfect dog for you."

Not all possible sources of dogs are of equal quality, though, and you may be in for some unbargained-for troubles if you are not careful. Let's look at some of the issues to consider when you are trying to pick your next family dog.

Purebred dogs and

puppies are readily available from a variety of sources these days. Years ago only a small minority of folks would actually consider paying for a dog. Now people from all walks of life pay hefty sums for purebred dogs and it's not considered at all unusual. There is a problem created by this increased demand for purebred dogs. Too many greed-motivated persons who care little about the health or genetic background of their dogs are producing too many puppies... solely for the sake of money. This is not to say that good purebred dogs are hard to find, just that it's lamentably easy nowadays to find weak and poorly bred ones.

If you've decided you'd like to adopt a purebred dog, ask around until you locate an experienced and respected breeder of the type of dog you want. A good breeder will have the knowledge and facilities necessary to breed and raise healthy, strong, sane puppies. He or she will also care a great deal about the pups even after they are adopted into their new homes. This type of breeder will be glad to advise you on any matters pertaining to a dog from his or her kennel... even years later. The purchase price of a dog from a reputable breeder is money well-spent.

Puppies Sold In Stores

Avoid buying your new dog-friend from a store that keeps puppies for sale on the premises. Often that type of pet store obtains their "stock" from "puppy mill" kennels where dogs are bred only to make money. The conditions at those puppy mills are often quite terrible. The operators of those kennels and the stores that buy from them think of puppies as merchandise and nothing more.

Chain pet stores buy up whole litters of purebred puppies and force them to be taken away from the mamadog several weeks earlier than is psychologically healthy... and sometimes even before they're old enough to be weaned. Breeders (or should we say "greeders") who sell baby puppies to stores like this are neither knowledgeable about the needs of the dogs nor caring and humane. Don't help this abuse and neglect to continue. Refuse to support these stores and the puppy-mills that supply them!

This sounds like hard advice when you're looking into the sad and lonely eyes of some innocent little babydog locked in a tiny pet store cage. Just try to remember that as soon as some softhearted person "rescues" a pup from one of the big pet store outlets, ANOTHER PUP OF THE SAME BREED WILL BE SHIPPED TO BE SOLD AT THE

SAME STORE. You will not really "save" puppies by buying one from a retail chain store, because another poor puppy will immediately be shipped in to take his place in the vacated cage.

The price of a poorly-bred dog from a puppy chainstore is often higher than the price asked by a reputable and caring breeder for a well-bred pup. Long and elaborate "guarantees" offered by most of the puppy stores are worded carefully for the protection of the store, NOT the buyer and certainly NOT the puppy.

Reputable Breeders

Buy your purebred puppy from a reputable breeder who cares about the breed and follows up on each pup produced by his kennel. You'll be glad to know a good breeder. His breeding stock will have been certified clear of hereditary problems before being mated. Puppies will be healthy and well-socialized. An ethical breeder likes to keep in touch with his puppies' new owners and is happy to help them with information gathered over years of experience. Buy from an experienced breeder! You will NEVER regret it.

The serious breeder will probably ask you quite a few questions about yourself... to determine whether you can provide a suitable home for one of his puppies. Don't be offended by this, a caring breeder should always screen potential puppy buyers. He needs to be sure his pups will be properly cared for. Not everyone is suited to every breed of dog. A good knowledgeable breeder tries very hard to know where his pups are going. A good breeder cares!

Breed Rescue

Pure breed rescue groups are operated by volunteers who put out special efforts to save dogs of their favorite breeds. When word reaches a rescue group that a dog of their breed is being abused or neglected, has been abandoned, or is otherwise in need of shelter and protection, these folks step in. Breed rescue volunteers provide loving foster homes for the dogs until permanent placements can be made. Many rescue groups concentrate on rescuing only one breed. Regional all-breed rescue groups may refer callers to the appropriate single-breed rescues.

Many reputable breeders have become involved in breed rescue. They feel responsible for their breed's welfare. It hurts them to see the many puppy-mill pups sold into inappropriate homes by chain stores. The ethical breeders are not the cause of this problem, but they take a very active and responsible role in the solution.

Rescue folks care a great deal about the dogs. Most groups have all rescued dogs vetted, neutered and sometimes trained before new placements are made. Most rescue volunteers donate quite a bit of their own resources to the rescue effort. The moderate adoption fee charged by rescue groups helps defray only a small portion of the costs of the rescue work.

Pure breed rescue folks really care about the dogs and try very hard to find appropriate permanent homes for them. If you especially love a certain breed, get in touch with that breed's rescue group. You may find a wonderful dog to adopt and at the same time help out your special breed.

Animal Shelters

If you're not attached to having a registered dog, you can find a wonderful pal by visiting your local animal shelter. There, unlike the pet stores, you WILL be able to rescue an innocent pup or adult dog. Many fine, loving, healthy dogs are to be found at shelters. It's usually best to have a pretty firm idea in mind of what you're looking for when you go to the shelter... or you might want to adopt them all. It's hard to say "no" to those big sweet eyes. If you know what sort of a dog you really want, you may find a great companion to take home.

Some shelters are privately run and some are operated by municipalities. Some shelters are affiliated with or approved by national humane groups, some are not. Quality of care may vary considerably from shelter to shelter because of this.

Adoption costs at shelters are usually quite reasonable. Many shelters now include (in the adoption fee) a veterinary health check, vaccinations, spay or neuter operation, license or I.D. tag and even a leash. Think seriously about adopting your new dog or puppy from a humane animal shelter near you. It's a great deal for you and gives you a real chance to do a good deed for "Man's Best Friend."

Classified Ads and Bulletin Boards

The newspaper classified ads are another resource to explore whether you're looking for a mix or a purebred. It's possible to connect with some very reputable breeders by calling the phone numbers in the ads. You may, just as easily, come up with some real "Lulu's" who couldn't care less about the welfare of their animals. Be discerning. Learn as much as you can about the breed of your choice BEFORE you go shopping. That way you'll know which questions to ask.

Classified ads and bulletin boards are often used to place unwanted pups and dogs "for free." Some are purebreds and some are
mixes; most are young pups, but older dogs sometimes need new
homes too. Again, be discerning. Even if your heart will hold all the
dogs who need love, you won't be able to fit them into your house.

Some "free" dogs and pups will make terrific pets, while others
have been damaged psychologically or physically and may have
severe bad habits or health problems. Each case is unique. Look for
the right dog, not for a bargain. Keep in mind that there is really no such
thing as a "free" dog anyway, because as soon as he is yours there will
be responsibilities and expenses to bear.

HOW TO PICK THE RIGHT DOG FOR YOU

Whatever dog you select, you will be happiest if you've planned
and made proper advance preparations for his "homecoming." When
you bring a carefully chosen dog into a well prepared home you'll
greatly increase the likelihood of getting off to a good start in a long-
lasting relationship.

Troubles can arise when people choose (or are chosen by) the
"wrong" dog. These problems could be avoided if people would first
carefully consider what type of dog would be most appropriate to their
lifestyle. Too often the decision to adopt a dog is made impulsively,
with insufficient information about the individual dog and its background. Age, sex, breed, and the dog's basic "personality" must be
considered if the relationship is to be a happy and longlasting one.

Dogs As Gifts

If you are thinking of giving a dog or puppy as a surprise gift to
a loved-one, please reconsider! A new pet will require much time and
attention, which your friend or relative may not be ready or able to
provide. Companion animals can be a great joy... or a heavy burden.
If you're thinking of giving a dog to someone you love, first ask if they
really want a dog. Then, if they're certain they're ready for a pet, be
kind enough to let them select the dog or puppy themselves. They'll
be living with that dog for years and years and should choose their own
companion. Adopting a pet is a serious long-term commitment, not a
choice to be made impulsively (or for someone else.)

A Dog For The Children

Many people believe that giving a dog to a child helps teach responsibility and nurturance. While it is quite true that most children enjoy having a dog in the family, very few children under 15 years of age are mature enough to take proper full care of an animal as complex as a dog. It is extremely unfair to an innocent animal to entrust its entire health and well-being to a child.

Children who wish to take part in the daily responsibilities of the family dog's care may certainly be encouraged to do so, but they'll need appropriate guidance to assure their success. An adult MUST regularly check to be certain all animal care tasks have been done properly. A caring adult can set a good example of responsibility for children to follow. Be sure a child's natural immaturity never becomes the cause of suffering for an innocent pet.

WHAT AGE?

Puppies are cute! (This is one reason there are so many dogowners.) Most people who consider acquiring a dog think immediately of a fuzzy roly-poly pup. For some people, starting with a puppy really is the best way. For others, a mature dog would fit better into the household... without the schedule-disrupting problems typical of life with a pup. The advantages and disadvantages of pups and adults are matters to weigh in each individual case.

Young Puppies

A young pup will not have yet bonded strongly to a human family and will be ready to form a relationship with you. This is very appealing to many folks, so lots of people opt for a young puppy. Baby dogs can be very time-intensive but they progress through the learning process rapidly. And... puppies ARE very cute!

To avoid some major difficulties, be sure the puppy you are considering for adoption is old enough to leave his mother. Mama-dogs usually wean their pups at about five or six weeks of age. Be sure that your puppy has been weaned completely, otherwise he will not be ready for a normal feeding schedule when you bring him home.

If you do find yourself caring for an unweaned puppy, ask your veterinarian about feeding goat's milk or a commercial milk-replacement formula. Either of those will help provide the nutrition an infant puppy needs while his digestive system matures enough to handle solid foods. You may be involved in midnight feedings for awhile, because little babydogs must eat frequently. Raising an orphaned or rejected pup is quite an undertaking in terms of energy and patience. If you become involved in such a project be sure to seek help from your veterinarian. She will be able to advise you on health matters vital to your infant puppy's early growth period.

Even if your new puppy is already weaned he will need to be fed more frequently than a mature dog. Also, of course, potty training young puppies is more time-consuming than with older dogs.

Once your pup has been vaccinated to protect him from communicable diseases, you will be wise to start socializing him with other dogs, preferably well-behaved ones. He needs to learn proper doggie etiquette while he is still young through regular social contact with his own kind.

Mama Dog's Job

In addition to taking care of her pups' nutritional and sanitation needs, a good mother dog (dam) gives her pups quite an education before they are ready to venture forth into the world. Starting shortly before weaning time and continuing up to about ten weeks of age, puppies learn about proper dog society etiquette.

Puppies learn to show respectful submission to Mamadog and other elders and dominant dogs. They learn to inhibit the force of their own bite, lest they accidentally injure a littermate or their mama's sensitive parts. They learn when to fight for a chew-bone, and when it's smarter to give it up. These lessons are very valuable, so normally it's not advisable to bring home a puppy until age eight or nine weeks. That way not only will he be already weaned but he'll also have started learning the canine social graces.

Puppies learn about status hierarchy within the pack structure while they are very young. In the pup's first social unit, the birth-litter, the dam is quite naturally in charge. The littermates wrestle and tussle for the best spot at Mama's milkbar. The strongest and most persistent pup dominates the choicest nipple. The other puppies take positions according to their strength and persistence. In this way a fairly stable ranking order is established.

This basic introduction to power hierarchy will be useful when the puppy begins to interact with people. If Mama-dog has laid the right groundwork with her puppies, they will have a dutiful respect for authority and will happily seek their places in their new permanent adoptive families.

When To Start Training A Puppy

At about seven weeks of age, puppies enter a developmental period when they learn how to act around people. With a good background from the Mamadog in etiquette and hierarchy, it's not be too difficult for a pup to learn proper behavior around his new human "family."

Many people mistakenly believe they should wait to train Little Fido until he reaches the age of six months. This is a serious error! A puppy learns most of what he needs to know about being a dog on this planet before he turns four months old. He is naturally inquisitive and open to new information at that young age and will respond readily to kind leadership.

Be patient and use only gentle training methods with your puppy. Encourage him, keep lessons up-beat and fun, and praise every bit of cooperation. You'll have a bright and willing student. Your puppy can begin to learn good manners and obedience at a surprisingly young age. Utilize his rapid-learning period and he will learn eagerly. If you procrastinate training your dog he'll most certainly pick up some bad habits you'll later have to undo.

Adolescent Puppies

One advantage to starting with a young puppy is that he is like a brand new blackboard -- smooth and easy to "write" on. Of course that means you'll have to teach him everything. A puppy will not have already formed persistent habits. With an older dog, some messages will already be "written" on his slate and you'll have to do some "erasing" before you can "write" anything new.

If you are thinking of adopting an older pup try to choose one that has been well handled and is already confident around humans. A puppy that has not received sufficient socialization before sixteen weeks of age will be likely to be uncomfortable around people. House manners may come with difficulty, potty training could take awhile, the dog may be shy or over-bold, there could be trouble with barking or biting.

From about seven to fourteen months of age, dogs go through

adolescence. Pups in this age group need steady guidance and regular vigorous exercise. In this period of development your pup will attain his adult height and will look more mature than he actually is. He will act as if he thinks he's pretty grown up, but you can see that he's really not. During this maturing process a dog's mind is still "puppy" even though his body starts to look "adult."

Early adolescent dogs (seven to nine months) may remind one of "skateboard kids" because their behavior at that age parallels the rambunctious and limit-testing stage human children go through from about seven to eleven years of age. Late adolescent dogs (ten to fourteen months) are "teenagers" with behaviors analogous to those of teen-aged humans.

Like human adolescents, dogs in this developmental stage naturally seek to raise their hierarchical position within the family. They test authority figures and may casually disregard rules. This happens predictably, even with many individuals who've been cooperative and respectful when younger. It's just a natural phase of growing up and developing a position in the pack hierarchy.

An adolescent dog may try the family's patience and may be more difficult to live with than either a younger or an older animal. This stage could pass fairly smoothly if the dog has received good guidance all along. However, when training is put off until an energetic young dog has gotten out of hand, some dogowners become frustrated and give up. In fact, if you take a look at the "Free Pets" listing in your local newspaper you may see ads like the following one:

> **"Free to good country home:**
> *ten-month-old dog, loves kids,*
> *good watch dog. Needs room to run."*

That ad might have been more accurately worded as:

> *"Untrained, unmanageable dog, wild and rowdy;*
> *barks at everything, jumps on children, tore up the house,*
> *now digs up the yard and runs off when we call him.*
> *We liked him when he was little and cute,*
> *but now we don't.*
> *Please, somebody... anybody... take him."*

Truth in advertising?

There may still be hope for the adolescent described above, but only if his new people can correct the damage done by the neglectful first home. You may find a perfectly wonderful "diamond in the rough." However, if a dog has not been socialized properly AND has already developed certain VERY bad habits (chasing livestock, biting people, running amuck in the neighborhood) his rehabilitation may be a long and challenging project.

Although it is possible in many cases to change a dog's attitude about people-in-general, it requires a great deal of patience and commitment. If you are the type to handle it, this can be a very rewarding project; if you're not, it could be a sorry situation for both you and the dog. Consider your personal time and temper limits before deciding to start a rehabilitation program for an improperly socialized skateboarder or teenager dog.

Although this adolescent stage can sometimes be difficult to manage, there will also be a lot of exuberant fun. It IS possible to get a fine companion when you adopt a "teenaged" or "skateboarder" dog. Just be prepared for high energy and some occasional impudence. Be patient, stand firm... and be sure to keep your sense of humor. After a few months of maturation, kindly attention, and proper education, Teen-age Fido may become a model citizen.

Mature Adults

Some people are hesitant to adopt a mature dog. They worry that the dog will not be able to bond with them. There is usually no real reason to be concerned about that. Dogs, even mature dogs, are very adaptable and optimistic creatures. They have a great desire to belong, a great desire to please. Mature dogs can be re-homed fairly smoothly.

Dogs who have passed their first birthday are often less trouble to their adoptive families than are slightly younger animals. Mature dogs normally have good control of their eliminative functions, which makes them much quicker to potty train than puppies. Adult dogs already have their permanent set of teeth, so the teething stage and resultant property destruction have already passed. Adult dogs usually know a few standard command words too, so you can start right off with a common vocabulary. They will also have established some habits, both good and not-so-good.

Adult dogs can be lovely companions right from the beginning of your relationship with them. This is especially true if they've already learned to appreciate a relationship with a nice person. The mature dog will usually try very hard to fit into your home routine. Be aware of how hard the dog IS trying, and remember to be appreciative and patient.

Many an adult dog has been given away or sold because his human family's living situation suddenly changed. Some of these dogs have been well-loved pets all their lives and it may be hard for them at first to make the transition of loyalty to you. Some mature dogs will "mourn" their previous families for a while. This is a normal stage which will pass soon enough. It may take about three weeks for a mature dog to accept the new home and family as his own. Once this transition has been made, the dog will let you know he's yours for keeps.

Most dogs WILL form a new bond if you are patient with them and give them reasons to trust and respect you. If you include the dog in your family activities and patiently teach him the rules of your household, the transition phase should go smoothly. Patience is important; your new pet will naturally miss his former family for awhile, but eventually his affection and loyalty will turn toward you.

If you adopt a grown dog directly from the former owners, be sure to ask what words the dog understands. Write them down so you'll remember, some dogs know quite a few. Also ask about the routines of feeding (when, where, how much, what kind, etc.) and sleeping. If the dog came from a happy home, try to keep at least a few things the same for the dog if you can. If the dog came from an unhappy home, feel free to change the previous routine as much as you like; the dog will be glad for the differences.

Sometimes mature dogs will have "flashbacks" of their former situation. If it was not a happy time, your dog may need help to get over the emotional trauma. Some of the dog's old "coping mechanisms" may have included running off or even biting. If you see serious problems like these surfacing, it would be wise to engage professional help. A professional dog behavior consultant could help you understand the dog's problem and devise a rehabilitation program.

WHAT SEX?

Another choice to be made is whether to adopt a male ("dog") or female ("bitch"). Some people say that one sex is more aggressive or better with kids... or whatever, than the other. I have found, when properly socialized and trained, both males and females make terrific pets and reliable protectors. My own dogs have always been chosen for their sterling personal qualities, not because of their gender. And as I review the gallery of my dogs I notice that the "bitches" column and "dogs" column balance just about evenly.

To Neuter... Or Not?

Now is a good time to discuss spaying and neutering options. Puppies are darling... and almost anyone's heart would swell with pride to see a litter of sweet little baby "copies" of their own beloved dog. That emotional vision has a negative counterpart... the reality of the present canine population problem.

You have probably heard the startling statistics related to the enormous numbers of pets destroyed for lack of adoptive homes. Literally millions of dogs and innocent puppies will die this year because nobody wants them. Each one of those dear-hearted dogs could have made a wonderful, loving companion for some person... if only there really WAS a person for each one of them. Some basic arithmetic would show us that there really ISN'T a kindly lifelong home waiting for each and every puppy born. Not even for all the purebred pups of registered parents... and you'd think SOMEONE would certainly be eager to adopt THEM!

So MANY nice puppies... just not enough homes.

PLEASE NEUTER YOUR PETS!

So, if you're thinking a litter of pups would help "pay for keeping" your dog, or that the "miracle of birth" would be great for your kids to witness, or even if you believe the old-wives-tale that having at least one litter of pups is necessary for a bitch to mature properly (which, by the way, is hogwash)... think again, please! Think of what would be best for the innocent puppy-lives you'd be inviting to come into this world.

Whether you are a breeder of show dogs or simply a proud pet-owner, if you decide to let your dog reproduce there is more to think about than putting down pans of food and picking up reams of soggy newspapers. You really owe a lot of thought to what kind of futures those puppies will inherit. And once they're weaned and have left your home what will their lives hold for them? Could you assure each of those babies a welcoming niche on this planet for their whole natural lives? Every "being" has a right to a good life, and if you're considering allowing your bitch to produce puppies, please look at all sides of the issue before you decide.

Owners of male dogs also have some options and responsibilities in limiting the exploding population of unwanted pets. If your dog is of mixed ancestry, or even if he is purebred but not a show champion, he will not be highly sought after as a "stud dog." He will, if not neutered, seek out bitches "in heat" wherever they are. He'll become involved in dogfights, property damage, paternity suits (you think I'm kidding? I'm not!), and possibly traffic fatalities (his own and other's.) Your male dog will stay home better if he has no hormonal "ring in his nose" to lead him off into temptation. Neutered, he'll quite likely live a longer, healthier and less frustrated life.

Your veterinarian is the person to talk with about the details of spaying or neutering your dog. She can advise you of the best age for Fido's surgery. Veterinarians differ in their preferences on this matter. She can also tell you of numerous advantages to spaying and neutering besides the population problem.

Spayed bitches and neutered male dogs are wonderful pets, companions, and protectors. They won't get fat and lazy (the old-wives-tale warning) unless their ONLY exercise before neutering was motivated by their sex hormones. Dogs normally retain their person-alities after neutering and will become even more loyal to you if you involve them in a consistent training and exercise program.

Spayed bitches (and their owners) are spared the cyclic stresses of seasonal "heats" and unplanned pregnancies. Even a hoped-for litter can seriously tax the physical reserves of a bitch. Certain diseases and cancers occur much more frequently in bitches that have NOT been neutered. These are good reasons to have your female dog spayed.

Neutered male dogs are still definitely MALES. Contrary to popular ignorance, neutering a dog does NOT make him a "sissy." He would, in fact, actually be a better guard dog (or lap dog, if that's his profession) if his hormones didn't get in his way so easily. Fido can smell Fifi's pheromonal perfume on the breeze from MILES away, and he will forget about everything else he's doing. Fido's quest for Fifi will throw him together with all sorts of hooligan-dogs, all seeking cheap thrills with no permanent attachments. Male dogs with excited hormones fight terrible battles with one another, resulting in wounds that are frequently serious enough to require surgical attention. Some fun, eh?

Fido will <u>not</u> turn wimpy or become a coward after being neutered. He won't have so many fights though, because he will not be "driven" by that hormonal compulsion to seek out conflict with other male dogs. If "gelded" before sexual maturity, a male dog will not develop the dangerous and obnoxious "addiction" to male dominance fighting. He will be able to have more dog-friends that way. Also, neutering will protect him from prostate cancer and certain other health problems. These are some pretty good reasons to have your male dog neutered.

CHOOSING A SPECIFIC BREED OR MIX

Heredity is very important. Many more traits than size and color are determined by a dog's genes. Most everyone knows that physical soundness is hereditary. This includes how well the dog's organs function, how smoothly his joints move, how resistant he is to certain diseases and conditions, and even how long he is likely to live. Less well-known is the fact that temperament is highly inheritable. This includes the tendencies towards serious shyness and aggression.

Whenever possible, arrange to meet both parents of your prospective puppy. If either parent shows extremes in temperament you may reasonably expect the puppy (or, later, the puppy's puppies) to inherit those same traits. It's easy to see how closely a pup may resemble his sire or dam in physical ways... be aware that his mental and emotional makeup also come from those same individuals. Pups are certainly not identical to their parents or siblings, but if you observe serious temperament or physical problems in the pup's close relatives, you should think twice before choosing a pup from that bloodline.

Mixed-breed Dogs

When you look at a mixed-breed dog you'll notice that he has mental and physical characteristics typical of the several breeds in his genetic background. Some doglovers prefer mixed-breeds because of their potluck ancestry and resultant unique looks. You could get a surprise when a mixed-breed puppy grows up, however, because you may only be able to guess at the size and shape of his ancestors.

A mixed-breed "mutt" could have more genetic weaknesses than a purebred dog... but, on the other hand, he might actually have fewer. That depends largely on the dog's genetic "luck of the draw." There is quite a variety of lovely and lively mixes out there; so if that's what you're looking for you should have no trouble finding one who'd love to go home with you.

Purebred Dogs

A purebred dog has specific qualities of body and mind that were intentionally bred into his ancestors for hundreds of generations. When you select a purebred pup you will already have a fair idea of what he will be like when he grows up. You will know approximately what size he will attain, what texture and length his coat will be, and you may have a good idea as to his basic temperament qualities. All the pure breeds have been designed with specific purposes in mind. Knowing the ancestral purpose of the breeds which attract you will provide important clues to consider when choosing a purebred dog.

Many people don't realize that all the pure breeds came from mixtures of other breeds. They may just assume that dog breeds have always existed in the forms that they're now known. Of course that's not logical.

Each pure breed originated from a mix of two or more breeds. Early breeders intentionally mated dogs with traits they wished to combine in the offspring. As the desired qualities were attained by breeding, pups who showed the traits most strongly were mated. A standard of perfection for each breed was decided upon and recorded. Breeders worked to produce generations of pups who embodied that ideal.

Even those ancient breeds which have bred true to type for thousands of years evolved from blended ancestry. Then there are modern breeds, like the Doberman Pinscher, which was developed during the 20th century. New breeds of dogs are being developed even today. Some will stand the tests of time and popularity and eventually become well-known... others will not.

Each breed has a club formed by breeders which maintains breed records and holds events to encourage interest in that type of dog. There are also larger organizations which maintain registries for numerous breeds. The American Kennel Club (AKC) is one of the best known of those registries. The AKC classifies the many diverse breeds into seven groups for show purposes. These groups are designated as: Sporting, Hound, Working, Herding, Terrier, Toy, and Nonsporting. Although breeds within each group differ from one another in many ways, certain similarities of purpose (and therefore "personality") do exist within each specialized group.

Sporting Group

The Sporting Group is the classification for setters, pointers, spaniels, and retrievers. These dogs generally have lots of energy and stamina, as is necessary to hunt all day. They usually need quite a bit of exercise, especially in their early years. Most of the Sporting dogs are fairly friendly to people, even to strangers. They may be good as watchdogs though, because they like to announce visitors. Some Sporting breeds are more protective than others, so note how aggressive the parents are when you go to choose a pup.

Sporting dogs often make good pets for active children aged six and older. Most Sporting dogs tend to be quite exuberant when young, and so can sometimes be too rowdy for small children or frail elderly persons. Sporting dogs lacking proper exercise are likely to take up such pastimes as incessant barking, hole digging, and perhaps escaping the yard and hunting "out-of-season." They take well to training, though, and when properly educated make some of the most pleasant family pets and all-around companions. In fact, both Labrador and Golden Retrievers are among the preferred breeds trained as guide dogs for people who are blind.

Hound Group

The Hound Group is made up of dogs which hunt by scent or sight. They are mostly pack-style hunters and enjoy the company of other dogs. Some hounds are heavy-boned and have pendulous lips and ears; these are mostly the scent-hunters, such as the Bloodhound, Basset, and Beagle. Other hounds are slender and streamlined with long narrow noses; these are the sight-hunters, such as the Greyhound, Afghan, and Borzoi.

Some of the oldest known breeds of dogs are included in the Hound group. Hounds have been working for humans since ancient times. These dogs have a well-developed instinct for the chase and require little direction from the humans on the hunt. Most of the time, while the hounds ran down the prey animal, their masters were far behind in the distance. For this reason hounds have not been bred for unquestioning obedience. They know their "job" is to hunt down the quarry; it is the job of their human caretakers to catch up with them when they have the prey cornered.

Most Hounds are funloving and energetic. These breeds need plenty of exercise, but if allowed to run loose and unsupervised may be gone for days at a time, following animal trails. This natural inclination can seriously endanger a dog. While on a trail Fido may not notice such deadly hazards as cars and trucks, or may actually lose track of the way home and become lost.

Hounds are likely to be fairly vocal (bark, howl, sing, or yodel) as this trait was selected in their ancestors to provide a means for the owners to locate the hunting pack when out of visual contact. Because of their strong pack hunting instincts, most hound breeds are socially inclined to enjoy the company of other dogs. Hounds tend to be gentle family members, playful, love an outing, and are rather independent-minded. Although hounds are not famous for precise obedience, they are certainly quite trainable and are very loving to their masters.

Working Group

The Working Group dogs have been bred to help with their human masters' work. They learn very rapidly and many of these dogs seem to really enjoy taking orders. Working breeds can be good watchdogs and guards. They are alert and energetic, and most will bark an alarm when visitors are near. They tend to be quite loyal to their masters and may take a little while to warm up to strangers. Some Working breeds tend to be gentler than others; all are more reliable when properly trained and well exercised.

Many of the Working breeds are somewhat large, but most are fairly docile when properly trained. Some have weather-resistant haircoats that allow them to live either indoors or out, but they're happiest when they live with their masters. Several of the Working breeds are known specifically for their ability as guards, so it is important when considering a dog from this group to be certain that the individual is not overaggressive for your particular purposes. Some examples of dogs in the Working group are Rottweilers, Akitas, Malamutes, and Saint Bernards.

Years ago the Working Group also included all the breeds that herd. It was a very large group of rather popular breeds and was unwieldy to judge at shows. The American Kennel Club solved that problem by dividing the old Working Group and creating a new group for the herding dogs.

Herding Group

The Herding Group is composed of dogs such as Collies, German Shepherds, Briards, and Belgian Sheepdogs. These and the other breeds in this group have traditionally worked as responsible caretakers of sheep and other livestock.

Herding breeds have fairly weatherproof coats and can work or play outdoors year-round, but they are happiest when included in family life. They tend to be playful and energetic but are usually gentle and naturally obedient. Herding breeds take well to training and need a job to keep them busy and satisfied.

Herding dogs without proper training sometimes become "addicted" to chasing cars and bikes, or perhaps birds or livestock. Remember, "chasing" is basically the same activity as "herding," just less precise... and can easily lead to trouble. Herding dogs also tend to be a bit barky sometimes, as this was bred in originally as a useful trait for convincing the flocks to "get a move-on."

In this day and age very few of us keep herds or flocks in our backyards, but Herding dogs are just as happy to be our constant companions and help out as "babysitters" for our children. When the children are infants, the Herding dogs may watch over them, protecting them as the master's possessions. When the children get a bit bigger, the dogs can be reliable and gentle playmates for them, following them everywhere and joining in their games.

... ABOUT DOGS AND CHILDREN!

This is a good time to mention that NO dog should actually be left "in charge" of a child or infant. In fact, dogs and young children should not be left alone to play together at all. This is such sensible advice that it should not need to be mentioned.

Nevertheless, romantic media portrayals of dogs as heroic babysitters have been popular for a number of years, so maybe there really are some folks who cannot see the danger in those lovely fantasies. Tragic mishaps can and HAVE occurred.

An adult human should always chaperone the play between dogs and little children.

Terrier Group

The Terrier Group was bred to hunt and dig out varmints such as rats. The word "terrier" is derived from the Latin word "terra" (meaning "earth") and implies digging into the earth. Terriers are quick, bright, active and alert, and in fact DO enjoy digging holes and chasing small animals into hiding places. Some breeds in this group are the Airedale, Bull Terrier, Fox Terrier, and Miniature Schnauzer.

Terriers are very playful dogs and will often initiate games of their own and entice people to play. For this reason they are fun pets for active children. These dogs have an abundance of energy and may be a bit rough with their mouths while they are still pups. It may require some patience and persistence to teach them to play gently.

Terriers need proper socialization around other dogs while they are growing up or they may become fighters later on. It's a good idea to get them used to cats early too, or the dogs may consider felines as "varmints" and deal with them harshly.

Terriers are easily excited and sometimes rather vocal if not properly trained early in their lives. They are clever, very energetic, rather territorial, have a "mind of their own," and most are quite strong for their size, whether small or large. For these reasons it is a very good idea to begin training a terrier when it is quite young, using a pleasant and gentle method which seems like a game to the puppy. If training is put off for too long, the dog may resent the controls when finally imposed and won't be very interested in obedience or manners at all.

Toy Group

The Toy Group breeds, as the name implies, are all rather small dogs. Any of them would fit in your lap, and some weigh less than ten pounds. Examples of the Toy breeds are the Pug, Papillon, and Chihuahua. However, even though they are tiny, they are full-fledged REAL dogs, just as much as German Shepherds or Cocker Spaniels. In fact, most Toy dogs do not think of themselves as small at all. They have all of the same behaviors in their genetic background as any other dog. They are just as loyal, protective, playful, clever, obedient, or naughty as the biggest dog on the block can be. Believe it!

Toy breeds make wonderful housedogs, especially for persons with limited space. The area required for a medium-to-large dog to get proper exercise may just not be available to everyone these days. All dogs need fresh air and sunshine for good health of course, but the Toys can get sufficient exercise to stay physically fit by running to fetch a ball inside the house or apartment. Toy dogs can be easily carried by their owners up and down in an elevator in a city highrise and require very little space to do a "potty" at the curbside. The Toy breed's "poop" is small and simple to scoop; or for that matter, the dog can be trained to "go" on papers or even in a litterbox. Folks who do not have the energy, strength, or space to manage a large pet can get great pleasure from owning a Toy dog. On the other hand, these little fellows can feel right at home in the "country" too, and love to romp in the great outdoors... as does EVERY DOG.

People who travel a lot may find the Toy breeds easily adaptable to "life on the road." They take up very little space and are wonderful company. I remember one huge, burly truckdriver whose constant companion was a tiny Pomeranian named Rosie. She was a sweet little finger-kisser when she was introduced by her owner, but I'd say it wouldn't be very smart for anyone to bother that driver's "rig" while Rosie was on guard in the cab. Toy dogs are REAL DOGS!

Young children are often careless and rough with these tiny dogs, treating them like stuffed teddy bears; this must NEVER be allowed. Toy breeds are very sensitive to noise and to pain, and when they are frightened or overwhelmed the little dogs may defend themselves by biting. Although they are not very large, their teeth and jaws are strong enough to do some damage. If you have rough-and-tumble children in your household, perhaps you should consider a larger, more durable dog than the Toy breeds.

Toys tend to be protective of their owners and their territories, sometimes to an excessive degree. Many people think of the Toy breeds as "yappy" or "nippy," but those problems generally stem from a lack of proper training. With correct training and socialization the Toy breeds make wonderful companions and are just as enjoyable and reliable as any larger dog.

Nonsporting Group

The Nonsporting Group includes such diverse breeds as the Chow Chow, Miniature and Standard Poodles, Dalmatian, and English Bulldog. Within the Nonsporting group the different breeds vary more in appearance and personality traits than in most of the other groups. What this group of dogs seems to have most in common is their "peopleness." Ask anyone who lives with a Nonsporting dog, they may tell you that their pet actually thinks he IS a person. Better yet, ask the dog himself!

Most of these dogs have a real "mind-of-their-own" and expect their opinions to be considered in family decisions. They tend to be quite bright and enjoy doing tricks and being the center of attention. If properly socialized and trained (don't TELL them it's "dog-training" though, or they may be insulted) these dogs are most charming companions. If not properly educated, these dogs can turn into arrogant, spoiled snobs.

Nonsporting dogs generally learn new things very quickly and like to show off how clever they are. They like being part of the family and assume they have every right to be, after all, they are "people"... remember? So, if what you want is a Dog-In-The-Yard, forget the Nonsporting breeds... unless YOU are planning to live outside in the doghouse WITH Fido!

NAMING YOUR NEW DOG

A name is an important part of identity; in the case of a dog, both his identity and your own. What you call your dog will affect how you feel about him. How you feel about his name will affect his behavior and response to you.

Registered Names

If your dog is a purebred and will be registered, he will have an official name (and number) recorded by the registry. If this name has not already been filled in on the registration application which you should receive when you purchase your dog) you'll get to choose one for him. Some breeders require that you include the name of their kennel in your dog's registered name. Some also require that all pups of a certain litter be given registered names that begin with a certain letter. These breeder requirements are to help people know, if your dog is shown, that he came from Such-and-Such Kennels. This furthers the breeder's good reputation.

You may wax creative when you make up the "official" name for your dog. Some people choose titles of movies or songs as names for their dogs. Some registered names include clever puns or plays on words. Others are lovely and poetic. Some are as simple as one word, but that's rare. Registered names are limited to a certain number of letters; be sure to read all the fine print instructions before you get your heart set on a name you've selected. Also, once registered, a dog's official name cannot be changed, so be sure that you pick one you'll still like in a few years.

"Call" Names

All dogs, registered or not, need a "call" name. That is, of course, the name the dog is called. Pick a name for your dog or puppy that's easy to say and pleasant to hear.

You will say your dog's name often and you'll say it in public, so make it a positive one. Never saddle a dog with a name having negative connotations. Dopey, Stinky, and Bummer don't sound like dogs one would like to share a room with... and in fact, dogs with icky-sounding names generally manage to live up to them. This is not their fault. It's because names, being an important part of identity, carry with them expectations. People tend to perceive what they expect to perceive. This is very well-known in the advertising and marketing industries, where names for new products are chosen with utmost care. It is a serious truth to consider when selecting a name for your dog.

Stay away from bad-behavior names like Nippy, Yappy, or Digger. Why name your dog after something nobody likes? If your dog <u>does</u> happen to have one of those those tendencies, DON'T perpetuate it by naming him after his worst quality!

Avoid "tough" names, even in jest. The name you call your dog will give people an impression of his personality and attitude. This is especially true with large dogs, but even tiny dogs may be suspect with names like Fang, Cujo, or Ripper. A mean-sounding name is likely to prejudice people against your dog, even if he's really a sweetie-pie. Give your dog a break and name him something that would make people WANT to meet him. He'll have many more friends in life that way. With today's emphasis on stricter dog laws and harsher punishments for breaking them... a dog could use plenty of friends.

Be creative when naming your dog. Try to avoid choosing one of the most popular dog names in your locale. If you call your puppy Max or Lady, don't be too surprised if another dog in your pup's play group or training class answers to the same name. That can be confusing for a dog. Consider this if you plan to compete in obedience trials. Imagine what might happen if your dog named Buddy was on a long sit-stay... and in the next ring another competitor called <u>her</u> dog, "Buddy, COME!" Uh-oh!

It's also wise to refrain from naming a dog anything that rhymes with or sounds like one of the command words. You will be using his name paired with commands. If the two words are too similar it may be difficult for your dog to understand what you mean.

Teaching A Dog His New Name

A dog can learn a new name very quickly. This is true of puppies and adults. Always use the name when you speak to your dog. Preface commands with it. Say it while you pet him; call him to you using the name when you have a little tidbit for him. Tell him he's good, using his name in the phrase. Praise him by name. Pretty quickly he'll hear that sound and know that you mean him.

Don't use your dog's name when you're talking <u>about</u> him, only to him. Along the same line, don't use his name much when you're upset with him. Nobody, your dog included, likes to hear their special name spoken in an angry tone. Leave his name out of the sentence when you scold your dog. When he hears "Fido!" he should WANT to listen to the message that follows, not feel like cringing away.

New Names For "Previously-Owned" Dogs

If you adopt a dog who already has been named you still have a choice. Although many people decide to keep the name a dog has been given by previous owners, it's sometimes better to change it. If your dog's former family was angry with him alot, he may not like the sound of that old name by which he'd been scolded. It's also a good idea to change a new dog's name if you personally happen to dislike his old one. A new name will give him a fresh start with you. He needs a name that makes <u>you</u> feel happy and warm when you say it. That's something nice you can do for your new companion.

The dog you choose will be a member of your family for quite a while, so take your time, keep your eyes and your mind open, and make a careful decision. "Look before you leap." If you've already chosen your dog before you read this chapter, perhaps the information here will help you to better understand him.

Chapter 3

HANDS ON

One of the things we really enjoy about our dogs is petting them. A clean and healthy dog's coat feels nice to the touch. Petting not only feels good and soothes the dog, it may actually make us "petters" healthier

Scientific studies have repeatedly demonstrated biological and psychological health benefits for pet owners who spend time stroking their dogs or cats. These benefits include relief from life's stresses and a health-bringing normalization of both heart rate and blood pressure. Thanks to this research we now know that petting our dogs is actually

GOOD FOR US, as well as pleasant for them. Isn't that great!

Communicating by touch is natural to both humans and dogs. It's the "language" we can share most clearly with our animal friends. When we touch our dogs we transmit feeling messages to them through our hands. They can tell if we are tense or tired, they know by our touch if we are happy or sad. We, in turn, can tell if our dogs need quiet affection or a playful game to boost their spirits.

As we know, certain voices have a calming action on a dog, while others may excite him. The same is true of touch. Different ways of touching will bring about different moods and responses in our furry friends. How we touch a dog can influence his behavior as much or more than anything we could say with words.

Exciting Hands

When you are ready for a round of vigorous play with your dog, you probably communicate that to him by the way you touch him. Exciting touch might include rubbing your dog's fur rapidly forward and backward, with and against the "grain" of his hair. Most dogs also get excited and playful when someone briskly ruffles their ears or pats them on the rump.

Some dogs become overexcited and may grab roughly at hands or sleeves to join in the game. Your dog has no hands of his own to return your touches, so he uses his mouth. This can become a problem in excitable young dogs. DON'T let him develop the habit of grabbing at you in play!

The use of Exciting Hands is often too stimulating for already-energetic dogs. For them this touch should be held in reserve to pep up response to commands. When, occasionally, Fido needs an energy boost to improve his focus on a lesson, Exciting Hands can be the perfect touch.

Rough Play-Hands

DON'T EVER allow or encourage your dog to become rough with your body or clothing... and don't let anyone else teach him that bad habit either! It can be difficult at times for a responsible dogowner to convince friends or family members that it's unwise to play roughly with the dog. It is extremely important that no one be permitted to teach a dog the annoying and dangerous habit of biting in play.

When a dog plays he is not just playing, he is also learning. One of the lessons learned from rough play is that it's okay for him to treat us as if we were dogs. This is NOT acceptable, and here's why: When a dog learns to treat a person the same as he'd treat another dog, he will do so not only during play but at more serious times as well. A dog allowed (taught!) to bite people in play will think it's okay to apply the same rules to us as to other dogs. A dog would naturally use his teeth to punish another dog for trespassing. "Trespassing" may constitute something as commonplace as walking by while he's eating something or bumping him slightly while he's resting. While he may get away with nipping at another dog, this kind of behavior towards people could get a beloved pet into lethal trouble.

Rough-handed, wild play will make a dog much more likely to put his mouth on people "for real!" Rough and aggressive play behavior is difficult to change later on.

If your pup starts to mouth your hands in play, say "OW!!!" as if he'd truly hurt you. "OW!" sounds a bit like a dog sound. It sounds enough like what Fido would say if he was hurt, he'll understand he's been too rough with his "game." Be sure to sound serious, not whiney, or he won't believe you. The dog should stop mouthing your hand and "apologise." Offer him a puppytoy to chew on instead of your hand.

*** Important Rule:
<u>NEVER</u> ALLOW HAND-BITING, EVEN IN PLAY!
Habits of mouthing develop easily and
may later turn into dangerous biting behavior.

Calming Hands
When Fido is OVEREXCITED, calming strokes will relax him. Calming Hands touch begins at Fido's head or neck and flows smoothly toward his tail, following the natural direction of hair growth. Stroking against the "grain" is NOT relaxing, it will tickle the dog and makes him want to wiggle around.

The Calming Hands stroke is most effective when it takes a LONG, LOOOOOOOOONG time for your hand to go all the way from Fido's head to his hindie. One calming stroke should take at least five to ten seconds, depending on the length of the dog's body. These strokes are probably much slower than you'd normally pet your dog.

Use a VERY SLOW stroking rhythm. Go WITH the lay of his hair. This will smooth Fido's fur and soothe his nerves at the same time. This touch will also relax the person petting the dog.

Reassuring Hands
If your dog is AFRAID or ANXIOUS the Reassuring Hands form of touching will help brace up his courage. This touching rhythm helps your dog release anxiety. It's done by pat-patting Fido on his side or shoulder with your hand and wrist quite loose and relaxed. This is the "Ol' Houn'dog Blue" method of patting. It's best to accompany the touch with a laid-back, relaxed voice to match... as if saying "Good ol' feller, you ol' houn'dog, you."

This loose-and-hearty style of petting will help Fido let go of anxious body tension. Your happy-go-lucky voice tone will also help

relieve his worried mind. Also, pay attention to your own breathing
rhythm while you do this. You should breathe full, even breaths. The
combined effect reassures your dog that you are not a bit worried, so
he doesn't need to worry either.

The Ol' Houn'dog Blue method of Reassuring Touch gives Fido
the message that you, his Fearless Leader, have the situation well in
hand.

A relaxed hand and confident attitude will reassure your furry
friend. You won't have to try very hard to convince him that things are
okay. Your air of leadership will make Fido feel braver because he
knows you are.

Massage

Speaking of relaxing, there are few things more effective than a
good massage. Massage is as healing and calming for dogs as it is for
us. Not only can massage relax your dog, it can also make him healthier
and more attentive.

A tense dog is not able to absorb lessons properly. He's more
interested in protecting himself from an imagined danger than in
learning. Tension like this in a sensitive dog at an obedience class can
sometimes be misinterpreted as rebellion or aggression. Viewing the
situation as a contest of wills ("You WILL listen to me; you WILL do
what I say... or I WILL make you!") some trainers rely on pain and
force to get the dog's attention. This is unnecessary and counterproductive to a good learning experience.

Instead of resorting to punishment, use massage and Calming
Hands to relax and re-sensitize a tense, shut-off dog. Massage can help
a dog become responsive to subtler signals and allow training by much
gentler methods.

Start the massage at the side of your dog's neck, where the
shoulder and neck muscles come together. Feel the muscles with the
pads of your fingers. Use only one hand at first. Gently, slowly and
rhythmically slide the dog's skin in small circles over the muscle tissue
beneath. Do not rub the hair back and forth, just move the skin. Your
dog may be fidgity and jumpy at first, but that won't last very long.

Slow circles of massage on the neck and shoulder area will
smooth those tight muscles. Your dog will relax noticeably and most
dogs will yawn after a little while. That will let you know it's working!

Dogs enjoy massage. It encourages them to become more
tolerant of touch, even in their sensitive, ticklish or "private"

areas. This, in turn, makes it easier to examine or groom them. Regular massage will also deepen your dog's bond of love and trust for you.

The Language of Touch

Communicating with our dogs through the language of touch is very natural and so rewarding. Not only does it make a dog feel better, it also helps him understand us. Messages we send to Fido through our hands are more readily translated than verbal ones. Awareness of what we "say" to our dogs when we touch them will improve our skills at interspecies communication. Our dogs' lives and our own will be enriched by this better understanding.

Chapter 4

THE DEN & THE DOG

In the wild, wolves dig dens for themselves and their cubs. They make those dens snug and secure. There is only one entrance and the den is only large enough to comfortably turn around and lie down. They can relax then, knowing that nothing can sneak up behind them as they rest. Our pet dogs also like cozy and private places, just as their wild ancestors did.

Left to choose their own sleeping quarters, most dogs prefer the privacy and security of dens or cave-like areas. A dog appreciates a comfortable place to rest undisturbed. He might curl up with his back to the wall, under a table, or in the corner of the couch. Some dogs try to dig a little "nest" in the sofa cushions to make an even cozier "den." It's possible you would not appreciate what Fido could do to your furniture in the name of comfort. Both you and your dog might be happier if you provide him with a nice ready-made "den" of his own.

There is a modern-day equivalent to the ancestral wolf's den designed especially for today's dog. It is most often referred to as a crate, travel kennel, or pet carrier. These dens come in two main styles, the molded plastic "airline" crate and the collapsible wire-mesh type. Your pet supply store may stock them or could order one for you. Crates are also available through mail-order catalogs.

The airline-approved style is made of sturdy opaque molded plastic. The door is strong wire mesh and there are air vents along both sides of the crate near the top. These

dens are safe and comfortable for dogs. The plastic crates come in a number of sizes, several different colors, and are sold under various brand names.

Dog crates are also available in a collapsible wire-mesh style. The wire crates are better ventilated but not as smooth and cozy as the plastic type. They are also noisier, tending to rattle when Fido moves around. Wire crates have some advantages though, as they fold flat for storage and are available in a wide variety of shapes and sizes. If you decide on a wire crate, drape a towel or blanket over the top, back, and sides of it to make the den feel more secure and private for your dog. The drape will also reduce the draftiness and noise of the wire crate.

WHAT IS THE RIGHT SIZE?

Your dog should be able to lie down comfortably in his den, and he should be able to stand up and turn around. If the crate is much larger than that, it won't be as cozy for your dog. On the other hand, if it's undersized, Fido will be too cramped to enjoy "his own room." Choose the appropriate size for your dog.

If your dog is still just a small puppy but destined to become a large dog, purchase the size den he will need as an adult and let him "grow into it." If the den is much too large, however, some pups think that the excess space is the crate's "backyard"... the place to go potty. That's JUST what you DON'T WANT! If you find your puppy toddles to the back of his adult-sized crate to go potty, block off the extra space with a barrier that can be removed when he gets bigger. Be SURE the barrier is fastened securely to the crate so it doesn't fall over onto your pup!

WHERE SHOULD THE CRATE BE?

Your dog's portable den should be located in an area of the house where the pup will be near you, able to see you, yet not be under foot. You could keep the crate in one spot during the day and another at night. The kitchen or family room may be the best spot for the crate in the daytime, then in the evening you could move it to your bedroom.

The crate-den gives Fido a secure and private place without isolating him. A dog can take naps in the crate nearby the family's activities, yet not be in the way. He can keep his favorite toys there. He can lounge there. The den is a nice private "bedroom" for a dog.

Use the Den Kindly and Safely

Any time you leave a dog in his crate with the door shut, be sure that the den is in a safe place. A cool room in the morning may, in your absence, heat up excessively. This can happen if the sun beats down on that side of the house in the afternoon. In his crate, a dog would be unable to move away from that heat. A dog would suffer badly (or worse!) in the inescapable heat. Do be careful where you place your dog's crate-den during the day. Be safe and be sure! Your dog counts on your good sense.

The crate will be a cozy haven for your dog without him being in constant trouble or danger. It's a cozy bed that will keep Fido (and your furnishings) safe at night or for a few hours during the day. Make it a secure and private resting area for your dog, but don't over-use it or make it a prison.

HOW LONG CAN YOUR DOG BE LEFT IN HIS CRATE?

Dogs are very social animals and need companionship. Mature dogs can normally spend time alone better than puppies can, but still they need some quality time and attention from you every day. If a dog is kept isolated too much of the time he'll be likely to develop some severe behavior problems. Frustration is expressed through such misbehaviors as barking, inappropriate aggression, destructive chewing, digging, and even self-mutilation. Be fair and realistic in your use of the crate.

Never leave a puppy in his crate for more than three or four daytime hours at a time. DON'T expect your puppy or dog to spend half his life locked up! He needs exercise, fresh air, education, playtime, and physical contact with you... none of which he can get while confined to his crate. You will need to explore other options if you must leave your dog alone all day.

Other Options

If your dog must stay alone all day, every day, while you're off earning his next bag of kibble, it won't be healthy for him to spend all that time in a crate. If you possibly can, fence your yard and let Fido wait there for your return. By the way, it is wisest and kindest to arrange this fenced yard to include one of the doors of your home.

When your pup's house manners are trustworthy, consider installing a dog-door, so he can go from the fenced yard into the house on his own. Your dog will feel like he's part of your pack," even when you're away. He won't be as likely to develop the behavior problems commonly associated with isolation.

If Baby Fido MUST remain indoors for long hours while you're away, puppy-proof an area of your kitchen as his "play-room." If your schedule keeps you away from home all day, you might have to make temporary provisions to keep your young puppy from going stir-crazy while you're at work.

Little puppies have a hard time spending long hours alone, just as little people do. Look into hiring a dogwalker or pet-sitter to visit your puppy daily or leave Little Fido at a doggie daycare facility. Your veterinarian or groomer may be able to recommend one of these services in your area. When Baby Fido grows up a bit he'll be better able to tolerate full days alone.

TEACHING FIDO TO ACCEPT HIS CRATE

It's best to allow your dog to get used to his new den gradually, letting him have time to think of it as "furniture." His den should represent safety, not feel like a prison or a trap! The first day, just let him sniff and explore the open crate. Hide a few little tidbits of something delicious inside the crate every so often. Make it a fun new place to explore. Take the door off the crate or tie it open, so Fido doesn't accidentally clang it shut behind himself when he ventures inside the new den. Be careful not to scare your dog.

A folded towel or blanket in the crate will make it more comfy and can be easily washed. Any bedding used in the crate is likely to be redesigned by the dog, so don't give him your best guest towels.

Put puppy toys and a few tidbit treats in the crate and let your dog decide for himself that his new den is a nice place. This low stress introduction period will greatly reduce Fido's anxiety when the time comes to actually close the door. This may also work to relieve any nervousness <u>you</u> might feel about it.

Getting The Dog Into The Crate

Get your dog a nice chewtoy (or a big knuckle-bone if your veterinarian approves) and put the chewie in the crate. Then put Fido into the crate. He may not cooperate with you on this matter at first, but help him into the crate somehow. You might try putting your dog into his crate hindie-first if he won't go in frontwards. Be gentle and be friendly, but be firmly decided... he IS going into the crate.

Closing The Door

Take Fido out to potty before you get started with the first closed-crate lesson. DO NOT have a big play session or obedience lesson right now; you'll want Fido to form as few "superstitious" associations about the crate-training as possible.

Once he's in, praise him, then shut the door of the crate. Wait about ten seconds, then open the door and call the dog out. He may not seem to need that invitation, but call him out anyway, he needs to hear permission from you.

Pet him, give him a little treat, then put him back into the crate. Praise, then wait ten seconds and let him out. Praise again. Repeat this sequence a few times, then, while your dog watches, place a small treat inside the crate and walk a few steps away. Don't try to urge your dog into the den, but if he goes in on his own, praise him. Leave the door open this time. Then go do something else with your dog for awhile.

Leaving Him Alone

After two or three sessions of in-and-out practice with the crate, it will be time to teach your dog to accept spending time in the closed crate. Take him outside for potty before you get started with this part.

Begin by telling your dog to get into and out of the crate several times, praising him each time as before. Then put a chew toy in the crate, put the dog in, praise him, then calmly latch the door. Be kindly and natural. DON'T apologize or sound like you feel sorry for him, or he'll think something's wrong!

In a matter-of-fact voice, tell Fido he's a good dog, he should wait for you, and that you'll be back in a few minutes. Then leave the room.

If your dog cries or barks when you first leave him (and he probably will) return to him only ONCE to reassure him. Keep your voice pleasant and try to stay relaxed. Don't open the crate, just tell him he's a good pup and that you will be back. Then leave him alone for awhile and busy yourself around the house. Twenty or thirty minutes is about enough time for the first experience. It may help your pup to relax if some mellow music is played while he is in his crate.

If Fido barks, whines, yells, yodels, howls, and/or sings the blues... try to ignore his protests. He's really NOT in pain. Steel yourself! If you were to let him out now he would learn that screaming and carrying on is a good way to manipulate you. You DON'T want him to think you will let him out when HE "commands" you to. If you absolutely can't stand listening to his threats and pleas, just leave the house. Go weed your garden or visit a friend. Or maybe go to the library for awhile, it's quiet there. Most dogs quickly figure out that crate confinement is safe, secure and only temporary.

Leave Fido alone for about half an hour, then return and CALMLY let him out of his crate. Tell him what a GREAT dog he is and how much you like him, but DO NOT APOLOGIZE to him for leaving! That would confuse him. Take him out for potty or a walk, be his nice friend. Don't make too big a deal of the crate experience; the more casual you are about it, the better. He really WILL get used to it, then he'll LIKE his crate-den.

If Fido spends some time in his new den every day he will soon be comfortable in it. In about a week or so you will probably notice him napping in his crate voluntarily. The crate is a secure spot for your dog. It provides an out of the mainstream place for him to retreat from family hubbub and resembles the comfortable den atmosphere dogs like. Although most dogs are a little suspicious of crates at first, they genuinely like these dens once they've had a little time to get comfortable in them.

What If There's Really No Time For Gradual Introduction?

If for some reason you MUST teach your dog to accept the closed crate immediately, with no time to get used to it, he will almost surely object rather loudly. It's always preferable to give Fido time to become comfortable lounging in his crate before you close the door, but in some situations that is simply not possible.

If you absolutely must quickly teach your dog to stay in his crate, just go ahead and gently put him in. Let him go in and out a few times. Give him some special tidbits and a favorite toy in the crate.   Then shut the door.   Do so in a pleasant, matter-of-fact way. Your calm attitude will minimize your dog's fears about any new experience.

CRATES & POTTY-TRAINING

Little Fido's crate can be a wonderful help at housebreaking time. A puppy naturally prefers a clean bed and normally will not potty in it. Crate-training will help your puppy learn to gradually increase his bladder control.

When your puppy has been relaxing in his crate and suddenly has to go potty, he'll become restless. Pay attention when this happens. You should take him outside, stay with him while he potties, and praise his good job. When you bring him back into the house afterward you can probably trust him to stay dry for awhile, if you're sure he's pottied-out.

Puppies need to urinate quite a few times during the day, usually at least once every two hours. If your puppy must stay in his crate for more than a couple of hours he will need to relieve himself as soon as you let him out. This fact is helpful when you are potty training Little Fido, because it gives you predictable opportunities to praise him for a job well done.

Most pups up to six months of age also wake up during the night, needing to potty.   This generally happens about four hours after the pup goes to bed. You will need to get up and take the little darlin' out to do his duty.   Afterwards, calmly return him to his den for the rest of the night. He may be fairly wide-awake after his trip outside and may complain for a little while. Ignore him, he'll quiet down and go back to sleep in a bit. Some soft music may help relax him (and you.) Older pups and adult dogs normally can make it through the night without pottying and do not need this mid-sleep outing.

REMEMBER:

◆ **ALWAYS give Fido a chance to potty before you close his crate, and...**

◆ **BE SURE not to leave him in the closed crate too long.**

ANOTHER BENEFIT OF CRATE-DENS

Crate training can help prevent much of the destructive chewing done by unattended young dogs. Besides the mess and expense of ruined furnishings and personal effects, there are some real dangers for puppies that chew... electrical cords, household chemicals, etc. Teach Little Fido to spend time in his crate with the door shut while you're unable to chaperone. This will protect both the puppy and the furnishings.

Little Fido should NEVER be abandoned for long periods of time in his crate! But when you are too busy to keep a hawk's eye on him, the crate can keep your pup safe and out of trouble.

ON THE ROAD

Your dog's portable den will also be useful for traveling. The den makes a safe area for your dog while he rides in your family car. In case of sudden stops the crate will protect the dog from being injured if thrown suddenly forward. A crate will also keep Fido's sandy little paws, smudgy nose, and shedding hair from messing up the interior of your car.

Dogs In Trucks

A dog riding loose in the bed of a truck is very vulnerable to injury. He is endangered by sharp turns, abrupt stops and traffic accidents. The dust and debris that blow into his eyes, nose and ears can create serious health problems. Fido could even become overexcited and jump out of the moving vehicle after another dog by the roadside. In some areas it is now illegal to carry an unrestrained dog in the back of a truck.

If your dog rides in a well-anchored crate he will be safer (and legal) while traveling in the back of your pickup. In wet weather, turn the crate upside down so the air vents are on the bottom half. That will prevent rain from dripping into the crate and will keep your dog dry and comfortable.

When You Arrive

When you arrive at your destination, Fido's den will be a welcome and familiar bed for him in the new surroundings. He'll sleep better in his own bed... it will remind him of home. An additional benefit is that some innkeepers will welcome dogs who sleep in travel crates but reject dogs which might be left loose in the rooms. Some of your own friends or relatives may feel the same way when you visit their homes with your dog. Vacationing with Fido is certainly more pleasant for everyone when he brings along his own bedroom.

Cozy Comfortable Cave

Considering all the benefits crate dens provide dogs and their human families, it's hard to imagine why some people balk at using them. Perhaps it is because they do not understand their dogs' natural preference for cozy dark places. Most dogs like their crates and are completely at ease in them whether the door is open or shut. It is not a "cage" to Fido, it's his own cozy private comfortable "cave."

Chapter 5

COMMANDS & REWARDS

Our dogs respond in predictable ways to the various tones we use when we speak. A playful, lilting voice has a quite different effect on a dog than does a sharp, harsh tone. Certain voices attract Fido's eager affection and others may cause him to cringe away or growl.

You may have heard it said that dogs can't understand the words you speak, only your tone of voice. Well, that's just not true. For many years that old idea was so well accepted that no one really thought to question its validity. When we bother to think about it, it's pretty obvious that dogs DO learn words or they wouldn't be able to tell one command from another. Our spoken language is not Fido's natural one, though, so when you teach your dog to obey commands you are teaching him a foreign language. Most dogs can learn to UNDERSTAND quite a few words, even though they are not able to pronounce them.

Many of us who share a household with dogs have found it necessary at times to spell out words like "W-A-L-K" or "B-A-T-H." This we do to keep certain conversations private from Fido's eavesdropping ears. We notice that our dogs have no trouble at all remembering the words that interest THEM!

BOTH tone of voice AND the words we speak can be used to communicate with our dogs. To make things clear when we teach our dogs commands, we must be sure that we use words and tones in a consistent way. If we make the command-message easy to understand, Fido will try very hard to please.

Dog Language

Dogs "talk" with each other in several ways. They vocalize as a way to call attention. They use voice tones mainly to communicate general mood or emotion, rather than specific information. Another form of communication used by dogs is body posture and tension. This also clearly establishes mood and is used to encourage or prohibit further social interaction. Touching is also a method of "talking" among dogs. Touch-talk ranges from the caresses and nudges that Mamadog gives her newborn pups... to the packleader's aggressive rush-and-crash treatment of intruders.

Fido's natural "language" is postural, tonal, and tactile. Our human languages have all those qualities plus symbols (words) that give specific information about objects or actions. We humans rely so heavily on the use of words for our communications, we rarely consciously notice the more subtle body-language we "speak." Dogs DO notice it. It makes more natural sense to them than the word-symbols we use. Dogs are not born understanding human speech (well, neither are we); they have to learn what it means.

COMMANDS

Commands are the signals we give Fido when we want him to start or stop a particular action. Commands can be verbal signals, hand signals, whistles, or any other way we can get the dog's attention and relay a message. Both voice and handsignals are used in this book to teach the commands.

When we say "SIT" to an untrained dog he does not automatically know what we're talking about. He may sincerely wish to understand

and please us, but he doesn't yet realize the sound's significance. The dog cannot understand until we teach him what the sound means.

When you teach your dog a new command it's important to be clear, patient, and consistent. Don't scare or confuse him with roughness and gruffness. Teach Fido the meaning of a command word by easing him gently into the commanded position, then rewarding him for his cooperation. Help your dog learn the words. He wants to please you and needs to know how. Help him as much as he needs and NEVER punish him for something he doesn't yet understand.

THE COMMAND PHRASE

You can make the command words pleasant and easy for your dog to learn. Speak clearly and simply in a confident voice. There is no need to speak sharply or any louder than you normally would, dogs have excellent hearing. Don't use a questioning or pleading tone for commands or your dog won't believe that you really ARE the "Leader." Leaders don't whine or plead, so your dog won't understand if you do.

Speak in a pleasant voice. Say your dog's name first, before the command word, so that he will know you're talking to him. Use the same command each time, so your dog can learn to recognize it and understand what it means.

Simple Commands

Keep commands as simple as possible at first. Introduce only one or two new words in a lesson. Imagine how your dog feels, trying to understand this unfamiliar language; don't overwhelm him. We humans make a lot of different sounds, a few of which will come to have specific important meanings for our dogs. Other sounds we make are just random filler-noises to the dogs. Fido needs to learn which are which. Be clear and consistent.

Begin by teaching your dog single-word commands. Gradually add more words, then phrases. After Fido has learned that individual word-sounds have meaning, he will start to pick them out of sentences.

Give The Command

To help your dog understand which words to listen to, isolate the command phrase from the rest of your "conversation." Say your dog's name first in the command phrase ("Fido, SIT"), so he'll know to pay attention. Speak the command clearly and confidently.

If your dog seems confused, gently help him do the right thing. He will learn most easily when his teacher is clear, patient and encouraging.

Tone of Voice

Old-time dogtrainers taught people to use an ultra-firm "military" tone to command their dogs. That style is unnecessary and gruff. Most people today would prefer to use a more normal "conversational" tone to give commands. This is fine. Dogs will learn to respond to the command words in any tone you use.

It's not necessary to sound tough or stern when you tell your dog to do something. Just speak the command phrase in a clear, normal, confident voice. Reserve the super firm tone for when you must REALLY grab your dog's attention. A normal voice will do well for ordinary times.

Repeating Commands

Never repeat a command. Your dog will lose confidence in your leadership if you do. Be sure to say the command so your dog can hear it the first time. If he doesn't respond, gently assist him to obey the command. When he's in the correct position, praise him for his "obedience."

REWARDS

Remember to reward your dog when he tries to please you. The reward is your dog's "paycheck" for good work. If he does his job well and is "paid" well he will be a happy and obedient worker. If your dog works hard for you and you forget to pay him, eventually he'll go on strike or quit his job altogether. Could you really blame him?

When your dog obeys a command you MUST reward him. Otherwise he will not know when he has done the right thing. Rewards communicate to your dog that he has pleased you. If you reward him when you're pleased with him he'll be motivated to continue to obey.

The most commonly used rewards for good-dog behavior are verbal praise, petting, food treats, and playtime. These rewards work differently with dogs of different ages and temperaments. A good reward must be something Fido enjoys, yet it must not distract his attention from the lesson. Use rewards that are appropriate for your dog... and always include praise!

Verbal Praise

Verbal praise is very important. It is a reward you can give to your dog from either up close or far away. Your pleased sounding voice is music to his ears. Fido will listen more closely to the words you say when he knows some of them are praise for him. To encourage your dog and help him learn faster, "Use A Praise Phrase When He Obeys."

The Praise Phrase

· To make commands easier for your dog to remember, pair them with praise when rewarding obedience. The praise phrase connects the command to the praise. A praise phrase, like "Good SIT!" will help your dog learn to recognize the command word. Dogs learns more rapidly when happiness and success become associated with the commands. (Doesn't everyone?) The combination reinforces the dog's correct decision to obey.

Remember, your dog is studying a foreign language! Encourage him with praise as much as you can. Use the command in a praise phrase each time you reward Fido. Hearing the praise phrase encourages a dog to learn and helps build his self confidence. A positive association is formed between the command word and your happy praise. The next time the dog hears that command he'll remember how good it makes him feel to obey.

Petting

Petting is a pleasant reward for most dogs. Gentle touch is relaxing to dogs and vigorous touch is exciting. Most dogs enjoy being lightly scratched, having their ears rubbed, or their head stroked. Petting your dog in a way he enjoys is a good reward for good behavior. If you stroke or pat Fido while you praise him, he will be doubly rewarded. He'll like that.

Petting is not the reward-of-choice for all dogs. It's too stimulating for some. Very high-strung dogs become too excited to hold still when they are rewarded with petting. Other dogs are so timid that a hand reaching to pet them may be interpreted as a threat. If your dog has either of these problems just use verbal praise and maybe food treats as rewards at first. Later, as Fido learns, his confidence level and attention span will both increase, along with his bond of trust with you.

He may then be able to enjoy petting as a reward without being overwhelmed by it.

Food Treats

Food treats are good attention getters and especially efective with young puppies and shy or timid dogs. The food diverts Fido's attention from his immediate surroundings. The yummy in the trainer 's hand keeps Fido's mind off other distractions. The dog pays attention because he' s attracted to the food. We must be careful in our use of food rewards because this attraction can become an addiction if tidbits are improperly used.

Use food treats sparingly . Give just a "flavor-bit," not a mouthful. Smaller is <u>better</u> when it comes to food rewards. Give TINY tidbits, no larger than 1/4 to 1/2-inch pieces. If the treats are too big the dog will think they're less valuable. He may also become so involved in the eating process that he'll not be interested in his lesson, only the food.

To prevent your dog from becoming a tidbit-addict, be sure he learns to enjoy other rewards besides food. When you use food treats as rewards ALWAYS pair them with verbal praise and/or petting. That will simplify the process of weaning Fido from the food-motivation to the higher purpose of pleasing his teacher.

Weaning From Food Lures

Start to "wean" Fido from tidbits before he becomes too dependent upon them for motivation. Gradually reduce how often you give tidbits; only give a foodie every other or every third time. Use petting and verbal praise whether you give a food treat or not. Eventually you can reserve food rewards as special bonus treats for only the best work and your dog will work enthusiastically with or without a yummy.

Food works well for motivating Fido to learn new commands and other "tricks" but it's really best if he works to please you, rather than because he wants something to eat. Even when a dog is well fed and full he still enjoys his beloved leader's voice and some nice petting. There's "always room for" petting and verbal praise.

Surprising as it seems to some, not all dogs can be motivated by food. That's okay. If you try a couple of different yummy tidbits and your dog turns them down, the solution is simple: quit using food rewards. Praise your dog, pet him, play with a toy... choose a reward that he agrees <u>is</u> a reward. You can be glad your dog's not a foodaholic... he'll never be troubled by obesity.

Playtime

Playtime as a reward has good points and drawbacks, depending upon how it is used. If you keep training sessions happy and up-beat with lots of praise and fun, the training itself will be like play. That will be a lot more pleasant for both you and Fido than if schooltime were just a boring series of gruff-sounding commands. Make the training fun in itself! It's top quality time to spend with your dog.

If playtime is used as a ruff'n'rowdy release from training, some problems may be created. If your dog thinks his "schoolwork" is dull and "recess" is the only fun event to look forward to, he won't be very motivated to learn.

Another problem with a playtime reward is the contrast between hard concentration on a new lesson and cutting loose with a play session. An abrupt switch from control to out-of-control can cause a dog to completely forget the last few minutes of the lesson he was learning. It's better to give your dog about five or ten minutes of "quiet time" (gentle petting or rest time) following each training session. Wait for the lesson to "sink in" before sending your dog off racing after the stick or ball.

When Fido responds to your commands with correct action, ALWAYS be sure to REWARD him. Use plenty of praise and some nice petting. Give him a food tidbit once in awhile as a bonus. He will work happily, knowing he can please you and earn a reward.

Be clear, be confident, be encouraging. Use a praise phrase to help your dog know specifically what he did to please you. Your dog will be counting on you to teach him. Clear communication is not difficult to achieve and it's so rewarding for both partners in the dog/master team.

Chapter 6

DISTRACTIONS
&
MAGNETS

Many of us can remember being told to turn off the radio or TV while we did our school homework. Our parents warned us it was "too distracting" and detrimental to our powers of concentration. In most cases they may have been correct. It is also true for our dogs that TOO MANY distractions can make it hard to learn a new lesson or skill. On the other hand, it's beneficial to have SOME distractions. Fido must learn to focus on you, his Fearless Leader, instead of the rest of the exciting world.

TO KEEP YOUR DOG'S ATTENTION
you must have the strongest magnet.

MAGNETS

It's as if everything in the world, including us, has magnets inside.   Dogs are attracted by some magnets and repelled by others.   Distraction-magnets are everywhere.   Although they can cause a dog's mind to wander there are actually ways to use magnetic forces to build Fido's concentration.

Most magnets exert an attraction-force; the effect of a kittycat on many dogs is a familiar example of this type.   Other objects, like scary vacuum cleaners or wide brimmed hats, have "fear magnets" in them which repel some dogs. Both types of magnets may be utilized for training your dog.

The strength of the magnet and how near it is influence its effect on your dog.   You can increase your own magnet's force while decreasing the distraction-magnet's by practicing with your dog near the distraction.   Working closer and closer to the magnet's forcefield you will build up Fido's ability to focus on you.   It will improve his concentration and increase his faith in your good leadership.

When you first introduce your dog or puppy to any new lesson it's best to work in a calm environment without too many distractions.   After he understands the new lesson, start introducing magnets.   Keep a fair distance between Fido and any really potent magnets until he learns to focus his attention on you.   When he is able to do that, work closer and closer to the distractions.   Don't expect perfect concentration from Fido at first; you may even find YOURSELF somewhat distracted by the same magnets that push and pull your dog.

USING MAGNETS TO BUILD CONCENTRATION

Start off with low-power distractions and work up to stronger ones.   The normal sights, sounds, and scents in your livingroom or backyard will be plenty distracting for your dog at first.   Later on try some training sessions at the park or other interesting place.

Be SURE to use a leash when you begin working around strong magnets.   The idea is to teach your dog to concentrate on you instead of wavering from enticement to enticement.   If Fido is on a six-foot training leash and you are holding the other end, you will be able to prevent him from chasing after a forceful magnet. The leash will also enable you to surprise your dog by changing direction frequently, which will make him want to pay closer attention.

What To Do
(See Chapter 11 "Schooltime For Fido) for instructions for WALK.)

Work with your dog on a loose leash on the "WALK" command. As you gain his attention, move toward the distraction until the dog seems to be drawn by its magnet.

When Fido begins to be pulled towards the magnet's force field, don't say a word, just turn <u>suddenly</u> and go in the opposite direction.

Praise your dog for turning with you.

Keep walking away until your dog is no longer controlled by the magnet's power. Then turn and walk toward the magnet again.

Praise Fido when he turns.

When your dog is pulled by the magnet, turn suddenly and walk briskly away again.

Do this as many times as you need to, until Fido gets the point he's supposed to be WITH you... and that means paying attention to where you go.

What NOT To Do

Do NOT warn your dog with his name or a command or by clearing your throat. ("Ahem.")

Do NOT wait for him to give you his attention. If you wait, he won't.

Do NOT tug on the leash. Do not jerk on the leash. It's not necessary and it will spoil the "organic" timing of this correction.

Do NOT scold or nag. He won't want to pay attention if you do.

Just turn and walk off as if you'd completely forgotten him.

When you do this properly, your inattentive dog will feel an unexpected pull that will turn him around and automatically move him in your direction. You should, of course, then **praise him delightedly** for being with you... as if you hadn't noticed his lapse of attention.

There will be no need for you to jerk the leash if you use this method. The lead will tighten automatically. When the dog's focus wanders, you merely change directions... not to punish the dog, but to teach him to <u>watch</u> you. It's the packleader's prerogative to change the activity. The rest of the pack is supposed to be paying attention to the leader so they don't get left behind. The leash only tightens if the dog is inattentive to the leader.

YOU'RE THE FOCUS OF FIDO'S ATTENTION

As you work with your dog, changing directions and praising him for paying attention, he'll learn to focus on you instead of on distractions. Formerly exciting magnets will lose their power as Fido's ability to focus on you grows stronger. As this happens, you'll have to really search for magnets strong enough to distract your dog. Before long you'll be able to hold your dog's attention regardless of whatever enticing distractions the world offers.

Chapter 7

CRIMES & PUNISHMENTS

Dogs, especially puppies, naturally engage in a variety of behaviors we humans would prefer they'd avoid. Some of the things dogs do for fun (and profit) can be quite destructive to our possessions and to our peace of mind. Dogs sometimes place themselves in danger without even being aware of it. Canine "crimes" can create some tense situations for the dog and for the family.

WHAT ARE CRIMES?

Without being taught acceptable behaviors, a dog is going to just act naturally. If he doesn't know what constitutes a "crime" it's not fair to punish him for that behavior. Of course he must be shown what IS right, so he'll know the next time. If Fido doesn't know what the rules are it's not his fault. It is our job to TEACH our dogs "right" from "wrong."

Sometimes people become frustrated and angry when a dog chews something valuable or goes potty on the rug. To an uneducated dog, chewing what he finds is NOT a crime. To an uneducated dog, one place is as good as another to go potty; doing it on the rug is NOT a crime to him. We must NOT assume that a dog has acted willfully to annoy us just because we don't like what he has done. We must first patiently teach our pups and dogs what we consider proper behavior.

This is NOT to say that a dog may never be held responsible for "breaking the law"... he certainly can be. But first we must be certain to give him proper and clear instructions. That is the fair way.

Once we have given our dogs some good education we'll be able to expect them to follow the rules. Remember to keep those rules clear and consistent. If one member of your family teaches the dog to play rowdy games and then the dog gets in trouble for being too rough... who has committed the "crime"? We humans fancy ourselves to be smarter and wiser than our dogs. That may be truth or just self-flattery, but it's a responsibility we ought to take seriously.

"Spite" Crimes

Spitefulness is rare among dogs. Dogs are usually quite direct about what they want. They seldom attempt to get an angry reaction from their leader if they understand how to get a pleased one instead. Some dog owners are especially offended by certain misbehaviors and may feel personally insulted by something Fido has done. "Spite" may be assigned as the motive for the dog's actions. This conclusion is usually not accurate.

An example of the type of dog behavior often labled "spiteful" is urinating on the master's bed. This is a distressing and particularly icky misbehavior. It is also, oddly, a symptom of infection or irritation of the urinary tract. A number of unfortunate dogs have become dangerously ill with a growing infection while their misguided owners tried to punish away the "bad" potty behavior.

A common reason for "deliberate" misbehavior is anxiety. A dog, anxious about something stressful in the environment, may exhibit stubborn refusal to obey or cooperate. One four year old Springer Spaniel whose owner consulted me was suddenly starting to potty in the house at night. She would refuse to leave the porch after dark, then would defecate on the kitchen floor after the family went to bed. The dog had been scolded for this behavior and punished by banishment to a doghouse in the back yard. The problem only worsened. At my suggestion, a bit of investigation showed that a huge old nasty-tempered raccoon had staked a claim on the innocent dog's outdoor foodbowl. This dog feared for her own safety. No wonder she didn't want to go out after dark!!! The dog had no better way to explain the situation to her owner, so she pooped on the floor.

Before deciding that a dog has acted spitefully, analyze the behavior. First, did the dog know it was "wrong"? When a dog does something he <u>knows</u> is wrong, there is often a compelling reason. Sometimes dogs do try to send us a message with inappropriate behavior, but spite is usually not the point. Often the dog who suddenly backslides behaviorally has a health problem or is experiencing intense anxiety.

If your dog behaves in what seems to be a deliberately spiteful manner, check all the other motivational possibilities for the behavior. There is usually a more rational explanation.

Correction or Punishment?

The words "correction" and "punishment" are often spoken as if they were interchangeable. They are really NOT the same thing. Although corrections and punishments may be used together in a supportive way, they are different.

If, after learning the rules, your dog "commits a crime" you will need to correct him. That is how to teach him what's right. Sometimes, to dramatize your point, you may also need to use punishment.

♦   A CORRECTION stops your dog from doing something inappropriate and then helps him do the right thing.

♦   A PUNISHMENT is used to dramatize the leader's disapproval of a particular behavior and helps the dog remember the lesson.

To teach your dog to become an enjoyable companion it will sometimes be necessary to both correct and punish. Remember, punishment is NEVER to hurt or intimidate a dog; it is dramatic, not violent. Minimize punishment, help your dog learn with gentle and understandable corrections and reward all cooperation with praise.

CORRECTION

We correct a dog to help him understand and obey a command. For example, if you tell your dog "Fido SIT" and he just gazes off into space, you can help him understand the command by correcting him. Gently maneuver his body into the right position. You could help him go from standing to sitting, for example, by gently raising his chin and tucking under his hindquarters. The dog has now been shown the correct position... or "corrected." You should then <u>reward</u> him with praise for his cooperation, "Good SIT!"

In a training situation like this there is no need for punishment. Gently <u>correct</u> to help your dog understand the command. The same is true for teaching all new rules, whether potty-training, house-manners, or obedience commands. NEVER punish to teach a new concept! It would frighten your dog, diminish his trust and give him a terrible opinion of the new lesson. Instead, gently correct his body position to help him understand what you want, then reward him for cooperation. Gentle correction builds trust and is <u>far</u> more effective than force or intimidation.

PUNISHMENT

Let's suppose, though, that you are SURE your dog knows what you want him to do (or not to do). Perhaps you have already corrected him a number of times for some particular canine crime. Maybe you've caught him digging up your prize azaleas again and <u>again</u>. You've corrected him by assigning him an approved place to dig and filling all his old holes, but he stubbornly undoes all your good work. You're getting frustrated and even a little angry. How can you get your point across to Fido clearly and humanely? You may have to dramatize your message with "punishment."

NEVER punish your dog for
something he does not <u>know</u> is wrong.

What IS Punishment?

First of all, a punishment NEVER has to hurt the dog. In fact, it will be much more effective if it does <u>not</u> hurt or frighten. Painful or excessively scarey punishment causes a fear reaction. That reaction actually causes chemical changes in the dog's body and brain that, at least temporarily, make it impossible for him to think about anything but defense or escape.

An upset and frightened dog is so busy trying to get away or fight back that he is not learning how to please his leader. When the "fight-or-flight" mechanism is activated survival becomes the main goal. This allows little attention for anything else.

Puppies learn from their mothers and other "power figures" in the pack how much force is appropriate to use in a disciplinary action. Later, when the pup grows up, he will apply this same degree of severity to his own interactions with others. This will include four-legged and two-legged "others." If you use harsh punishments with your dog you will teach him, by your own example, to deal harshly with others. Setting that type of example would be a serious mistake.

Remember when you discipline your dog:
HE is learning from YOUR behavior.

Appropriate Punishment

Punishment is meant to be a dramatization of your displeasure at your dog's behavior. A mild dramatization, even a sharp glare, will suffice as punishment for some dogs. Others need more award-winning drama to convince them that you are "not amused."

In dog society there are standardized, almost ritualized, punishments. They are crystal-clear dramatizations of one dog's feelings about another's actions. Within the pack, except under unusual circumstances, punishment is dramatic but not damaging. Punches are pulled, so to speak. Outside intruders will meet with much rougher treatment when caught trespassing on another pack's turf. In those cases it is common for combatants to come away wounded... sometimes mortally. Physical punishment of intruders is completely different than the ritualized "dance" that occurs within the pack.

Within our own family "pack" it is better to use persuasive drama with our dogs than resort to harsher punishment. Our dogs instinctively know punishment is meant to be tempered within the family-pack. We need to get our point across without hurting or cowing our dogs. It's confusing and terrifying for a dog to be punished more harshly than a canine higher-up in his pack would do. Dogs understand a symbolic representation of punishment.

Violence simply does not help.

DOMINANCE & AGGRESSION

Packleader types, human or canine, are easy to spot. They have a certain inner confidence and matter-of-factness about their leadership position. If your dog considers himself dominant to you, you may not be very convincing in your display of packleader power. The following section is to help you better understand some of the communications dogs use with each other.

If your dog is still a puppy, or if he already thinks of you as his "Fearless Leader," you should be able to utilize the following "ritualized" dog communication methods to help your dog understand.

Overly Dominant Dogs

If your dog has been behaving aggressively toward you, your family members or friends, you should seek the help of a dog behavior specialist. Aggression can have a number of causes and each case must be treated differently. It can be dangerous to work with some types of aggression in dogs, so the support of a qualified professional is recommended. Ask your veterinarian or groomer to give you the name of a behavior specialist experienced in working with temperament problems.

If you have a dog who is actually dominant over you, you should not try to use even the following gentle, symbolic, Mamadog-like discipline techniques. If you are at all afraid of your dog, for whatever reason, you will convey that to him. If you compound the matter by trying unconvincingly to "show who's the boss" (when it's clearly him anyway) some dominant-type dogs may bite.

Dogs quite naturally feel justified in punishing an "underling" who acts "uppity." This situation sometimes presents itself quite unexpectedly, especially with "second hand" dogs whose history is not known. Bear this in mind when deciding how to discipline your dog.

Children and Doggie Discipline

Children should never attempt to "boss" or dominate a dog. This is doubly true if there are no adult "Authority Figures" around to referee. A disagreement between a dog and a small child over status hierarchy could lead to a dangerous confrontation. Parents or other adults, not children, should carry out any necessary correction or punishment with the family dog.

DON'T HIT THE DOG!

The controversies still rage: "Is it better to spank a dog with a rolled up newspaper or with your hand?" and "Is it better to hit his nose or his hindie?"

The answers to these questions are "Neither!" and "Neither!" Hitting a dog is not instructive, it's frightening. And it's counterproductive as well.

Spanking, slapping and swatting produces nippy, hand-shy dogs that seldom come when they're called. Hitting generates fear of the "master" rather than respect. Dogs do not instinctively understand hitting, because their species doesn't do it.

SO... DON'T HIT THE DOG!!!   OKAY?... OKAY!

Hit The Object!

Although you should NOT hit Fido, you CAN make a lasting impression on him if you hit the object involved in the crime. If you happen to find your fuzzy bedroom slipper "customized" by Little Fido's teethmarks again, what should you do? First, show the chewed slipper to him, then scold him and HIT THE SLIPPER, NOT THE DOG!

He will be awed by your behavior, but won't feel directly threatened or personally endangered by you. Your dog will not have to defend himself from you if you hit the object he chewed. He WILL be VERY glad not to have that awful, BAD, slipper-thing in his mouth, though. He will learn that he has no business stealing your slippers, but he will NOT fear you or your hand.

What Would Mama Do?

Dogs are both dramatic and physical with each other. Mama dogs and dominant pack members growl and nip to keep pups and other subordinates "in line" but they very seldom actually hurt them. Disapproval is conveyed through body posture, tension, facial expression and voice tones. Both instinct and early training by the mamadog prepare Little Fido to understand certain types of reprimands.

We can do a few things that remind a dog of how a superior pack member would discipline a pup or underling. We cannot, of course, become dogs, but we can follow some of their standardized patterns in our own human way. There are several punishments that may be used which are naturally understandable and reasonable for dogs.

Appropriate "punishment" should be a dramatization of your personal power as your dog's packleader. Drama is the key to a punishment's effectiveness. You'll want Fido to remember your display and to think about it the next time he feels that ol' criminal urge coming on.

Mamadogs and pack leaders use body language and vocalization to "maintain order in the ranks." Like the dam with her pups, the packleader must sometimes discipline "underlings" to preserve pack order. Although he may be more abrupt and stern with his discipline than Mama, a good packleader is able to uphold the "law" without injuring the other dogs. There is much more DRAMA to natural canine disciplinary actions than there is pain.

Physical Discipline

If you were to observe a bitch with her pups you could see her discipline them in several ways. She might simply stiffen and glare or growl at a naughty pup to remind him to behave properly. If Little Fido doesn't "shape up" right away, Mama might bite his muzzle lightly or nip him gently but firmly on the side of his face or neck. The bitch is dramatic with her pups but not abusive.

Contrary to popular myth, Mamadog does NOT pick up her puppy and shake him by the scruff of his neck! This would be an excessive punishment. Shaking the pup could injure him severely and would certainly terrify him. Mama dog doesn't need to do that. Neither does she grab her puppy and pin him to the ground, as some "experts" recommend. The dam can communicate much more subtly and clearly than that... and without compromising her pup's safety.

Mamadog merely tags the pup. She taps her naughty pup's nape or cheek quickly and lightly with her teeth, often vocalizing sharply as she does. To make a STRONG point, Mama might tap him two or three times with her open mouth, then firmly (but carefully) hold his head or muzzle in her strong jaws.

The dam doesn't need to hurt her pups or even use much physical force. Her dominance is expressed symbolically and convincingly through posture, gesture and tone. Mamadog is the established and accepted high-ranking packmember in all interactions with her pups. She rules with drama and dignity. Her pups respect, obey and adore her.

BITE MESSAGES

We humans can utilize some natural canine communication methods to teach our dogs how to please us. When we observe ways dogs express dominance we note that they don't normally need to be violent with subordinate dogs in their own pack. A quick tap-tap "bite" with an open mouth or a sudden hard stare is usually sufficient to arrest most disrespectful dog behavior. Very seldom is harsher punishment used by dogs within the pack and very seldom is it necessary for us to use in training them.

To simulate the drama that works so well for dogs, we humans can use voice tones and facial expressions to communicate our approval or disapproval. We can also "bite" a dog with our HANDS, as if they were dog mouths... tap-tap or quick-grab/freeze, similar to the way Fido's Mama would have done.

The Tap "Bite"

There are several "bite-messages" we can convey to a dog with our hands, allowing us to communicate with Fido in a way he can easily understand. The tap-tap "bite" is used for minor infractions and is the punishment most appropriate for puppies and sensitive dogs.

To do this "bite," curve and stiffen your fingers; try to imagine you're holding a steel grapefruit. Tap Fido with your stiff, curved fingers two or three times, briskly and abruptly on the side of his shoulder or neck. Just tap, do not grab. The tap tingles and gets the dog's attention but does not pinch or hurt.

The Freeze

Another gentle dramatic punishment is the "Freeze." Abruptly put your hands on the pup and hold him still for several seconds. Your hands should be flat and firm, holding him without squeezing his skin or frightening him, but firmly enough to keep a grip. Remain motionless for four or five seconds, then gently and gradually release your hold. If the dog squirms around while you hold him, wait to let him go until he's been still for four or five seconds.

When you let go, if your dog starts dancing around, he's trying to lighten your "bad mood" with play and frivolity. Ignore his antics. It's important NOT to accept his invitation to play at this point or he won't take you seriously. Also, do NOT attempt to catch hold of him as he bounds by. Instead, remain dignified and aloof; ignore his silliness and don't give him any energy until he calms down.

When he notices you aren't "playing" he may come over to see what you'll do. Calmly look at him, once he's "turned himself in" then tell him to "Sit" (if he already knows this command). Praise him in a low-key way when he responds.

If he does not sit, simply gaze off into space and ignore him. You may be surprised when he DOES come over and sit by you in a few moments... just to get you to look at him again. If he does this, calmly praise him, "Good Sit."

Scruffs & Stares

As a more severe punishment, give the loose "scruff" skin at the nape or side of Fido's neck a quick grab or a firm but gentle shake (just his skin, NOT the whole dog).

For an even sterner message, hold the dog's cheek skin (which is stretchy) on both sides of his face and glare into his eyes for three to five seconds with a serious expression.

Caution: Physical punishments such as these which involve holding the dog still, a hard stare or a shake of the scruff skin are serious discipline. This is especially true for pups and sensitive dogs. Be very careful not to overdo it or a dog may fear or resent your touch. Watch your dog's reaction, each dog is a unique individual. What works well for one dog may be too much or too little for another.

Growling

Dogs growl as part of their natural vocal communication. Growling is usually a signal to stop, a warning or threat of impending attack. If your dog growls at you it could mean several things. It could denote fear or anxiety in some dogs. A growl can be a request or a threat. Some dog trainers suggest that people use this form of communication to discipline their dogs. This is not a wise practice. There is too great a potential for mistaking the precise tone needed to convey an intended message.

It's difficult for most humans to accurately simulate the exact tone of growl a canine would use to discipline a subordinate. A wrong "pronunciation" may elicit playfulness or even aggression from a dog instead of respectful submission. It's usually wisest to leave the growling to "native speakers" of dog language.

Instead of trying to growl like dogs, we can use words. Disapproval is convincingly shown by speaking in a low monotone through clenched teeth. Nearly any words uttered that way have a convincing "growl" to them. Try saying "Please pass the butter" aloud through clenched teeth in a monotone and notice how serious it sounds. If your discipline words have this type of dramatic sound to them most dogs will really pay attention.

Temporary Banishment

Another natural form of discipline is temporary banishment from the pack's activities. Dogs are extremely social animals and do not like to be excluded from their group. A brief Time-Out for naughty Fido, away from the rest of the family, can be quite effective.

Put the dog into his crate or confine him to the backyard where he cannot see family activities for about fifteen minutes. If Fido barks or carries on while in banishment, do not bring him back into the activity area until he has been quiet for five minutes.

Don't leave your dog in Time-Out for too long, or he'll forget the reason for his banishment. Ten or fifteen minutes is normally enough. Time-Out also allows you space to cool off if your dog's latest escapade was anger-provoking for you.

Be sure the place you select for Fido's Time-Outs is safe and has proper shade and shelter. Your dog will be punished enough just being

sent to his "room," you needn't send him to a desert island. Deprivation of social acceptance is the point of banishment. It is neither necessary nor fair to cause the dog physical misery as well.

As with any punishment, banishment should not be over-used. A dog will not make the connection between his "crime" and the punishment if you make it too extreme. Be rational and fair. NEVER punish your dog to indulge your own anger. A good packleader is a fair packleader.

Intensity and Duration of Punishment

Punishments should be brief and dramatic. They should vary in intensity to match the individual dog's temperament and the seriousness of the crime. A tap on the side of the neck with your fingers is a mild punishment, very mild, but quite effective for sensitive dogs. Tougher-minded dogs or "repeat offenders" might require more to get their attention. "Serious" crimes such as running out into traffic or harassing livestock have potentially lethal consequences. These crimes could merit a firm skin shake or double-handed "grab-and-freeze" AND a fierce dominant stare. As always, pay attention to your dog's response and modify the drama to make it right for that individual and situation.

Harsh force is not necessary if drama is properly used. If you run into trouble with a dog or pup over-reacting to punishment, you may have gone too far. Over-reaction is often expressed as fear or aggression. Use good sense and avoid roughness, there's no need to go overboard, dogs are normally pretty sensitive. Gentle but dramatic displays of leader-power are readily understood by most dogs.

Punishment, properly applied, is dramatic but NOT painful. Its purpose is to remind Fido of your rightful position as pack leader. This, when done justly, is reassuring to your dog... NOT frightening.

A "Second Chance"

After any punishment a dog needs a short period to absorb the message. Then help him do what he was supposed to have been doing ("correct" him) and praise his cooperation. After that, he will need a way to start over again "on the right foot" with you.

Always offer your dog an opportunity to get back into your good graces after a dramatic scene. Wait a moment or two after your dramatization, then give your dog a command he knows and can easily obey. ("SIT" is a good one for this purpose.) Praise him for his obedience to that command. Your dog will appreciate this chance to please you and renew his place in your pack.

DON'T apologize to your dog for having punished him He'd become confused and wouldn't take the discipline seriously. He might even think he could just "wind you around his little finger." (If he actually <u>can</u>, don't let him know!)

CORRECTION & PUNISHMENT "RULES"

◆ ALWAYS REWARD Fido's cooperation and obedience with praise and petting, even if you had to help him get it right!

◆ Follow every "crime" (whether it's chewing on shoes or not coming when called) and every "punishment" (even banishment) with a "correction." <u>Correct</u> your dog by helping him to do what he's been told. This is how your dog will learn what you want him to do. Give him a chance to do the RIGHT thing by helping him fix his mistakes.

◆ NEVER over-punish your dog! When you DO need to use "punishment" to dramatize a correction be sure to keep it clear and appropriate to the "crime."

◆ NEVER take out your own anger or frustration on Fido!

Care and Kindness
Use "punishments" kindly, carefully and rationally to help TEACH.

Use drama, not pain and fear, and BE SURE to watch your dog's response so you don't overwhelm him.

Some dogs have been harshly over-punished by someone in their past. This often makes a dog afraid of anything that reminds him of those earlier experiences. You will need to be especially careful not to overwhelm these dogs with excessively heavy drama. Modify your actions to the individual dog and the individual situation.

♦ **Important Caution:** YOUNG CHILDREN SHOULD NEVER physically punish a dog. Most dogs, even puppies, consider children peers or underlings, NOT "Authority Figures." A dog may be "offended" by a child's attempt to assert physical power over him and may "punish" the youngster by biting. This is especially true when no adult is present.

Only adults and some older children should dramatize their authority over the family dog. Disciplinary measures should be used only by those "pack-members" who actually wield GREATER power of authority than the dog himself. If a dog acts aggressively toward any members of the family, the services of a professional behavior consultant or trainer should be obtained.

When Is A Crime NOT A Crime?

Not every misbehavior is intentional! Sometimes Fido will simply make mistakes or misunderstand your commands. You should gently CORRECT his behavior when that happens, so he can learn. However, you should NEVER PUNISH your dog for an "honest" mistake. That seems pretty obvious, but it's not always clear whether an incident was deliberate or accidental. Examine all the evidence, not just the first pieces you see when you walk in the door. We've probably all heard or known of cases where the wrong "criminal" received the punishment.

Dogs love to please, so try to be patient and understanding with your dog as he learns HOW. Give him the benefit of the doubt. Be clear and consistent with corrections, fair and dramatic with punishments and generous with timely praise. Your dog will learn rapidly and will be happy to obey you... once he understands how.

Chapter 8

RAISING A PROPER PUPPY

Sometime in January, when the holiday hubbub has subsided, folks suddenly realize that the darling "Christmas Puppy" has grown into a rather different animal. They marvel at the pup's increased size and energy level. Just the other day they'd sat beaming fondly at the sweet little fella as he lay dreaming in that adorable (expensive) wicker basket-bed. Now the basket lies shredded and splintered as the pup (barking in gleeful defiance) cavorts on the half-devoured remains of his master's favorite easy chair.

What has happened? It seems impossible! How could that cute little fluffball have become transformed into this needletoothed terror with such flagrant disregard for private property? Babydog is growing up!

Puppies grow rapidly and go through many developmental changes as the early weeks go by. During their first year of life puppies mature from infants into adolescents. Each month of Little Fido's first year is roughly equivalent to one year in a human child's development.

When a puppy is one month of age he still nurses and isn't very mobile yet. By two months of age he's weaned, walking well, and ready for potty training (as is a two year old child). At age four years a human child begins to assert some independence from mother; at age four months a puppy begins to explore farther from the porch and yard. At eight or nine months a pup may try out some fairly rebellious behaviors, testing his own power and self-efficacy, just as an eight or nine year old child might.

At about one year of age a puppy enters his "teens," which (thankfully!) only lasts for about six or seven months instead of six or seven YEARS as in humans. By eighteen months of age your "puppy" is nearly an adult and will be expecting "voting rights" soon. He may even be hoping for a leadership position in your pack. The dog's most rapid growth period is finished by that time and his "personality" (temperament) and "self-image" (dominance rank) are well established.

Early Puppyhood Education

Many people put off training Little Fido until he is six or eight months of age. This delay is unwise for two important reasons. Not only does it permit the formation of bad habits, it wastes the early, ultra-cooperative, rapid-learning period. Improper behaviors formed during this period will be difficult to correct later on.

A dog learns most quickly from birth to about age five months, so it's best to start your puppy's education as early as possible. Gently and persistently teach Little Fido your rules. He wants to know what pleases you because he desires acceptance in your

pack. Many lessons, for better or for worse, will be learned by your puppy between the ages of five weeks and five months. The earlier you start guiding him into approved behaviors, the easier he will be to train.

During Little Fido's first five months he will learn much of what he'll need to know for social success with other dogs and with people. The rules he learns while young will be the ones that guide his interactive behavior for the rest of his life. The curriculum for "Early Puppyhood Education" includes understanding of dominance and submission, feeding rules, territory and boundaries, good sportsman-ship, communication, and personal hygiene. This is information every dog needs to succeed in the world.

The young puppy is naturally eager to explore and discover. We can utilize this early period to teach him some important rules and tips about enjoying life with people.

POTTY TRAINING

Puppies take their first lessons from the Mamadog. She teaches them what constitutes proper canine cleanliness. The dam licks her pups to bathe them as soon as they're born and then at frequent intervals after that. Her insistent yet gentle touch is vital to the pups. In fact, if not cleaned and stimulated by the mother's licking an infant puppy will be unable to urinate or defecate and will sicken and die.

A good dam licks her pups spotlessly clean of food and debris. She maintains sanitation in the nursery in the same manner, so there is no buildup of feces or urine around her little pups. The smell of "potty" is not there, so the puppies learn that their sleeping area is not a "potty place."

When the pups are a few weeks old they begin to follow their dam around. She may take them several steps away from the den and then urinate. This marks the edge of the "family territory" and by smell and by example gives the puppies an indication of where they're supposed to potty.

Once the pups have been weaned to solid food their dam no longer cleans up their body wastes. The dam's owner (the "breeder") must then take over housekeeping chores to maintain sanitation in the puppy area. By that time, however, the pups have become accustomed to toddling away from the sleeping nest to do their potties. Seldom will a weaned and healthy puppy soil his own bed.

A puppy comes to his new family with a few clues about potty rules already, if his dam and the breeder have done their jobs. Little Fido knows not to "mess" in the sleeping and eating areas. He may not understand at first that you'll expect him to go all the way out to the distant backyard to go potty. It's not uncommon for a young puppy to seek a potty place just beyond the main activity area of the home. If you spend a lot of time in the kitchen, for example, Little Fido might figure that the livingroom is the "indoor backyard" and far enough away to use as a potty place. Be patient... he's TRYING to be "clean." At first he may just underestimate the size of your territory. He'll need your help to understand the finer points of good potty behavior.

Your new puppy's age is an important consideration when potty-training him. Puppies younger than ten weeks of age don't get much advance warning from their body's plumbing system and may not make it to the door before they have an "accident." It's pointless and cruel to punish a young puppy for a potty accident. It's really up to you to anticipate his needs and help him learn where to "go." Success in potty-training, especially with a young puppy, is highly dependent upon the vigilance and patience of the humans in the household.

Observe your puppy and note his normal daily potty cycle. BE READY for your pup at those times and MAKE IT EASY FOR HIM TO PLEASE YOU. Most puppies' potty times are dictated by their eating and drinking schedules. It takes a certain amount of time for Little Fido's dogfood to travel through the length of his digestive system, then... what went in must come out.

A Regular Schedule Makes Potty Training Easier

Puppies fed by the free-choice "help-yourself" method usually eat and drink at irregular intervals. This can make it hard for you to anticipate the timing of Little Fido's potty needs because those functions will occur at irregular intervals also. If you experience this problem with housetraining, try feeding your puppy at scheduled times. The same holds true if you're attempting to housebreak a recently adopted mature dog.

Put your pup's food bowl down for him for only twenty to thirty minutes at each meal. Let him eat what he wants in that time, then take the food away until the next mealtime rolls around. Puppies from two to five months of age should be fed three or four times a day. Older pups and adult dogs do well with two meals per day. Pups accustomed to free-choice feeding may take a few days to adapt to the new schedule. They'll soon learn to eat the food when you give it to them. See if this helps your little buddy develop a predictable rhythm for his pottying times.

Be consistent! Be prepared! Know your puppy's habits and patterns. Young pups usually need to potty right after: 1) Eating, 2)Drinking, 3) Playing, and 4)Waking up.

Also, any time you happen to notice Little Fido walking in a circle while sniffing the floor, or dashing back and forth with a worried look, leaving the room with a backward glance over his shoulder, tippy-toeing off behind a piece of furniture, or actually starting to squat...TAKE HIM IMMEDIATELY TO THE "POTTYING GROUNDS!"

Tell Your Puppy Where To Go...

A puppy from eight to sixteen weeks of age catches on quite readily to potty training. Your job is to make it easy for him to get outside when he needs to. Watchfulness and consistency on your part will have an excellent effect on your puppy. He'll learn that he can rely on you to let him out for potty and praise him for a job well done. He may even start to come to you and whine when he needs to relieve himself, or go to the door and sniff or scratch. If you see him do this, praise him and take him outside. "Good Fido... let's GO OUT, GO POTTY." Take him out to the potty place and wait for him to "go" then praise him. "Good POTTY Fido!"

It would be helpful to leave one or two of Little Fido's "poops" in the area you WANT him to potty, to indicate the right spot to "go." The approved potty area should be cleaned DAILY, except for the "re-minder poop," or your puppy may decide to find a less "yucky" place to relieve himself. Most dogs dislike having to soil their feet with poop and really appreciate a well-maintained potty yard. (Note: a good commercial poop scoop makes the job easier and less odious than the old shovel-and-hoe method.)

... And When!

By telling your puppy to "GO POTTY" and then praising him "Gooooood POTTY" when he goes, you will be teaching him a command. Yes, your dog CAN learn to do his business ON COM-MAND! This is very handy at times, as you can easily imagine. You'll actually be able to stop at a rest area, point to a likely spot, tell Fido to potty there... and he WILL. (Amaze your friends!)

What To Do

When it's time for potty, ask your pup "Want to GO OUT? Want to GO POTTY?... Let's GO OUT, GO POTTY." Call him or carry him to the door, then take him out right away. Take him to the area you've chosen for him to use and tell him "GO POTTY, Fido." Don't stare at him, just be casual. Some dogs prefer a little privacy: turn your back.

The best progress will be made if you go outside with your pup and wait there with him until he goes potty. That way you'll be able to "catch him in the act" of doing the RIGHT thing. This method of potty training sometimes requires a raincoat and a flashlight, but it's the surest and quickest way to get the correct idea across to your pup.

The BORING WALK

A problem might arise if your puppy goes outside for potty and forgets what he went out there for... so he starts to play and explore the yard. If this happens, you can remind Little Fido what he's supposed to be doing by repeating the command "GO POTTY" when he gets sidetracked.

Limit your pup's potty outings to a certain area of the yard. Long walks around the block or romps in the park are often too stimulating for a puppy to "remember" to potty. A dog can get so involved in the myriad of scents, sights, and sounds that he becomes too distracted to think about potty until he's back inside the house. The Boring Walk is very useful to keep the dog's mind on his "business."

How To Do The "BORING WALK"

First of all, don't do anything that might "jazz up" your puppy once he's in the potty area. WALK with him to a likely spot then STOP. STAND STILL. Give Little Fido a low-key command to "GO POTTY." Allow him to sniff around and find a good spot. If he starts to play instead, just mill around a bit to redirect his interest away from the distractions he finds. Take a SLOW step to the side... or backwards... then STOP. You could, perhaps, turn your back to the pup and take a small step sideways. Relax and act as if you're staying there and have all the time in the world. Showing impatience at this point would excite your puppy and NOT speed up his potty process at all.

Move slowly and DON'T give your pup the impression that you are going anywhere. If you move fast or frequently, Little Fido will interpret your activity as an invitation to play rather than a reminder to sniff and potty. Occasionally repeat the command "GO POTTY" in a calm and bored-sounding voice. Don't fidget, BE BORING... that's the idea. Then the most interesting thing for your puppy will be his own urge to potty. Praise him calmly when he does "go."

Be Sure He's Finished!

Some puppies need to potty several times before they're done. Make a mental note of your pup's potty "pattern" and be sure to give him all the time he needs. A potty outing should take exactly as long as it takes... but a dog in good health who delays more than ten minutes may be stalling.

When he "does his duty" praise him SOOTHINGLY, "Goooooooood Potty." Keep this praise low-key or Little Fido may get so happy and excited from your enthusiasm that his muscles will tense up. He'll stop piddling in mid-stream, only to finish his business after he's gone back into the house... OOPS!

If your pup is one who has some trouble with potty training, continue to keep an eye on him for a short while after he comes back inside. If he "forgot" to do something he will probably "remember" within five minutes of returning indoors. If he looks restless or anxious, take him back out for another few minutes chance to finish up.

DON'T PUNISH YOUR PUPPY... TEACH HIM!

It's best if an "accident" is still in progress when you discover it. However, if it's still fairly "fresh" your pup WILL remember having gone potty there if you point it out to him. A dog can recognize his own distinctive scent where he has gone potty.

If Little Fido does have an "accident" on the floor, ask yourself what clues he gave that you might have missed. Or maybe you forgot to take him out after the four important times: wake-up, feeding, drinking, or playtime? If this is possibly the cause, the solution is simple: next time try to be more in tune with your pup. He needs your help to make this project work.

Meanwhile, get some paper towels to collect the mess, then go pick up your pup if he's small enough to carry (otherwise use a leash) and take him to the "accident" site. Point to the spot and in a stern voice tell the pup "NO, NO... BAD POTTY!" You don't need to yell, just speak firmly.

Show him the mistake up close, but DON'T SPANK HIM and NEVER NEVER NEVER put his nose in the mess. (He wouldn't understand why you did it, and it WON'T teach him that you value cleanliness.) Then take the pup AND the "evidence" to the approved potty area, set the "accident" (soaked up or picked up in the paper towel) on the ground. Don't leave the paper towel in the potty area, dispose of it. Just drop the poops in the "good potty" place or smear the pee on the ground to leave the scent. Then tell Fido, in a pleasant voice, "GOOD POTTY OUTSIDE." If he sniffs at the potty you put there, praise him again in a friendly tone.

Your puppy might not have any more potty left to do, since he just emptied out on your floor, but stay outside with him for a few minutes anyway, just in case he "goes" again. If he does, praise him lavishly, "Gooooood Potty Outside!" After that you can both go back indoors, if you like.

Helping Your Puppy Tell You When

Many puppies can't seem to figure out how to let someone know when they have to go potty. They stand by the door, staring hopefully at the door knob. If nobody happens to notice them in time they just potty on the floor by the door. These "accidents" may frustrate or possibly anger the humans in the household. Some people might wonder if Little Fido messed on the floor to be spiteful. They don't realize the pup had been standing by the door for five minutes, staring helplessly at the unmoving doorknob... waiting and hoping, silent and desperate.

The problem boils down to Little Fido's inability to communicate his needs to his human family. There is something you can do to help him solve this dilemma. Teach him to ring the doorbell!

The "Magic Door Bell"

Hang a small bell (not TOO tiny, you'll need to hear it) by a cord from the doorknob at puppynose level. The door should be the same one that leads to the pottying grounds. Ring the bell each time you open the door to take your puppy outside for potty. He will learn to associate the bell ringing with the door opening.

Your pup will probably try to ring this "door bell" on his own in about a week or so if you encourage him by ringing it yourself every time you take him out to potty. He'll deduce that the "magic bell" makes the door open. Be LISTENING for that bell! The first time Little Fido rings it on his own you can appear INSTANTLY to take him outside to relieve himself. The bell is a handy signal for Fido to communicate his potty needs to you, and is neither as noisy as barking nor as destructive as scratching on the door.

Some clever pups, after learning to operate the magic door-bell, decide to ring it just to get attention or to go play outside. This is NOT what the bell is for. If your dog rings the bell just for fun, you'll need to help him realize he is to use it for potty outings only.

If you suspect the bell is being used to send false alarms, respond as is it was a true potty call. Go outside to the potty place with your puppy and give him a chance to "go." Do the Boring Walk if necessary. If he potties, praise him. If he only wants to play around, take him back inside after a few minutes of the Boring Walk. Watch him carefully for awhile, just in case he remembers that he DID need to "go" after all. If you do this a few times your pup should quit misusing the door-bell to send false alarms.

Keep Potty Time Just For Potty!

While it is very important to praise your puppy for successful pottying, it is a mistake to engage in exciting play with him during potty sessions. If you turn potty time into game time your pup may forget to "do his business" in his eagerness for play. Little Fido may then go back indoors after an unproductive potty/play session and blithely urinate on the kitchen floor. A puppy doesn't do this to be ornery, but he may get sidetracked and forget what he went outside for. Back inside the nice warm house he suddenly remembers... OOPS! To avoid this problem and the frustration it causes, keep potty sessions FOR POTTY ONLY until your puppy is <u>well</u> <u>housebroken</u>.

Some people think they should reward their pup with a food treat for pottying in the approved area. It is not necessary to do that and can be counterproductive. The relief the pup feels after emptying out is a physical reward in itself. When you praise him, "Good Potty!" that is a psychological reward. Fido really doesn't need a cookie too. Also, he may be overly eager for the yummy and, forgetting to finish his business, rush inside to claim his reward tidbit and end up peeing on the floor. Don't bother with a food reward for pottying.

Indoor Paper Training

Some people prefer to train their puppies to potty outdoors right away. Others might decide (because of horrible weather or some other reason) to start their pups out on potty papers indoors and later switch to outdoors. Still other families choose to have their dogs potty indoors on papers on a permanent basis. This decision is an individual one, a puppy can learn whichever spot you choose for his potty area.

If you prefer to indoor-train your pup to potty on newspapers or a piddlepad, you can follow the same basic procedures as for outdoor potty-training. Carry Little Fido to the papers, gently set him down there, and tell him nicely to "GO POTTY." Praise him when he does his potty in the approved place.

If you leave your pup in a safe "playpen" area at night or while you are away, be sure to place his newspaper potty-pad as far away as possible from his food, water and bed. It's unfair to force a puppy to eat and sleep right next to his "toilet" area.

Sometimes paper-trained pups miss the right spot by a few inches or more. This is usually an honest mistake. Little Fido's FRONT paws could have been on the papers, but his hind paws were not... so the puddle missed its mark. Try to be understanding about this. It may be necessary to expand the target area of papers until your puppy develops a better aim.

LEAVING YOUR PUP BY HIMSELF

A puppy's natural energy and curiosity can get him into a heap of trouble when there are no chaperones around. It's sensible to restrict your pup to a safe and easily cleaned area of your home when you are unable to watch him.

Part of the kitchen, walled off with a baby gate, makes a good "playpen" for Little Fido. It's a spot where he can be safe and secure when alone yet well-socialized when the family is home. You must NOT expect your pup to keep that area clean and tidy, though! You CAN expect him to use a corner or more of the playpen for his potty if he's there when nature calls. He can't help it if you're not there to let him outside in time! Accept that fact and put a thick pad of newspapers in one corner of his area. Put a little smear of puppy pee on the papers so Little Fido will get the hint when he needs to potty.

ISOLATION PROBLEMS

Be careful not to leave your puppy alone in his playpen too much of the time. He needs your company and attention to learn proper conduct, including house manners and potty behavior. If you abandon your puppy in his playpen for much of the day and all of the night, he will be forced to educate himself... and, obviously, he wouldn't amount to much that way.

The limiting size of the playpen is hard on a growing pup with overflowing energy. His need to exercise may result in overactive behavior when he's turned loose again. You can solve this problem by making sure that the little fellow gets plenty of supervised exercise outside the playpen several times each day.

The main problem that can arise with overuse of the playpen is the strain of isolation. Dogs are very sociable creatures. A lack of sufficient time with people takes its toll on a puppy or mature dog. While it's true your pup does need to learn to spend time by himself, too much time alone will prevent proper development. Confinement alone for long periods every day, whether in an indoor playpen or an outdoor yard, will create loneliness, boredom, and frustration.

Isolated dogs develop neurotic patterns. Among these are destructive chewing, digging, poor potty habits, and excessive barking.

Those habits result in thousands of dogs each month being abandoned or relinquished to animal shelters. The exasperated owners, not realizing they've <u>caused</u> their pet's predicament by isolation, most often blame these problems on the poor dog. The lonely dog is just expressing how anxious and miserable and isolated he feels. Don't let this happen to YOUR dog!

Double Trouble

Adopting two puppies at once so they can keep each other company while you're away may seem like a good idea, but it can easily backfire. TWO isolated, untutored, unsocialized pups-in-a-pen are at <u>least</u> twice as destructive as one and more than twice as much trouble to housetrain. Two pups, often littermates, become a pack on their own and may not bond as strongly to you as to each other.

If you really want two dogs, first get ONE. Train him well, THEN get the second puppy. Dogs learn a lot by imitating other pack members. When your first pup knows the ropes he'll be able to HELP you train the second one. They'll both be easier to manage and train that way and will make better companions for each other and for you.

Crate-Den May Help With Potty-Training

A useful tool for housetraining is the dog crate or "shipping kennel." A crate enables you to teach your pup to "hold it" for a gradually increasing time and to "go" immediately when you take him to his potty spot. Your dog will become quite comfortable in his cozy private "den" once he gets used to it. It's comfortable and represents safety and privacy to a dog.

Like the playpen, a crate-den will keep Fido safe when left alone. Unlike the playpen, however, the crate should NOT have a potty area in it. A dog cannot stay in a crate as long as in a playpen which includes a potty area. Refer to "The Den & The Dog" chapter for crate training suggestions and directions for the proper use of this helpful tool. Again, don't abandon your pup too long at a time in his den or he'll develop problems.

Housebreaking The More Mature Dog

If you adopt an older puppy or an adult dog who has not yet been potty trained, you will have to teach him what he needs to know. The same routine suggested for younger puppies will be helpful. You'll need to be watchful and consistent to housetrain a mature dog, just as you would with a puppy, until he learns the rules. There's a bit less urgency than with a young pup, because the older dog can normally "hold it" longer. Consistency and praise for a good job will help your dog to quickly understand what you expect of him.

SPECIAL PROBLEMS WITH POTTY

Normally potty training should go smoothly if your pup is healthy and you are vigilant and consistent. There are a few problems that can make potty training more difficult with some dogs. If you do run into problems, remember that most any behavior has a logical cause and a logical cure. Some potty problems may require medical treatment by a veterinarian, some may respond to behavioral intervention by an experienced trainer, still others may simply require more time and understanding. Special problems with potty are usually solvable, although they do demand an extra measure of patience.

If your dog or puppy is slow to housetrain, look for a logical cause. Don't jump to the conclusion that your pup is trying to "spite" you. Dogs are not spiteful by nature and rarely use potty to "punish" their people. Sometimes the dog's health may be the root cause for a potty problem. The dog's background with previous owners may also have something to do with troublesome potty behaviors.

Lack of Control for Health Reasons

Physical problems can make a dog unable to control his urine or feces. If you follow the potty training methods described in this book for more than two weeks without seeing definite improvement, there is reason to suspect that there may be an undetected health problem.

Several health problems which are curable in their early stages can do permanent damage if left untreated. Infections and parasites commonly cause problems which show up first in the dog's potty behavior. If it seems at all possible that your dog could have a health-related potty problem, take him IMMEDIATELY to your veterinarian. She'll examine your dog and run the necessary tests to detect or rule out physical abnormality. The doctor may want to you to bring a sample of the dog's stool to check for parasites. When you call to schedule Fido's appointment be sure to ask what items or information you should bring to the clinic with you. By staying alert to changes in your dog's physical condition you can greatly aid your veterinarian in her quest to keep Fido healthy.

Urination as a "Greeting"

Some puppies (and some adult dogs too) have a problem with bladder control when they're over-excited or just glad to see you. This behavior stems from a natural submissive gesture. In canine society it's common and proper for a young or subordinate member of the pack to greet a dominant member by submissively crouching and urinating. The puppy greets his beloved leader by rushing up to him and piddling

at his feet. To a high-ranking dog this would be a well accepted token
of respect, but when it happens to us in our livingroom the gesture is
seldom properly appreciated. If your dog is one that greets you in this
manner there are several things you can do that may help.

First of all, even if you are shocked, frustrated or angry with this
situation, DO NOT raise your voice or punish the dog. Seeing your
disapproval for his well-meant greeting will only give your dog a
further reason to piddle submissively. Fido is not doing this wet
"hello" to annoy you; he actually intends to please you by demonstrat-
ing his great respect for your authority. So you see, if you become
MORE authoritarian by scolding the Little Piddler, he can only
respond MORE submissively by peeing again. The problem just gets
worse when disciplinary measures are taken.

An excellent way around this leakage problem is to greet the dog
OUTDOORS, when possible. If he's already outside when you get
home, greet him calmly and warmly and just ignore the puddle. If he's
indoors awaiting your return, open the door and call him outside for the
greeting before you go in. The outdoor greeting will help eliminate
your frustration at the annoying job of mopping up the "hello" puddle.

Be matter-of-fact and pleasant when greeting a submissive piddler.
DO NOT bend over to pat the pup as you say hello, that's a dominant
posture in dog body language and will elicit a submissive (and piddly)
response. Instead of bending or crouching, walk around as you greet
the pup. That will help keep the energy neutral and won't encourage
your dog to urinate submissively.

While you're at it, you can combine this low-key greeting with
some effective potty training. As your pup runs to you to welcome you
home, say "Hi Fido! Good Puppy. COME, GO POTTY!" as you pat
your leg and start to walk away from the dog. Stop when you get to the
pottying grounds, and praise him if he relieves himself there. Once
Fido's bladder is empty and you've been properly greeted, the pup can
go inside with you.

Another helpful training hint is to teach Fido to COME and
SIT on command. This is not difficult and it's fun and self-
esteem building for the pup. When your pup is SITTING on
command, confidently anticipating the reward (food tidbits are
good for this), he won't be trying to impress you with a display
of wet submission. He'll be proud of himself for obeying the
COME and SIT commands. The improved self-esteem and
confidencewill reduce your puppy's need to show postural

submission.

As the pup matures and becomes more confident in his relationship to you, the submissive-urination greeting problem usually is resolved. Be patient in the meantime and try to be understanding. Remember the reason Fido pees at your feet is because he thinks you're so awesome. Try to take it as a compliment.

DOGGIEDOO DO's & DON'Ts

♦ DO HELP your puppy get to the approved place in time.

♦ DO PRAISE your pup for potty in the right potty-place, whenever you see it happen.

♦ DON'T HIT YOUR PUPPY! He'd begin to fear and distrust you at just the time he should be learning to trust and follow your leadership.

♦ DON'T RUB HIS NOSE IN POTTY! He'd learn to be UNCLEAN by that example, and might even learn to HIDE his potty behind your couch in the future.

♦ Give your little buddy a break; help him out, allow him time to learn and develop. Be clear and consistent. Your patience will soon be rewarded by a "clean" puppy.

CHEWING

Puppies explore the world with their noses and mouths. It's natural for any curious pup to taste all new objects and substances... sometimes with disastrous results.

Puppies go through several teething stages during their first year of life: first when their puppy teeth are loosening to fall out, next as the big new teeth are erupting through their gums, and finally as they work to strengthen their jaw muscles when the permanent set of teeth is complete. These teething stages follow one another without much of a break from age four months to ten months, so it may seem like one long continuous chewfest. Don't despair! Really, Little Fido CAN learn to control his teething urge if you help him to choose some appropriate chew items.

But Why'd He Chew THAT?

A well-loved pup quickly learns to associate his master's scent with kindness, comfort, and security. This is as it should be, but problems may arise when Little Fido is left alone. A puppy may get lonely, bored, or frightened when his master is away. The scent of the beloved human is very comforting to a pup at a time like that, even though the scent may be only that faint whiff which still clings to the binding of the master's library book. First a good sniff... then a little taste too... pretty soon Little Fido is in much deeper than he ought to have gone. It takes no time at all for a puppy's needle-sharp milkteeth to cause irreparable damage to a library book.

This type of incident often leads to misunderstanding and frustration on both sides of the pet/person relationship. What may SEEM to be willful and wanton destruction could actually have been motivated by Little Fido's innocent ADORATION for you! Keeping that in mind can help puppy owners stay rational when they happen upon the aftermath of Hurricane Fido.

This is not to imply you should resignedly do nothing about indiscreet chewing. It's just to help you keep the whole situation in perspective. You'll need to teach your pup what he may and may not chew. He will make mistakes from time to time. If you're patient, consistent, and watchful, your babydog WILL get the right idea.

Puppies have a peculiar penchant for chewing ANYTHING THAT STICKS OUT OR HANGS DOWN. That includes, but is by no means limited to: tablecloths, stair corners, bathrobe hems, edges of carpets, electrical cords, and kittycats' tails. It is up to us to protect our young dogs from their own natural inquisitiveness. We must provide them with appropriate chew toys and prevent access to tempting but

dangerous items. It is also our responsibility to protect our furnishings and precious belongings from a teething puppy. Consider packing up your fine lace tablecloth and putting your favorite sandals away in the closet for the duration of Little Fido's teething months.

Puppy Toys

Your puppy should have about three or four toys. One toy usually is not enough, but more than three or four may confuse Little Fido and give him the wrong impression. It seems that dogs can "count" to three pretty well, but if they have more than three or four toys at a time many puppies think EVERYTHING is a puppytoy. It's as if dogs counted this way... "1, 2, 3, Infinity." If your puppy has a whole pile of toys, put most of them away and give them to him three at a time. You could give him a new toy about once a month if he seems able to keep track of "what's his" and "what's yours." Having too many toys is NOT more amusing for your puppy... it's more confusing.

The best toys are those chosen with both pleasure and safety in mind. A ball too large to swallow, a squeeze-toy with a non-removable built-in squeaker, a flexible nylon "bone," a knotted piece of thick rope about two feet in length... all make good puppytoys. NO OLD SHOES PLEASE! Puppies can't reliably tell which shoes are your old trashers and which are your new treasures. Try to avoid giving your pup a toy too similar to items he's not permitted to chew. For example, if you have a young child in your family there will very likely be plastic squeeze-toys that are Junior's only... NOT for Fido. Be sure your puppy's toys are easy to distinguish from Junior's.

Dealing With A Little Bandit

When you DO happen upon Little Fido gnawing away at something he shouldn't have, take it away from him. It would be a good idea (right now, BEFORE you have a problem) to turn to the "Fun & Games" chapter and read how to teach your dog to play "Thank-You/Take-It." That game will help a lot when you need to reclaim your belongings from Fido's sharp little teeth.

**NEVER ALLOW YOUR PUPPY
TO KEEP SOMETHING AS A TOY
HE "STOLE" TO BEGIN WITH!**

This is <u>VERY</u> important, and many people make this mistake. When your puppy takes something that is not his, don't let him keep it, even if he has ruined the item for its original purpose. If you give

it to him you'll be rewarding a young outlaw for taking what he wants -- when he wants it. Very risky business indeed!

Helpful Theatrics

If your puppy chews some particular item repeatedly, even after you've corrected him and helped him find a proper puppytoy, it's time for you to "make a scene." Squint your eyes and clench your teeth to give yourself the proper dramatic expression. You may find that it's not necessary to PRETEND anger, you might be pretty upset with your pup already. This drama will help you release some of your own real feelings of frustration in a positive way. Your puppy learns a memorable lesson without you hitting or hurting him. Everyone comes out a winner this way.

So, be DRAMATIC! It won't work to just "pretend"... you must really "ACT!" Feel the part... get INTO it! Your pup would EXPECT a dramatic power display from a trespassed-upon CANINE superior, so YOUR display of "rightful ownership" will be quite understandable to him.

If you play your part in this scene with gusto you'll really capture your pup's attention. However, if you are NOT believable this lesson will not work and MAY even BACKFIRE. If you are wishy-washy, Little Fido will think it's just a funny game and will try to play with you and the taboo item. Pay attention to your dog's reaction. You'll be able to tell whether your "audience" is impressed with your performance.

Now For The "Script"

Do all this with your eyes squinted and teeth clenched. Keep your voice low rather than high, it will sound more dramatic. You don't need to be loud either, a voice that's more of a growl than a scream carries greater power.

After you take a forbidden object away from the dog, hold the item close to your chest and "own" it. If the object is too large to do that, just grip it with both hands.

Now, here comes the really dramatic part. Focus your wrath on the object. You could even HIT the object (NOT THE PUPPY!) or pound the object on the floor. As you do this, say through clenched teeth something like "MINE, MINE, MINE! NOT FOR YOU! BAD!!!" Anything you say through your teeth will have a <u>very</u> serious sound to it; Fido will NOT ignore you.

After you've delivered this dramatic monologue, pause for about five or ten seconds to let the message sink in. Your puppy will probably have backed up a step or two and may be watching you very carefully to see what happens next.

Relax your posture and take a few steps AWAY from your pup and the object/crime-scene. Pause again for five or ten seconds, then turn sideways to your dog, pat your knee and invite him to come to you. Praise him sincerely when he comes. Obeying your command allows your pup to "save face" and get back into your good graces. Don't apologize for scolding him but let him know you still like him and that he's "Good to COME."

Now, in a pleasant, encouraging voice, say to your dog, "Where's YOUR good puppytoy? COME... let's go find YOUR GOOD PUPPYTOY!" Meanwhile, if possible, "disappear" the non-approved chewed item for a while. Out of sight, the object will hold less tempting magnetism for Little Fido.

Help your puppy find an appropriate chew toy and give it to him, commanding in a friendly voice, "Take It." Praise him when he takes it in his mouth. This will help him learn how to please you. The contrast between the scolding for "wrong" and the praising for "right" will add to the drama of the discipline. Focusing your wrath on the chewed object instead of the dog allows you to deliver a very dramatic message without making your dog fear he has to protect himself from you. This gives your dog an opportunity to redeem himself by obeying your command to "COME" and helps turn a negative experience into a positive one.

Drama is the key to impressing your dog, NOT physical force. Notice that you are NOT TO HIT THE PUPPY! You hit the chewed object instead. Remember, the idea is not to frighten the dog, but to display your disapproval in a memorable way. It's an impressive show for the pup, but because you do NOT hit him or hurt him, he heartily respects you without becoming afraid of you. He WILL remember the lesson.

By dramatizing instead of spanking, you won't risk harming your pup either physically or mentally. There are benefits to you from the drama scene also. It gives you a constructive way to vent the anger or frustration you might feel about the chewing situation. Plus, you'll be able to feel GOOD about yourself for not "blowing it" by flying off the handle and hitting your babydog.

Another Help

If your pup's chewing behavior is threatening to get out of hand, despite your consistent and patient efforts to guide him toward proper puppytoys, don't give up... there's yet another tool. You might be glad to know there are bitter tasting anti-chew preparations on the market which work to help a dog learn that he must not chew certain things. These products are manufactured by several companies and have different ingredients. AVOID the type that contains capsicum (red cayenne pepper), especially when using the product with puppies. Capsicum is an intense irritant to the sensitive mucus membranes of the eyes, nose, and lungs. It's overly harsh and cruel to use a product that hurts when just a nasty taste would be sufficient. The bitter spray is only intended to spotlight the lesson for your puppy.

To use, spray or smear the bitter stuff on the items your dog most persistently chews. A small taste of it is usually enough to change a dog's mind about eating furniture, shoes, plants, and other taboo items.

DO NOT put the anti-chew product into the dog's mouth, only put it on the OBJECTS. The instructions on the package of one of these products directs the user to force the dog to taste the yucky stuff. The directions suggest intentionally putting some in Fido's mouth before a crime has even been committed. This is cruel and unneccessary. DON'T DO IT!

The idea is not to PUNISH Little Fido for his natural need to teethe, but to CORRECT his choice of teething objects. If you have provided him with several appropriate chewtoys, your pup will have some safe objects to sink his teeth into. The next step is to apply the bitter stuff to items you wish to protect. If an object you plan to spray with the product is delicate or precious, test first on a hidden part to be sure it won't harm the finish or fabric.

Since it isn't feasible to slather everything you own with this bitter stuff, you should select things that are the MOST likely to be chewed upon. In that category is anything that sticks out or hangs down, and anything you'd wear close to your body or hold awhile in your hand. Put the icky tasting stuff on those items and try to protect the rest of your belongings the best you can during the training period. (Incidentally, DON'T put it on the kittycat!)

Some good news is that dogs translate new information into generalities rather quickly. After Fido tastes a couple of shoes (for example) that have an AWFUL flavor, he will be likely to stop thinking of ALL shoes as potential snacks. One manufacturer of an anti-chew preparation describes the product as "A dog's best friend." This claim may have some real truth to it, considering how many sweet little puppies have been abandoned or killed simply because they had ruined something "valuable."

Oh, How Quickly We Forget...

While we're still on the subject of puppy's chewing stages it should be mentioned that by the time Fido has become a decorous senior citizen you will probably have forgotten how destructive and rowdy he was back in his puppy days. You may not recall all the times you had to correct him for chewing your favorite belongings while he was teething. In fact, good old dogs seem like they were ALWAYS well-behaved... even saintly... even as puppies. They were NOT!

So, to keep History from being completely swallowed by Legend, it might be a good idea to keep one formerly valued possession your puppy has managed to ruin by chewing. (There are likely to be several items fitting this description unless you are SERIOUSLY vigilant during Fido's first year.) Put the chewed object away in a shoebox, along with your puppy's first outgrown collar. For that matter, you could go ahead and have the object "bronzed" and keep it on your mantelpiece. Take it down and look at it when you adopt another puppy someday! The "relic" will help you to put things back into perspective and avoid unrealistic expectations when you once again have a little teething puppy tyke in your home.

PLAYING WITH YOUR PUPPY

Puppies love to play! They learn by playing. In fact, that's what they do best. The game rules learned by a puppy will determine many of the behaviors he will exhibit as an adult. So, if you want your puppy to grow up to be a nice dog, teach him how by playing gentle cooperative games. Read the "Fun & Games" chapter to learn some enjoyable and educational ways to play with your dog.

Remember, Fido learns from the examples you create. Roughness TEACHES roughness... and fairness TEACHES fairness. Play gently, cooperatively, and fairly with your puppy so he can grow into a gentle and trustworthy dog.

Mouth-On-Hand Games... A BIG No-No!

Puppies naturally will mouth people's hands if they are allowed to do so. All dogs should be taught to permit examining fingers in their mouths, but must NEVER be allowed to play with people's hands or to bite down on them. A human hand is NOT an appropriate puppytoy! Playing mouth/hand games can be a difficult habit to correct later, so it's important never to encourage a puppy to play that way.

Many people, not realizing the future behavioral consequences, teach their little puppies to play-bite fingers and hands. As the pup develops stronger jaws and quicker reflexes he will play more exuberantly and may start to hurt the people he plays with. If he played that roughly with a littermate or any other dog, the injured playmate would either get angry and bite back (provoking an altercation) or would bark "OW!" and refuse to play any more until the rowdy one "apologized."

When a rambunctious pup bites hard in play many owners are inclined to react by spanking him. This is unfortunate because spanking actually provokes many pups to "protect themselves" by biting back FOR REAL. They lash out at the person in fear or in anger (usually fear), which greatly compounds the original problem of the rough play-bite. This is a situation to avoid. It is better to say "OW!" sharply and refuse to play any more until the pup settles down. Little Fido will understand and probably apologize to you as he would to an offended littermate, and he'll learn to be more gentle and careful next time.

All mouth-on-hand games should be discouraged from the very beginning. It's far more sensible to teach your pup to bite on an appropriate toy than on your flesh. If he wants to put his teeth on something, give him a puppytoy, NOT YOUR HAND. If you provide your pup with good toys and teach him gentle games you'll both enjoy playtime more and Little Fido's behavior will be much better.

JUMPING ON PEOPLE

Most puppies jump up on people to get attention. That was one of the ways they learned to get their Mamadog's attention and it's quite natural for pups to try the same behavior on humans. Some people encourage this bad habit by allowing or inviting Little Fido to put his cute little paws on them as they hug him and ruffle his ears. No wonder the puppy jumps up! Most humans would prefer dogs NOT jump on them. This habit becomes even more obnoxious when the weather is bad and Fido is muddy.

Knee-In-Chest & Other Not-So-Good Ideas
Most dogowners do try to teach their puppies not to jump on people. Some ways of working on this bad habit are more effective than others. Old-time methods included things like kneeing the dog in the chest, stepping on his back toes, squeezing his front paws, "waltz-ing" him backwards, or kicking his back legs out from under him. Some of those methods might work to a greater or lesser degree, but could do accidental harm to a dog. (For example, I've seen dogs with broken rear toes from having been stepped on by people trying to eliminate rude jumping behavior.)

The Sit Method
There is a better solution to the problem of jumping up. This method works to correct even stubborn jumping dogs and will not harm them. The command "SIT" is used to redirect the dog's exuberant energy. As your dog is about to "greet" you, give the "SIT" command. Be prepared to help him comply, especially the first few times. Keep your knees slightly bent if your young rowdy is big and heavy. When he crashes into your knees as he screeches to a SIT you'll be glad they weren't straight and rigid at the time.

If you've already trained Fido to COME & SIT using a tiny food tidbit as part of his reward, this new use of the command will be readily learned.

Toughies and Hard Jumpers

There is a tougher way to deal with confirmed jumpers. This method combines a quick grab or pull of the dog's chest to stop the jumping, with the command to SIT.

When your dog jumps up on you, instead of trying to push him away, pull him TOWARD you. As Fido leaps up, or if he's already standing with his paws on you, grab the center of his chest with one hand and quickly give a short pull toward you. Then immediately let go. Fido will probably get right off you! You won't have to grab him very hard, it's the surprise that does the job. DON'T OVERDO IT! It's better to go a little light and find out that you needed to give a harder squeeze than to do it too hard the first time. You'll need to pay attention to how much pull is necessary with each individual dog.

Reward your dog for getting off by petting him nicely on his chest. As you stroke his chest, tell him "SIT." Help him obey this command if necessary and be sure to praise him when he sits.

Some dogs (and most young pups) are quite sensitive in that chest spot. Some puppies have such a sensitive chest that the pull is not necessary. Just a little bump with your fingertips in the center of the chest of that type of pup will convince him not to jump on people. Puppies that sensitive rarely retain the jumping habit long enough for it to become a problem.

Some dogs will SIT without even being commanded to while you're petting their chest. Others will need to hear the command "SIT" or to have their chin elevated slightly before they'll SIT. If you've taught your puppy to SIT on command for treats you should have no problem teaching him to SIT now instead of jumping up. Be ready for him each time he starts to jump, then help him SIT and praise his corrected behavior. He'll soon learn that good things happen when he SITS instead of jumping.

Strengthen Good Behavior With Praise

Remember to acknowledge good behavior! If your dog comes up to you and SITS, looking for attention, he's doing some very good behavior without even being told. Praise him, "Good SIT!" Dogs jump up on people to get attention. Be sure to give your dog good energy for polite behavior, so he doesn't have to be annoying to get your attention.

COMING WHEN CALLED

A lot of dogs have a problem with COMING when called. This is an extremely important command and it's vital your dog learn to respond to it quickly and willingly. Early events in a puppy's life are linked to his later tendency to obey or to ignore this command. Puppies sometimes learn to run away from their master's call, either as a game or to avoid discipline.

Bad Game

To begin with, NEVER CHASE YOUR PUPPY! Not for discipline's sake and not even in a friendly game. If you play "chase" with your puppy he will learn to run from you. Dogs love a good game of Tag and don't much care who's "It." Tag is a harmless game when dogs play it with each other, but it's NOT a good game for us to play with them. If your dog eludes you in the chase he'll learn that you CAN'T catch him. When you don't catch him YOU LOSE STATUS!

Good Game

To teach your puppy to COME to you, play this game: Call, "Fido COME!" then clap your hands and run AWAY from your pup, encouraging him to follow. When he runs after you, make it easy for him to "catch" you by squatting or kneeling down to his level and holding your arms open to welcome him. Tell him "Good to COME! Good Fido. Good to COME!" and pet him.

Make a grand fuss over him to let him know how marvelous he is. If you sometimes give him a toy or a little food tidbit as a bonus reward, he'll like this game even better. ALWAYS praise your puppy enthusiastically when he COMES to you. The game becomes Fido RUNNING TO YOU. When he "catches" you, BOTH of you WIN!

If you gently help Fido to SIT while you're praising him for COMING, he'll also learn not to jump on you when he's excited. Stroke or slowly rub the center of his chest while you praise your dog for SIT. It feels good and will relax him and help him stay sitting instead of bouncing around.

The good game of COME WHEN CALLED is fun for your puppy. It's also much better for him than the bad game of RUN AWAY TAG. If Fido never accidentally learns it's "fun" to elude you, COME will be a command Fido will enjoy obeying.

Bad Discipline

NEVER-NEVER-NEVER CALL your puppy to you TO PUNISH him for any reason. If you do you'll have a dog who cringes and runs away when you call. When you have to discipline your puppy or adult dog GO TO HIM, don't call him to you. Fair's fair, and if you call Fido and he COMES to you he deserves a REWARD, not a punishment. He will not understand what he's done wrong or why you're angry if he COMES to you and you punish him. It will seem like a breach of trust.

Good Discipline

If you must discipline your puppy, WALK towards him, DON'T RUN. Try not to scare him into running from you. Gaze neutrally over his head as you approach him, don't stare right at him. A direct stare is a very threatening dominant message in dog body language and may activate Little Fido's fight-or-flight response. Stay calm, and when you get to the dog take hold of his collar gently but firmly.

Snap a leash on the pup's collar to give yourself a handle on the dog and some "room to move." Holding a dog's collar during this dramatic production could get you bitten. It is better and safer to have a leash.

Calmly lead or carry Fido to the scene of the crime and scold him there. If the offense involves a chewed object small enough to carry, you could take the object to the dog instead of bringing the dog to the crime scene.

After the scolding, end the drama by stepping away from the "evidence" and pausing silently for four or five seconds. Then call Fido to you, even if he's only a foot away. Praise him sincerely for COMING. It will not confuse him because the praise phrase you'll use is very specific ("Good to COME!") and uses words that you've already taught your pup. This gives him an opportunity to earn your praise by doing something that he knows is always safe and good... COMING WHEN CALLED.

What if your pup suddenly COMES to you while you're approaching to correct him for some misdeed? You should first calmly acknowledge the good behavior ("Good to COME...") then calmly take him to the scene of the crime. Show him what he did, then scold him. Pause afterwards to let the lesson sink in. Always finish up by calling Fido to you and praising him for his good response to COME.

SOCIALIZING YOUR PUPPY

Puppies learn what "normal" is while they're growing up. If they are not exposed to a variety of new situations while young, pups can become insecure around strangers or in unfamiliar surroundings. If the only people Little Fido really knows are you and your family, he may tend to be shy or overaggressive with strangers all his life. Your puppy will have to deal with all kinds of new people and situations, dogs, and various other animals in his lifetime. It's important that you help him learn to be confident. Introduce him to a variety of different safe and pleasant social experiences while he's still an optimistic and impressionable youngster.

Take Little Fido with you wherever you can. Use the commands you've been teaching him to help him learn how to behave properly.

Introduce your little buddy to lots of friendly nice people. Be especially sure your puppy meets nice children and persons wearing uniforms, as these are two "classifications" of people about whom dogs form strong generalized likes and dislikes.

Let him romp with pups his own age and well-behaved adult dogs. Be sure to keep up to date with all his vaccinations to protect him from dog diseases. Take him to fun and fascinating places. Give him a chance to see that the world really is an okay place. This will go a long way toward preventing antisocial behaviors and dangerous fear and aggression reactions later on.

ENJOY YOUR WONDERFUL PUPPY!

Puppies are cute and playful. Puppies are curious and sweet and naughty. Puppies can be darling... and frustrating at the same time. Bear in mind that puppyhood is a very short period compared to the rest of a dog's life.

Take some time to appreciate your furry little companion's

puppyhood, with all its joys and its trials. It's a precious time and passes quickly by.

Don't miss out! Enjoy your wonderful puppy!

Chapter 9

FUN & GAMES

Certain games played by dogs seem to be "programmed" by instinct. Soon after they open their eyes, little puppies start to tussle and chase each other in a very predictable manner. These natural dog-games serve as practice sessions for such important "real" skills as hunting. The events are acted out "symbolically" in games. For example, a playful ambush might be laid for a littermate instead of for a real rabbit. A dog's agility and reaction time improv through practicing these natural games.

GAMES & STATUS

Puppies learn many of Life's rules on the playground. They tend to grow up either gentle or rough, depending upon how they learn to play as youngsters. Some of the games we play with our dogs will teach them good social habits. Other games can make for troublesome behaviors. There are both positive and negative types of training through play.

Superior strength and intellect can be determined within dog games, eliminating the necessity of a serious fight to prove dominance. Similarly, we humans also use games to determine leadership; we honor our sports winners with respect and higher social status, at least temporarily. Both dogs and humans can resolve hierarchy issues through symbolic dominance attained by winning in competition. Because of this symbolic dominance, if we play win/lose games against our own dogs some misunderstandings and power struggles will inevitably result.

Winners & Losers

When Fido romps with his doggie pals, one of their favorite games is Keep-Away Tag. It's very competitive. Participants enjoy trying to roughly snatch an object out of each other's grasp. The goal is to take possession of the object by any means necessary and to retain it by any means available for as long as possible.

Because Keep-Away Tag is <u>such</u> a doggy favorite, your furry pal may try to entice you into this game. DON'T play it with him! Although Keep-Away may be fun at first, it tends to create some serious and persistent behavior problems. While there's no harm in dogs playing this game with other dogs, when <u>we</u> become players bad lessons are taught. Leave Keep-Away competition for dogs only.

Fido's willingness to come when called, fetch and release an object on command, and cooperate rather than compete with you are all badly affected by playing Keep-Away Tag. If you chase your dog, one day he'll to learn that you <u>can't</u> catch him. In dog society your weakness in this competition would raise Fido's position in the pack above yours. He wouldn't feel obliged to do anything you told him to, because your rank in the pack would be lower than his.

It's <u>much</u> better to teach your dog games which instill cooperation and good behavior. Playing this type of games with your dog will help teach him to be gentle and obedient. The following games will give you and your dog plenty of fun and good exercise.

GAMES TO TEACH GENTLE MANNERS

"THANK-YOU / TAKE-IT"

This game forms a solid base of cooperative trust and modifies a dog's natural grabby, competitive behavior. The purpose is to teach Fido to willingly give up any object when you ask for it. Tgame is fun for him because the object will normally be handed right back to him. When your dog realizes this game involves <u>sharing</u> an object back and forth, NOT losing possession permanently, he'll feel less need to "guard" his belongings. Fido will be more gentle and trusting and a safer companion for everyone, including little children. This lesson also protects the dog from hastily swallowing an object to guard it from being taken away.

Thank-You/Take-It is best taught while a puppy is still young, before he develops the dangerous habit of guarding possessions. However, mature dogs can also learn to play this game and enjoy the fun and the cooperation-building benefits.

When your dog learns to play Thank-You/Take-It, instead of running off to shred and devour a "stolen" object he'll be likely to bring it and drop it in your hand. Then you'll be able to praise him and give him a "legal" puppytoy to play with.

How to Play THANK-YOU / TAKE-IT

Start the game by holding a puppytoy in front of Fido and wiggling it a bit to make it interesting. A rope toy or a rubber bone works well in this game. When your puppy notices and approaches, hold the toy out to him and say (in a happy voice) "Fido, TAKE-IT." As he puts his mouth on it, praise him "Good TAKE-IT!" and pat him. Let go and allow him to enjoy the toy. After awhile, take hold of thetoy while Little Fido continues to play with it.

Then say "Okay Fido, THANK-YOU." Your tone should be pleasant and friendly but be sure the words sound like a **statement** and not a **question**. As you speak, sweep your free hand (open palm toward the dog) close by, but not touching, the side of his face. Move your open hand smoothly, past his eyes. Do it with a flourish, as would a stage magician to distract the gaze of his audience. The idea is to get your dog to watch your hand and lose his concentration on the object in his mouth. This is NOT to threaten him, it's only intended to distract him.

Most dogs will be curious and some mildly startled by this handsignal movement. Many will automatically loosen or release their grip on the object. If Fido lets go, praise him immediately and enthusiastically, "Good THANK-YOU!" After about two seconds hand the toy back to him with a friendly "Fido TAKE-IT!" Remember to praise him for obeying the "TAKE-IT" command with as much enthusiasm as for "THANK-YOU." Many people forget to praise the dog for receiving the toy, placing too much emphasis on giving it up. This makes the toy too valuable and the dog wouldrather keep it. Put the emphasis on the interaction and cooperation in this game rather than on the object. Remember, in "Thank-You/Take-It" the object is only a prop. This game is about cooperative exchange.

Be careful never to allow your dog to grab the object until you say the command "TAKE-IT." If he does, stop and remove the object from his mouth in a calm and matter-of-fact manner. Make him wait until you command him to TAKE-IT, then praise him happily for his obedience.

Repeat the sequence of TAKE-IT and THANK-YOU four or five times, praising and petting your dog each time he does what you tell him. End the game with "Fido TAKE-IT!" Award him the toy, praise him, pet him, and let him keep the object.

Remember to KEEP IT FUN!

Be friendly and enthusiastic, this IS a game! Praise and pet Fido for each command he obeys, both THANK-YOU and TAKE-IT, so he feels like a Winner. Quit before your puppy loses interest, and he'll be happy to play this game with you often.

Many dogs enjoy this game so much they'll initiate it with people and with other dogs. The lessons of gentleness, trust, and cooperation Fido learns from THANK-YOU/TAKE-IT make this game worth playing on a regular basis.

Potential Problems

When you first introduce Fido to the THANK-YOU command he may be reluctant to release the object. This is because he thinks you plan to KEEP his toy, as he instinctively knows another dog would. He does not yet realize that you will be giving the prize right back to him.

To teach your dog to release the object you may have to open his mouth. This can be done easily with most pups by simply touching the side of the tongue with your finger.

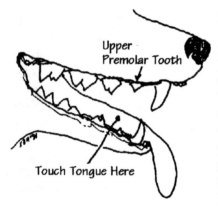

Upper Premolar Tooth

Touch Tongue Here

Behind Fido's fangs ("canines") are smaller teeth known as "premolars." Between the canines and the large back molars, is a place where the dog's tongue is visible when you separate his lips. If you touch your dog's tongue in that spot he'll probably start to release his grip on the toy. When he does, remove the object from his mouth gently, with a rolling motion. (Don't try to yank it straight out or you'll end up in a contest with Fido.) Praise him, "Good THANK-YOU!"

Some dogs are quite determined to keep the toy and will not yield to the finger-on-tongue method. If your dog doesn't release his grip on the play object right away, place one hand over the top of his muzzle, wrap his lips around his upper premolars and squeeze upwards quickly and firmly for just a second. This is uncomfortable for the dog, and he will probably release his grip right away.

If your dog is a real toughie who still hangs on, continue to press his upper lips against the premolar teeth while you roll the toy out of his mouth. Be firm, but be careful to use only as much force as necessary to do the job. Too much would certainly sour your dog on this important game.

Praising

Whichever technique works best with your dog, be sure to release all pressure as soon as you remove the toy from his mouth. Then, RIGHT AWAY, praise your dog enthusiastically, "Good THANK-YOU!" as if he'd given up the toy of his own free will. Soon he'll get the idea of the game and will confidently release the object when you ask for it.

REMEMBER...

◆ NEVER LET YOUR DOG GRAB the object until YOU tell him to TAKE-IT. Allowing him to snatch the toy away from you without permission teaches a very BAD lesson to the dog and will make his behavior worse instead of better.

◆ MAKE SURE HE ALWAYS GIVES YOU THE TOY when you command him "THANK-YOU." If your dog resists and you give up before he lets go, he'll assume you're not much of a leader. A dog may test you, be sure you pass. If you can't get him to let go of a mere puppytoy in a game, you surely won't get him to give up a REAL prize (your new wool mitten) without a major contest of wills.

◆ ALWAYS GIVE THE TOY BACK TO THE DOG after you receive it from him. The more times the "Thank-You" interaction ends with

"Take-It" and Fido being given his toy, the more trusting he'll become. The exception to this would, of course, be with something he'd stolen in the first place. In that case you'd substitute an approved puppytoy instead, giving it to him after you'd finished your "Mine! Not for you!" lecture about the stolen object. Be sure to praise him for "TAKE-IT" when you hand him his "legal" toy. Don't give him what he stole!

Teach your dog the Thank-You/Take-It game using a fairly neutral puppytoy at first, so the stakes are not too high. Don't use a juicy beef knucklebone for the first lesson, or you could "lose" the game (and maybe a finger!) AFTER Fido learns to gently take and release a "weakly magnetized" object, you can work up to more exciting items such as bones. Soon your dog will happily give you ANYTHING he has in his mouth. Thank-You/Take-It is fun for Fido. It also builds trust, teaches gentle-mouth, and lays important ground-work for more complicated and challenging games.

"COME-BRING"

COME-BRING, which is similar to "Fetch," is a game that develops obedience to the command COME while it teaches willing retrieval of objects. Many dogs enjoy running after thrown objects but prefer to tease you with Keep-Away Tag rather than retrieve the items to your hand. It may at first seem fun and harmless to chase after Fido as he dodges about, teasing you with a stick or ball. It may be amusing, but it forms two very bad habits: **running off** and **guarding objects**. NEVER encourage your dog to RUN AWAY from you, and he should NEVER refuse to give you what he has in his mouth. Bear in mind what he learns in play carries over in more serious situations later.

I prefer to teach COME-BRING with a command and reward for each step of the game, rather than the single word concept "Fetch." As Fido completes each of the four phases of this COME-BRING (going after the object, picking it up, bringing it back, and giving it to you) he receives praise. This way his "vocabulary" of useful word concepts is increased and he doesn't have to wait for his reward until the whole sequence has been completed. He'll like his "job" better and be more eager to do it when you "pay" him for each new step. After your dog learns the whole game you can switch to a single command for the entire sequence of actions if you like.

How to Play COME-BRING

Start the game by showing your dog a toy. Charge up the magnet in the toy by wiggling or shaking it and asking Fido, "Do you want this?!!!" When his interest builds, throw the object. Make it easy at first; throw it in plain sight and enticingly close to your dog.

As you throw, say "GET IT!" in an enthusiastic voice. When Fido noses or picks up the object, praise him "Good GET IT!" If he picks it up, praise him more. Smile and clap your hands.

Then in a happy voice (you're having fun!) tell Fido "COME-BRING!" Pat your leg or clap your hands to encourage him to come to you. Take a few steps backward, away from your dog, so he'll know you do not intend to chase him. NEVER CHASE AFTER THE DOG! As he starts coming toward you with the object in his mouth, praise him enthusiastically, "Good COME-BRING!"

When your dog is near you DO NOT REACH FOR THE OBJECT! If you try to take it now, you'll put too much value on the toy and make your dog want to tease you with it and play Keep-away. Always praise and pet the dog first, BEFORE you focus on the object. While you are petting Fido, take hold of his collar GENTLY BUT FIRMLY, so he cannot dodge away. Make a happy fuss over your dog for bringing the toy, then tell him "THANK-YOU" (you've already taught him this command) and receive the object from him.

Praise Fido for obediently giving you the toy, then hand it back to him with the TAKE-IT command, praise him and allow him to "own" his prize for a bit before you throw it again.

Possible Problems

If Fido runs out and picks up the thrown object, drops it on the way back to you, but does COME to you, praise him for COME and make a happy fuss over him anyway. After all, he did COME to you, and that's really more important than BRING. Then take him playfully back to the object, pick it up, "charge" it up, and hand it to him saying "TAKE-IT." Praise him and clap your hands as you step away from him a few feet. If he carries the object toward you, praise and encourage him, "Good COME-BRING!" If he tries to tease you with the object, turn your back on him and walk away... Game's over for now.

Sooner or later Fido will bring the object to you. When he does, tell him "Good BRING!" and pet him. Don't reach for the object at first, just make a nice fuss over the dog. Pet him and tell him how great he is while he just enjoys playing with his toy. His confidence will grow and soon he'll realize this game is FUN. Then he'll happily play the whole sequence by your rules.

It's wise at first to play only a few rounds of COME-BRING each time, even if your dog loves the game, then let him keep the object. Call a halt to the game before Fido gets bored with it. If you let him keep the toy after a few rounds of COME-BRING, the dog's interest in the game will remain strong. When your dog has learned to enjoy this game he'll bring the object for you to throw again and again.

Play COME-BRING with your dog as often as you both enjoy it, but teach him some other games as well. If Fido only knows how to play one game he might become "addicted" to that one activity. Addicted dogs do not make as good companions as those with a broader range of interests.

What If He Just Won't Retrieve?

Oddly enough, some dogs just don't care to play retrieving games, no matter how enthusiastic you are. They act as if they wonder why-in-the-world they should keep bringing an object back if you're just going to throw it away. Most of the dogs who hold this opinion are adults who, for one reason or another, never learned to play as pups.

This type of dog CAN be trained to retrieve on command, but it may seem more of a chore to him than a pleasure. Be patient and allow him time to learn the game. Some trainers believe in forcing an uninterested dog to retrieve. I don't. It's better to make the game more interesting, if you can. If your dog really doesn't care at all for COME-BRING don't take it personally. Not everyone enjoys the same sport. Play something Fido likes better. After all, some folks love a good game of chess yet have no interest at all in golf. Dogs have their preferences too.

The "NAME GAME"

If your dog enjoys COME-BRING he'll probably ask you to throw the object repeatedly. At that point you can make the game more complicated and more fun for both of you. One variation involves teaching Fido to bring back a variety of throwable objects. In addition to sticks, balls, and flying disks you could try some unusual alternative throw toys. How about a pop can, a ring of keys, a long blade of grass, a rolled newspaper...? If you teach your dog to retrieve objects by name ("COME-BRING the tennis ball" or "keys" or whatever) you'll be able to send him after specific items. Fido's obedience and vocabulary will grow rapidly.

You could be quite imaginative in your selection of objects for this game, but be sensible. Don't send your dog to retrieve items that could hurt him or that he could damage. Take care never to permit Fido to chew or tear these alternative "toys." They are YOUR belongings and he must treat them respectfully.

Multiple and Directed Retrieves

Another way to play COME-BRING is to teach Fido to "WAIT" or "STAY" while you throw the toy. After it lands, direct the dog to the retrieval object with a dramatic sweep of your arm toward the item as you tell him to "GO GET IT... COME-BRING!" Or you could name an item and ask for it specifically, "Fido, GO GET the KEYS!"

When your dog has mastered this new twist of the game, you'll be able to throw two or more items before sending him out to retrieve them. You could have him bring the items to you one at a time or several at once, if he can fit them into his mouth!

Scent Discrimination

Another challenging variation of the COME-BRING game is Scent Discrimination. This game teaches your dog to retrieve an object with your scent on it. He must find it "hidden" amongst a group of items which you've not handled. It will help Fido succeed if you have not touched the "unscented" items for at least one day. The only object with your "fresh" scent on it should be the one you've chosen for him to retrieve.

Hold the object in your hands for a minute so it gets your scent on it. Then place it among the group of others or have a helper put it there for you. If you'd like to be sure that Fido doesn't "cheat" and watch where you put the scented object, make him STAY around the corner while the item is placed. Let the dog sniff your hand to give him a clue before you send him out to find the scented object.

Start off with just one or two articles in the non-scented group until Fido builds his skill and confidence. If you make it too tricky at first, your dog might get discouraged and not catch on as readily. Soon enough he'll be able to discriminate your scent from others and select the correct item from a large group of articles.

It's a fairly easy trick for most dogs to differentiate one person's scent from another's, even in very minute concentrations. Fido's sense of smell is vastly superior to ours. He could pick YOUR brown glove out of a pile of hundreds of identical brown gloves. Although it's not necessary to use a set of look-alike scent articles for this game, it's more impressive to watch.

Special sets of identical items for use in obedience competitions may be purchased through dog training supply outlets. You could, for fun, improvise a less formal set of articles from same-sized blocks of wood or empty popcans. You may want to mark the scented object somehow so YOU can be sure your dog has retrieved the correct item.

Safety First!

When playing any of these retrieval games BE SURE TO CHOOSE ITEMS THAT WILL NOT HARM YOUR DOG! Examine an object for potential hazards before you ask your dog to put it in his mouth. Fido just wants to play the game; he has little concern for his own safety. That's up to you.

Rocks are BAD fetch toys because they're hard and abrasive, so they rapidly wear down a dog's teeth. Glass objects can break into knife-edged shards, so they're also dangerous. Certain types of trees and shrubs have poisonous bark or wood, so even sticks should be carefully examined before you throw them for Fido. Your veterinarian can probably provide you with a list of toxic plants to avoid in your area. Safety First! You sure don't want to hurt your buddy by sending him off to bring back something that could harm him.

And Remember...

◆ Be SURE to PRAISE your dog for each step of the game. It's so much more fun and more rewarding when he's praised for each good thing he does while learning a new lesson. The specific praise phrase for each action helps teach Fido to recognize several new words (Good GET IT, Good COME, Good BRING, etc.) When your dog knows and enjoys this game you can switch to one command for the whole sequence if you prefer.

◆ DON'T REACH FOR THE OBJECT until your hand is holding your dog's collar as you praise and pet him. Fido will be much more cooperative about coming to you with the fetch toy if he's expecting to RECEIVE something (petting) rather than LOSE something (the toy). Focusing on the toy too soon, rather than on the dog himself, gives the object too much ownership value. That will tempt Fido to KEEP it rather than hand it over to you.

◆ DON'T CHASE YOUR DOG! This is very important! Fido must NEVER learn to run away from you, EVEN AS A GAME. Games translate easily into much more serious behaviors. That's why it's vital to play <u>cooperative</u> and <u>obedience-based</u> games with your dog in the first place. Don't ruin everything you're trying to build by playing "Chase the Dog." You may not catch him unless he allows you to. He will lose respect for you when he discovers you really can't keep up with him. Don't teach him this regrettable lesson.

◆ The IMPORTANT GOAL of the COME-BRING game is to strengthen your dog's desire to obey and cooperate (rather than compete) with you. Once he understands the game your dog will happily give you the toy without a Keep-Away tease.

"TUG-OF-PEACE"

A traditional favorite game, "Tug-O-War," has come under some harsh and well-founded scrutiny among dog behavior specialists. Problems with canine aggression often develop when this game is played as the usual "no-holds-barred" competition. Tug-O-War is a very "ON" game with no "OFF-switch." The goal of the old tug game was to win by superior strength and toughness... you against your dog. It's unwise to place yourself and your dog on opposing teams this way in a Tug-O-War competition because he'll be trying to BEAT YOU.

A dog should NEVER be taught to pit his strength AGAINST his master. He could find out that he really IS tougher than you, which in dog society means HE's superior and should be the new packleader. Not a very good idea at all!

There is a sound alternative to the old Tug-O-War. The new game is "Tug-Of-Peace." When played properly this game will provide fun and vigorous exercise for both you and your dog without pitting you against each other as rivals. Tug-Of-Peace teaches Fido gentleness, obedience, and cooperation. If Fido has learned Thank-You/Take-It first, he'll be ready for this safe and enjoyable alternative to the old aggressive Tug-O-War.

How to Play TUG-OF-PEACE

Begin the game with Thank-You/Take-It. Interest your dog in a tug-object and tell him "Fido TAKE-IT" in an encouraging voice. Praise him when he does. Then, instead of letting go, start to gently pull and shake the object, encouraging Fido to tug on it. Tell him "PULL! PULL! Good PULL!" as you do this. Some dogs growl playfully as they tug; this is usually okay and can be allowed if it doesn't start to sound "serious."

After Fido has tugged on his end of the toy for a little while, you should stop pulling but maintain a firm passive hold on the toy. I call this passive hold the "dead hand." It's not as exciting to your dog as an active pull, but he still can't jerk the object away. When your dog gives you a questioning look about this change of pace, say "OKAY Fido, THANK-YOU." Praise heartily when he gives you the object. Then tell your dog "TAKE-IT!" and hand him his end of the toy. Praise him for taking it, then begin another round of Tug-Of-Peace. This is an instructional game, reinforcing the commands he has learned... and it's great FUN!

If your dog does not immediately release the toy when you give the handsignal and command for Thank-You, you should remove the object from his mouth. Praise the dog for giving it to you, even though you had to correct him first. Work a little while on Thank-You/Take-It practice before you make the object more exciting again with Tug.

After a few rounds of the Tug game, quit before Fido gets bored or addicted. Command "THANK-YOU" then take the toy and praise your dog enthusiastically. Then tell him "TAKE-IT" and gently give him his toy to enjoy by himself. If he tries to give it back to you, tell him "NO THANK YOU" and hold your hand up, like a "Stop" signal. Then make your hand passive and ignore the toy, even if your dog "pressures" you to take it. He'll soon realize the game's over... until next time!

When your dog has learned the rules of Tug-Of-Peace you can play hard together, as hard as you like, and he'll stop pulling and release the object instantly upon your command. It will be fun for Fido to play this game and it will NOT teach him to be competitive or violent. He'll learn instead to willingly and instantly quit a very exciting activity when commanded. This will help him become increasingly obedient and cooperative under other more serious circumstances as well.

◆   The rules of Tug-Of-Peace do NOT permit "warlike" competition, so NEVER try to yank the toy out of your dog's mouth and NEVER encourage him to rip it away from you, either.

"Wimpy Tug"

Tug-Of-Peace can be played with varying degrees of "muscle" once your dog understands the basic rules. One variation of this game is "Wimpy Tug." It involves pulling on the toy using VERY LITTLE STRENGTH. The dog learns to match his pull to yours so the game may continue.

When you teach Fido this mild form of the Tug game, hold the toy with just two or three fingers and pull only very gently. If your dog pulls too hard just let the toy slip out of your hand. Because you offer no resistance to his pull, Fido will not feel like he's "won" a contest if he ends up with the toy this way. He'll probably offer it right back to your wimpy hand. Have him give it to you, using the THANK-YOU command. Then begin again.

"Dance of Peace"

Tug-Of-Peace can also be played as more of a dance than a wrestling match. In fact, it's a lot of fun to play this game to music. One of our dogs, a Rottweiler, especially thinks so too. He likes musical Tug-Of-Peace so well that he brings his knotted rope toy to us when he hears his favorites on the stereo.

To do this dance with your dog, hold one end of a soft thick rope or other tug toy. Hand your dog the other end. To the rhythm of the music, pull and bob and turn with your dog. He'll catch on pretty quickly to the new moves. Our Rottie has even made up a few steps himself that we include in our "dance routine."

With a good foundation in Thank-You/Take-It, your dog will learn variations of the Tug game and enjoy playing at different levels of vigor. He'll match his pull to yours instead of trying to compete for the pull-toy.

Remember...

◆ RESIST the temptation to make this Tug-Of-Peace into a compe tition with your dog!

◆ As with any game, it's important NOT to OVER-PLAY it. Some dogs will become bored with a game if it is over-played, others become "addicted" and lose interest in other things. Vary the games you play.

◆ Played as described above, Tug-Of-Peace is safe fun and great exercise for dogs and their people. It also helps Fido learn to manage his excitement level. This game teaches very valuable control skills. Plus it's good exercise. So... let's give "PEACE" a chance!

"HIDE-AND-SEEK"

This game encourages your dog to keep you in sight when you take him for walks off-leash. It also improves his natural ability to track a person by scent. Hide-and-Seek is a lot of fun for everyone and helps build useful skills.

How to Play HIDE-AND-SEEK

You can play this game either outdoors or inside the house. Pick a time when Fido is in a playful mood. While he's not looking, duck around the corner or behind the couch and call out, "Fido FIND!" Snap your fingers or make a funny noise to attract your dog's attention and to give him a clue to your hiding place. Have a tidbit of food ready as a reward when he finds you. Praise and pet him enthusiastically; let him KNOW you're pleased! Then wait until he's not looking and hide again. You'll notice that it soon becomes difficult to sneak away from your dog. He will be expecting you to hide, and will try to stay "tuned in" to you more than he did before learning this game.

The next phase of Hide-and-Seek involves waiting until your dog is in another room of the house or around a bend in the path. Slip into a hiding place, call your dog's name ONCE... then be silent. He won't see you or hear you when he runs back in response to your call, so he'll have to seek you out by following your scent trail. If he runs past your hiding place without noticing you, make a funny noise or say his name. That will help him succeed when he's new at this game.

Pick uncomplicated places to hide at first. Make it fairly easy until your dog develops skill at this game. Soon he'll be able to find you no matter WHERE you try to hide.

Friends and family members may also enjoy playing this game with your dog. Children especially love to play Hide-and-Seek with a dog.

To teach this game, hold Fido while someone goes and hides. Once they are in their hiding place have them call out, "FIDO FIND!" When you hear their call, tell Fido "GO FIND Suzie" (or whoever) and release him. Go with your dog as he searches for the "lost" person. It might help at first if YOU already know where Suzie is planning to hide, so you don't end up on a "wild goose chase." You and Suzie should both give Fido some treats and hugs and pats when he finds her. Praise the dog enthusiastically, "Good Fido, FIND! Good to FIND Suzie!"

When your dog catches on to the idea of searching for a "lost" person, you can increase the challenge of the game. Instead of having Suzie call Fido, just have her go hide quietly. Then YOU tell Fido "FIND Suzie!" and go with him as he searches. Again, it may help in the beginning if you know where Suzie is hiding, but let Fido do the finding. Don't lead him to the hider or you'll spoil his fun.

If Suzie takes food treats with her each time she hides, your dog will search for her quite enthusiastically. Many dogs love this game so much that after awhile the food treats become less exciting than the joy of finding the hidden person. ALWAYS PRAISE YOUR DOG when he finds the hider; let him know you think he's fantastic! He really IS!

An advanced form of the "Find" game involves letting Fido smell a recently worn article of Suzie's clothing before you tell him to FIND her. After he gets the idea of this sniff-and-find variation, you can omit the name of the person who's hiding. Just let your dog get the scent from the clothing, then tell him "Fido, GO FIND!" Always praise and reward him for finding the correct person, and have that person give your dog a treat and tell him how great he is.

A dog loves to use his nose to find things. Teaching Fido this game is fun for him and for the whole family. It may someday also come in handy. Imagine if you and your dog happened to be off in the woods on a camping trip when another camper became lost in the woods. Who knows? Your buddy Fido might become a doggy-hero!

GROUP GAMES

One of the strongest magnets for a dog is another dog. You may notice that your well-behaved companion suddenly gets a bit wild when you meet another dog on your walk. It even seems as though your dog cannot hear your voice at those times, or has never received any education of any kind. A good cure for this dog-induced lack of concentration is to work your dog around and with other dogs.

If your dog is enrolled in an obedience class or puppy socialization group you'll already have some dogs to practice around. Exchange phone numbers with other folks in your group whose dogs are friendly toward yours. You could meet for a little extra practice and play outside of class.

If you teach your dog to pay attention to you even when he's having a great time with another dog, you've got it made! This is not as difficult as it may seem... especially if you make it a GAME!

"COME-AWAY"

This is a game that provides good attention practice. Your dog will enjoy it because he'll get a special reward and then be encouraged to go back to his fun with his dogfriends.

It's best to start this game with only two dogs at a time. After they've learned the game you'll be able to add players. Begin with the dogs on leash. At first you may need those "handles" to bring your dogs back to you. Be watchful to keep the leads from tangling as the dogs play together.

At first, just let the pair of dogs sniff and bow and start to romp a little. Before they get too fully involved with one another, the handlers say to their own dogs, "(Dog's Name) -- COME-AWAY." So saying, the handlers move apart. The dogs, on leash, go with them. Move playfully, don't be stern; this is a fun game. You're teaching your dog to give up his play with a friend, so you'd best make your own manner as interesting and fun as you can!

The handlers move far enough apart so the dogs are able to focus on them. Then each praises and pets his own dog and gives a tiny food treat. Then... and this is the part the dogs enjoy most... the handlers tell the dogs to go back to play with each other.

The special treat and then permission to return to play helps a dog learn that "COME-AWAY" is a fun command to obey. He'll think it's a great game to romp back to "master" to receive a prize, then dance back to dogfriend to brag about it. After dogs learn this game they can play without leashes. Caution: Some dogs will run in <u>huge</u> play circles off-leash.

"NOISY TOYS RELAY"

If you're looking for a way to practice STAY, this "Noisy Toys Relay" will be great. This is a race played with pairs of dogs and their handlers. It will work with as few as two dog/handler teams or may be played in a larger group or obedience class.

This game provides important hard-to-resist distractions... clackety-poppity noises, erratic motion, and handler-excitement. It's a "race" -- yet strategy is very important. Each handler must be aware of his or her dog's ability to withstand the types of tempting magnets used in this game.

How To Play

Draw two parallel starting lines on the ground, 10 to 50 feet apart (depending on skill level of dogs & handlers.) Long-lines, rope, or flagging tape may be used as starting lines if lines cannot be drawn on your "playing field."

"Teams" of two handlers, with their dogs at HEEL, face each other from behind the two starting lines. Noisy kid-toys on wheels are attached to six-foot cords or leashes which the handlers use to pull them. (There are some real noisy ones that you might borrow from someone with toddlers or purchase quite inexpensively at garage sales.) Each pair of handlers shares one toy-on-a-leash.

Teams can be of differing skill levels. Handlers decide which of their pair will go first. It makes sense to have the person go first whose dog is most solid on Stay.

At the "Ready, set, go!" the first handler of each team gives her dog a STAY command, picks up the leash of the toy and takes it across to her team-mate then stands behind his dog. Now the second handler tells his dog to STAY, then drags the toy back across and stands behind his team-mate's dog. When that's accomplished, both handlers on the team raise their hands to signify to the "judges" that they've been successful.

handler & dog

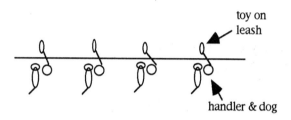

toy on
leash

handler & dog

The dogs are to remain on STAY during this "chaos." If a dog moves, the handler drops the toy's lead and returns to re-fix his or her dog. If a dog is not reliable off-lead, the leash or longline may remain attached. A handler standing behind the team-mate's dog may stand on the leash, but handlers should only correct thir own dogs.

Dogs who can learn to hold a STAY during the "Noisy Toys Relay" will be in GREAT shape for the long SITS & DOWNS at the next obedience match or trial!

BRACE WORK

If you live with two dogs, here's a way to give them some good obedience practice together. This "game" allows some really challenging obedience work. Each dog should already have received individual training and know the basic command words. When your dogs are confident working one-on-one with you, try training them together as a "brace." You may use one leash for each dog or connect the dogs together by their collars with a brace coupling or a foot or two of cord.

Some handlers like to use both dogs' names when commanding a brace. Other handlers prefer to use a "group name" like "Puppies" or "Boys" to command both dogs at once. Help your dogs understand that you mean both of them. The dogs will learn to follow commands in unison. Be sure to praise both dogs using the command phrase when they both respond correctly. If one dog is slow to obey, praise the one who obeyed by name for his response. Then help the slower one. Praise both dogs with a praise phrase once the slower dog gets into proper position. Let your dogs know how smart they are and how proud you are of them.

There is a non-regular competition called Brace Class at some obedience trials and matches. Titles are not awarded, but ribbons are and sometimes trophies too. It's fun to work two dogs together and is a skill that can come in quite handy at times.

"TAKING TURNS"

This is a great game for multiple dog households. It can be played with any number of dogs (well... within reason!) Your dogs are likely to compete for your attention at times anyway, so this game is good to help them learn to take turns.

Taking Turns is sort of the opposite of Brace Work, in that you'll give each dog a different command to follow. Again, the dogs must have learned their obedience lessons individually first, or they'll be confused by this advanced training game.

Pick simple commands first. For example, tell one dog (using his name before the command word) to SIT, then praise him (by name and with a command/praise phrase.) Then give the other dog a command to DOWN (by name and with a praise phrase after he obeys.) A tiny food tidbit is a nice reward for each dog as they obey the commands. The dogs will soon catch onto the idea that one is supposed to do one thing and the other another when you command. It's great fun!

As your dogs get good at this game you can make it more of a challenge. Try leaving both dogs on a STAY, then call them one at a time. Or have one STAY and the other HEEL away with you. Be sure everybody gets lots of praise for playing this game. Taking Turns is also good practice for the "real world," as when you might want one dog to go outside and another to stay in.

Taking Turns can also be a big help when two dogs have a status disagreement within the pack and get aggressive with each other. Any time two adversary dogs start acting up you can bring them back into your reality with a firm (not playful) round of Taking Turns. You'll have to be on your toes to keep both dogs focused on you instead of each other. They each, in turn, are given a command (say the dog's name first, of course.) Each dog has to stay in position while the other obeys your command. It's good practice, it de-fuses arguments between dogs, and it puts the "Leader Hat" back where it belongs: on YOUR head!

SERIOUS FUN

The games in this chapter combine fun with the business of training your dog to be a good companion. These are by no means the ONLY positive games you could play with your dog. They are intended to give you a good starting point and to inspire your imagination for other beneficial games.

Think of ways to use games in your training sessions and daily routine. Dogs love games and learn them quickly. Be creative in your play; your dog's mental and physical agility may amaze you. Just remember that games TEACH while they entertain. Always try to play with your dog in ways that will help him form GOOD habits.

Chapter 10

COLLARS & LEASHES

There is a vast array of dog equipment available. Some of it is very well made and some is not. Be a discerning buyer. Some equipment will be appropriate for your needs and some will not. When you have the right tools for the job, training your dog will be happier and more comfortable for both of you.

COLLARS

Little Fido's first collar should be a plain buckle-type collar made of leather or cloth. The first time your puppy feels it around his neck he may be startled. The new collar might tickle or itch. He'll probably scratch at his neck, shake his head or run in circles at first, but he'll soon get used to the feeling and accept this new wearing apparel.

For safety's sake and for comfort, be sure your pup's collar fits him properly. The collar should be loose enough for you to easily slide two fingers between the collar and the pup's neck (one finger for tiny dogs) but it must be snug enough so he can't slip out of it or work his lower jaw under the collar in front. It's frightening and dangerous for a puppy to be trapped with his collar through his mouth like a horse's bit. Beware of overly loose collars on puppies.

Be watchful as your puppy grows and check his collar at least once every week so it doesn't get too tight. Puppies' necks grow surprisingly fast and an overly tight collar can cause serious health problems. There have been cases where a collar has actually become imbedded in the neck of a rapidly growing young dog. Keep an eye on how your little buddy's collar fits!

Buckle Collars
This type of collar is good for daily all-the-time wear. Identification tags and licenses may be attached to the same D-ring used to fasten the leash to the collar. A buckle collar is adequate for training most young puppies and sensitive or timid mature dogs. If you only need

to correct your dog mildly or infrequently, the buckle collar will be best for that dog.

Buckle collars are not suitable for training dogs requiring strong or repeated corrections. When you pull on a buckle collar the pressure is all at the front of the dog's neck, where his trachea (airway) is located. Although it must be uncomfortable for Fido to have that pressure against his throat, a strong-willed dog can somehow get used to it and sort of become "immune" to correction by the leash. Hard or constant collar pressure against the airway can cause permanent injury.

Slip ("Choke") Collars

When used properly, this type of collar does NOT "choke" the dog. This piece of equipment has been called a "choke collar" because of a common misapplication of its use. Many kindly people hesitate to use a slip collar because they do not understand the proper use of this training tool. The collar should only be used with a quick tug-and-release and NEVER used in a manner that chokes the dog!

◆　**NEVER PULL THE SLIP COLLAR TIGHT FOR MORE THAN A HALF-SECOND.** Two or three quick tugs-and-releases in rapid succession are more effective than one huge pull.

The slip collar is a great help when working with a boisterous or headstrong dog, as it enables the trainer to quickly get the dog's attention using a minimum of force. Correctly handled, the slip-type collar is humane and effective.

A properly applied leash correction using a slip collar is distributed evenly around the dog's neck, so the pressure is NOT concentrated on the trachea. To get Fido's attention with a slip collar, quickly tug-and-release the leash. The pull you use should be appropriate to the size and sensitivity of the individual dog. A brisk snap of the wrist will give the right action to the lead. The sensation for the dog is an attention-getting tingle all around his neck, rather than a hard bump concentrated against his airway.

If you put this type of collar around your own arm and give it a quick pull-and-release, you'll feel the strongest sensation at the side, where the rings move. The slip collar actually places less direct force against the dog's throat than a buckle collar.

Slip collars are available in flat or rolled leather or nylon, and in various gauges and types of metal chain. The leather or fabric slip collars are quite mild and are a good choice for sensitive dogs. Medium to heavy chain is best for most dogs. Thin-gauge chain has more "bite" than thicker chain and will be <u>too</u> <u>severe</u> unless used with an <u>extremely</u> light touch.

Check to be sure the links of a chain collar are smooth enough to slide easily through the end-ring. If the links are too "lumpy" or the chain tends to twist, the collar will not tighten or release properly when you're training your dog. It's important that the collar work smoothly. Some brands are better than others, so check carefully before you buy.

Fitting the Slip Collar

The slip collar should be snug, but comfortable . The collar length should be the measurement around the lower part Fido's neck, plus two or three inches. If the collar is too tight it won't work properly. On the other hand, excessive length is to be avoided. DO NOT buy a slip collar too large, expecting your puppy to grow into it. If the collar is too long it will fail to release properly when the leash is loosened. This would confuse and frighten a dog.   Be sure the collar fits Fido correctly to begin with.

Putting the Collar On

For a slip collar to work properly and safely it must be put on the dog properly:

1) First slip the chain through ONE of the end rings (either one will do.)

2) Next, hold the collar up so its shape resembles the letter "P" (for "Proper Puppy.") Be sure it looks like a "P" and NOT a "9" or it will go on your dog the wrong way.

3) Face your dog and look at him through the opening of the "P." Slide the collar gently over Fido's sweet face and down around his neck. It may help to reach through the collar and cup your hand under your dog's chin as you slide the collar over his head with the other hand.

4) When the slip collar is put on as described, it will have the right tighten-and-release action. If you've made a mistake and put it on Fido as a "9" instead of the proper "P" the collar will not work correctly with the dog at HEEL to your left side. It would tighten but will NOT readily release.

◆ ALWAYS check your dog's slip collar to see it's on properly before you attach the leash.

SAFETY SENSE...

◆ **CAUTION**: A slip collar is potentially hazardous. Horrible accidents have happened when slip collars were left on unattended dogs. If something snags the working ring of the collar, the poor dog is helpless to escape. If he becomes frightened and twists around in a desperate attempt to free himself, he could be asphyxiated by the ever-tightening collar. DON'T let this happen! Use a slip collar for training-time only. Let Fido wear his buckle collar when he's "off duty," or switch his slip collar to the "safety" mode.

Switching The Slip Collar To "Safety"
1) First remove the collar from your dog.
2) Next, locate the "working ring" (that's the one you'd attach the leash to while training.)
3) Then feed the whole collar through the "working ring." Jingle the chain a bit to straighten out any twists.
4) Finally, CHECK TO BE SURE it's on "safety" by tugging at the ring... it should NOT slip.
    Now you can put the collar back on your dog. It will be as safe this way as a buckle collar.

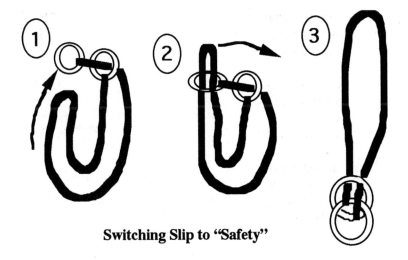

Switching Slip to "Safety"

Both Buckle and Slip Type Collars

When a handler uses the proper pull-and-release technique most dogs will quickly learn to walk politely on a loose leash. This works whether the dog is wearing a buckle collar or a slip collar.

To remind a dog to pay attention, quickly tug-and-release the leash. If you tighten and hold instead, it won't work properly. Most dogs feeling a steady pull or push will meet that force with steady resistance. (So will most people.) A quick tug-and-release will give Fido nothing to lean against, so he cannot resist your message.

Remember, the tug-and-release is meant to get the dog's attention, not to punish him.
- DO tug-and-release!
- DON'T pull-and-hold!

MISCELLANEOUS OTHER COLLARS

Several other types of collars are available. Some of them can be rather hard on a dog. Others, when used with care, can be helpful and humane.

Convertible Collars

A new style of collar now on the market converts fairly readily from buckle-type to slip-type. Some are made of leather and some of nylon. One brand is designed with a limited slip range, another has an unlimited slip range like a conventional choke-chain. These collars are good if your dog is not too hard and headstrong.

Convertible collars are adjustable, which allows the dogowner to safely buy a size too large for a pup and loosen it as he grows. This is also handy for dogs whose coats get thick and long and are then shed out or clipped short. That extra inch or so of hair around the dog's neck would ordinarily necessitate two different sized slip collars to accommodate seasonal coat changes.

These new collars can be converted from slip to non-slip with a simple refastening procedure. These versatile collars are a sensible innovation in dog training equipment.

Head-Collars

These are not exactly collars, as we'd normally think of dog collars, but more a cross between a muzzle and a horse-type halter. The head-collar has a slip-type band that encircles the dog's muzzle. The lead is attached to a metal ring on this band and, when pulled, steers or stops the dog. The leverage advantage with this apparatus makes it possible for a smallish person to control a largish dog.

A problem with these head-collars is that many dogs dislike the slip-band around their muzzles. When the handler pulls the leash the band tightens and closes the dog's mouth. If Fido happens to be panting (which is the dog's primary means of regulating body heat) when the muzzle band tightens he will bite his tongue. That could be quite uncomfortable and unpleasant for him.

In most cases an ordinary buckle or slip collar seems to be more comfortable for dogs than a head-collar. In the event that a person is severely overmatched by a very large and headstrong dog, a head-collar may be useful for training. Be gentle with leash corrections, though. The extra leverage available with a head-collar makes a pull on the lead more forceful than with an ordinary dog collar. A dog, even a friendly one, who overpowers his handler is a dog who may cause injury to people. Rather than using gadgetry to "even up the odds" with an overpowering dog, the owner would be wise to seek help from an experienced professional trainer.

Pinch or Prong Collars

The pinch collar, also called prong collar, is made of interlocking metal prongs. These poke and pinch the skin of the dog's neck when the leash is pulled. Although this collar has lately become rather popular, it is neither necessary nor appropriate for most dogs.

Unfortunately, some trainers and dog owners seem to be more interested in "quick fix" results than in kindly communication and understanding. They look upon this harsh gizmo-collar as the answer to their problems. A dog will certainly pay attention to his handler when this device is used, BECAUSE IT CAUSES THE DOG PAIN IF HE RESISTS. It's far more humane to get a dog's attention by being more interesting than by being more forceful.

Kindhearted doglovers naturally balk when a pet supply dealer or obedience instructor tries to sell them on the idea of a pinch collar. Promoters of this device try to convince the dogowner that the collar will not hurt Fido. They place it around the owner's arm and give a light tug or two. "See, that didn't hurt you," they say. What they don't say is that the collar has a completely different action when used on the dog. A dog's loose neck skin is lifted up and pinched between the metal prongs. It can hurt. It can and often does puncture the skin. The wounds, in pairs around the dog's neck, sometimes become abcessed and require veterinary care.

Trainers who routinely use pinch collars sometimes recommend them to beginner handlers with exuberant young dogs. This is a bad mistake! It is difficult, especially for a beginner, to use a pinch collar with any degree of subtlety or sensitivity. A small blunder by the handler can cause a dog unnecessary pain or injury.

◆   Many sensitive dogs become fearful of training when a pinch collar is used. This can cause sour, sullen attitudes about leashwork.

◆   **Some dogs even become aggressive toward their own masters in an attempt to protect themselves from this harsh training tool.** It is much too easy to misuse this forceful collar... with unfortunate results for both dog and handler.

An ordinary slip collar should be used instead of a pinch collar for most dogs. Give your dog a chance and time to learn. A wise handler avoids resorting to harsh methods. Massage may be used to relax and sensitize a "tough-necked" dog instead of using a harsher collar. Massage and relaxation allows gentler methods to be used for training. (See the massage section in the "Hands On" chapter.)

Electronic Collars

Another type of collar you may encounter is the electronic "shock collar." Used by a knowledgeable and sensitive trainer this collar can be a useful tool. In the WRONG hands this piece of equipment can spell psychological DISASTER for the poor dog.

This collar carries a battery powered device that delivers an unpleasant (but not physically harmful) mild electrical shock. The trainer operates the collar by means of a battery-powered hand-held remote switch. The strength of the shock can be adjusted by the trainer to suit the dog and the situation. The sensation is a light prickle at the lowest setting and pretty uncomfortable at the high end, much like the "zap" delivered by an electric livestock fence.

Once I <u>intentionally</u> shocked my bare moist palm with an electronic dog collar at the highest setting, just to know what it felt like. (Notice I said "ONCE.") I dropped the collar when it zapped me and wouldn't have been easily persuaded to repeat the experiment. It was more than a "tingle," but I really wouldn't describe the sensation as painful... just really unpleasant and a little "spooky."

Careful consideration must go into any decision to use an electronic collar. Some trainers use these devices for ordinary obedience lessons. I think that's unfair, unkind, and unnecessary. Dogs love to please, so there's no need to use unpleasant tactics to teach basics. Petting, praise, and tidbits are much better training tools!

Once a dog has been taught basic obedience commands in a kindly and patient way there is normally no need to use a harsh device like the electronic shock collar. However, in some cases of very dangerous and persistent behaviors. If used sensitively by a knowledgeable professional, this tool can cause changes for the better. Used improperly this device can quickly RUIN a dog. There's too high a risk of careless or accidental over-punishment with this training device.

As with any tool, the electronic collar takes practice to use properly. The problem for a dogowner is that any errors he makes while learning to use the controls on this gadget will confuse, frighten, and possibly ruin his own dog. Mistakes in timing or too high a setting may cause the dog's behaviors to worsen rather than improve. If your dog's behavior problems are serious enough to consider the use of an electronic collar, get help from a reputable professional trainer first.

Any dog must FIRST be given a good basic education in obedience BEFORE use of the shock collar is ever considered. It's unfair and cruel to punish a dog for breaking rules he has not yet been properly trained to obey. Once a dog fully understands the basic rules and commands, many distressing misbehaviors just go away. This often makes forceful training and equipment unnecessary.

A well-trained dog is happier, more responsive, less bored, and therefore automatically in less trouble. Only if a dog persists in a dangerous habit that refuses to respond to ordinary training methods, might the electronic collar be considered. The electronic collar is NOT a shortcut to basic obedience training... there are no shortcuts!

Harnesses

Collars are for walking on-leash, the dog learns not to pull and the leash is kept loose. A harness is designed for the dog to go ahead and pull as hard as he can and is useful for mushing (dogsledding) or tracking. A harness puts the pressure harmlessly against the dog's chest when he pulls, rather than on his neck.

Some people use a harness on a small dog because they fear a collar might harm the dog's neck. Most small dogs can quickly learn not to pull on the leash, so this worry is usually unfounded. They may be trained with a light slip collar, using a quick tug-and-release as described in other sections of this book.

There are, however, some tiny dogs with tracheal problems which may be worsened by even slight pressure on the throat. There are also larger dogs with neck problems who should not have any collar pressure used. Dogs with neck or throat problems should be thoroughly examined by a veterinarian before any leash work is started.

Some dogs, even tiny ones, may pull so hard in harness they put their handlers off balance. This is, of course, excessive! If the dog cannot wear a collar, there is a special type of anti-pulling harness that may help. Even a dog with neck or throat problems can learn to walk properly on a leash. This harness has cords that go under the dog's "armpits" and squeeze there when the dog or the handler pulls on the leash. The cords can cause irritation to that sensitive area though, so if you decide to use this piece of equipment check frequently to make sure it isn't chafing your dog. This type of harness can be used when a collar cannot, but it could be uncomfortable if overused. Be careful and be kind if your dog wears one of these halters.

TRAINING LEASHES

Leashes, also called leads, are available in a variety of materials, lengths, and widths for different purposes. To follow the training instructions in this book you'll need a six foot leash. The length is important. If your leash is too short or too long you will not be able to make corrections effectively using the pull-and-release method.

Most training leads are made of leather, cotton or nylon. They are available in several widths, to suit the size and weight of the dog. Cotton or leather leashes are more comfortable for most people than nylon. Nylon is slippery, which makes it more difficult to grip. This promotes the ungainly and dangerous habit of wrapping the lead around the hand.

The width of the leash will also make a difference in ease of handling. If the strap is too wide it will be difficult and clumsy to hold. Good manageable widths for training leads are 5/8-inch for large or medium-sized dogs, and 1/4 to 1/2-inch for dogs under 30 pounds.

The training leash should have a hand loop stitched into one end and a swivel clip attached to the other. The clip must be strong enough to hold the running weight of your dog, yet light enough not to pull a slip-collar tight on its own. The clip must be the swivel-type to prevent the leash from getting twisted up as you train.

HOW TO HOLD THE LEASH

The six foot training leash is a versatile tool. It allows the handler to adjust the length short for close HEELING or longer for the more relaxed WALK command. Both commands, briefly described below, are fully described in the next chapter,"Schooltime For Fido."

Leash Safety

For safety's sake, when you hold your leash DO NOT stick your wrist through the loop, because that makes it very difficult to change hands or to let go of the lead quickly. DO NOT wrap the excess length of leash around and around your hand. If your dog suddenly bolts, the wraps of lead around your hand can tighten severely. More than one handler has suffered injured fingers from this dangerous and awkward habit. It's also nearly impossible to let go of the leash quickly, should one need to do so, once those wraps have tightened around the hand.

The following illustrated directions will help you learn to utilize your six foot training lead to best advantage.

Holding The Leash for WALK

When you are using the WALK command to exercise Fido on-lead, allow him the whole six feet of leash-length so he can move around freely. WALK is a command that may be done with the dog on either side of you, so the lead may be held in either hand.

Hold the lead with the loop over your thumb, as illustrated. Close your hand securely on the leash. This method makes it easy to switch the lead from one hand to the other whenever you need to.

Hold the excess length LIGHTLY in your opposite hand, merely to keep it from tripping you or your dog as you walk along together. Some dogs prefer to walk close to the handler, others vary their distance, enjoying the casual freedom offered by the six foot leash.

Holding the Leash for WALK

WALK is the command to use when there is no need for your dog to be precisely positioned at your side. It's the most convenient command for exercise or potty times. For "formal" walking or in in situations requiring you to have greater control of your dog, the HEEL command would be more appropriate.

Fido will be learning to HEEL at your left side, so you'll need your left hand free to encourage and pat him and to make minor leash adjustments. For this reason it's best to hold the leash in your right hand. When your dog is in the HEEL position you'll need to shorten your leash from the less formal WALK command. When working on the HEEL command, if you need to give a quick tug-and-release to get your dog's attention, you can do so with your left hand.

Holding the Leash for HEEL

1) Hold the leash with the hand loop over your right thumb.

2) With your left hand, pick up the leash at about the midpoint of its length and "hang" that bend over your right index finger.

3) Close your right hand on both folds of the shortened lead.

4) To easily lengthen or shorten the leash during HEELING, adjust the bend of the leash that's held over the index finger.

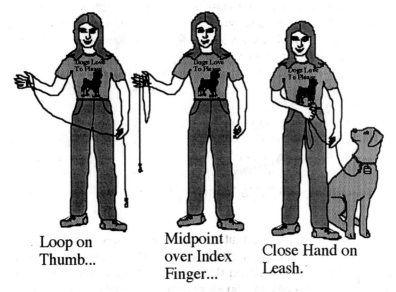

Loop on
Thumb...

Midpoint
over Index
Finger...

Close Hand on
Leash.

Holding the Leash for HEEL

Only pull the leash taut for the briefest instant with a tug-and-release correction when necessary to regain your dog's attention. The leash should at all times be loose enough that the clip hangs down from the ring on the dog's collar. At the same time it also must be held short enough so you don't get tangled or trip over it.

This method gives the handler good control of the training lead and permits quick adjustment of its length. At first the technique may feel somewhat awkward, but as you practice more with your leash the method will become very comfortable and natural to you.

MISCELLANEOUS OTHER LEASHES

The six foot training leash is a very versatile tool but it's not the only kind of lead available. There are a number of choices to consider for your dog's leash "wardrobe." Some may be more useful to you than others. Following are descriptions of a few different kinds.

Chain Leashes

Chain leashes are not suitable for teaching commands because they can't be held in the recommended way without hurting your hand. A chain leash could also accidentally flip up and hit poor Fido in the face, causing him some pain too.

Four Foot Leads

A four foot long leash may seem at first to be less cumbersome than the six foot training lead, but in truth the shorter lead is only less versatile. Whether you're working with Fido on the formal commands or just taking him out to smell the flowers, a four foot leash is really too short. Two feet more length makes a lot of difference in training maneuvers or when trying to keep your shoes dry on a potty walk.

Traffic Leads

These leashes are about two feet long. They may be useful in some training situations, such as agility work, because the handle can be dropped and not drag on the ground or hamper the dog's move-ments. Traffic leads are too short to be very useful in regular basic obedience training.

Some folks use a traffic lead when just out for a walk with the dog. When I see this it makes me wonder why the leash is on the dog at all, since there's nobody in charge of the "business" end. It doesn't make too much sense. If Fido's not in the habit of COMING when called, the short hand-loop will not help reel him in. On the other hand, if the dog <u>does</u> obey his master's call, a short dangling lead isn't really necessary for control. Anyway, a loose dog with a short handle hanging from his collar does not satisfy the requirements of most leash ordinances.

Retractable Leads

A leash on a self-rewinding spool is available in several lengths. As the dog pulls ahead of his owner, the tension placed on the lead unwinds it from the spool (which is inside a hard plastic case with a handle). When Fido moves closer to his handler the leash retracts. There is a thumb-button "brake" which can be pressed to stop the lead from lengthening or shortening. When the brake is released the leash reels in or out again.

These retractable leads are quite popular, but they have an inherent problem. They actually TEACH a dog to **pull** on the leash, by keeping it slightly taut at all times. This is the very opposite of what we want! A leash of this type is not useful to teach a dog to walk politely. The retractable leash may, however, work fairly well as a long line if the handler pre-selects the length and sets the thumb brake.

Long Lines

A light long line is another piece of training equipment you will need. You can easily make one from 30 to 50 feet of smooth round-braided nylon cord (which is available by the foot on spools at many hardware stores). Nylon is a good material for long lines because it's very strong, slides smoothly over the ground, weighs very little and doesn't absorb much water.

Use 1/8 in. cord for dogs under 30 lbs. and 1/4 in. cord for larger dogs. This thin nylon cord is very strong UNLESS CHEWED! Do <u>not</u> let Fido even nibble on your long line; stop him right away if he tries.

Tie a hand-loop into one end of your long line. Tie a single knot at the other end to prevent slippage when fastened to the dog's collar. It is best to TIE the line to the collar, rather than attach a leash-clip to it. The small extra weight added by a metal clip would remind Fido that he's wearing a control device. It's better if he isn't constantly made aware of that control during long line work. You should hope that your dog will "forget" about you for a moment while he's on the long line. Then you'll get a chance to demonstrate your "amazing powers" to control Fido from a distance.

Long line work prepares a dog for off-leash training while still allowing you to maintain safe control. Be sure to give your dog plenty of happy, enthusiastic praise for good work on the long line. You'll build your dog's trust and respect for your leadership as he learns to work farther away from you.

A long line will also allow you to give Fido some good running exercise without turning him loose. A 50-foot line gives your dog a 100-foot diameter circle around you. A dog exercising "freely" on a long line is in compliance with most leash ordinances. Even before he's reliable on the "COME" command, Fido will be able to romp and burn calories exercising on a long line without being endangered by the pull of new magnets.

YOUR DOG'S I.D.

Protect your dog from anonymity, give him an identification tag. A license or rabies tag can be used for identification purposes, but often that's not a sure enough way to find a dog's owner. City halls and most veterinary clinics are closed at night and on weekends and holidays. They can't always be reached to search through official records to identify a licensed or vaccinated dog.

For more useful "personal" I.D., purchase a "real" I.D. tag for Fido or have your phone number engraved on the back of one of his "official" tags. There are also dog collars which may be ordered with the dog owner's phone number embroidered around the band. Every dog should wear his master's telephone number on his collar. A readable phone number can help quickly reunite a lost dog with his worried family.

Travel I.D.
If your dog accompanies you on vacation, his tag should bear both your home phone number and a local contact where you'll be staying. Write the temporary number on a piece of adhesive tape and fasten it around the tag. Check every day to be sure the number is still legible.

A lost dog desperately needs a way to get home again... his family's phone number on his I.D. tag can make that happen. Don't ever think that YOUR dog would "never get lost" because you take careful measures to keep him safe. Any dog could become lost! An I.D. tag could make all the difference in how the adventure turned out.

Noisy Tags

Two or more tags clattering together can be an annoying racket to a dog's sensitive ears. Multiple metal tags can also sharpen each other's edges with constant rubbing. Wrap the tags together with strapping tape or electrical tape to mute their sound and prevent wear. If Fido ever became lost, his finder could easily remove the tape to read the tag.

Microchip I.D.

This new development in identification was in use at zoos for years before introduction to the companion animal industry. The I.D. is encoded on a tiny electronic chip, less than half an inch long and the diameter of thin spagetti. This little space-age ditty is implanted just under the animal's skin, usually between the shoulder blades. It's considered safe and does not seem to bother the animal once it's in place. The code can be "read" electronically and the lost pet's owner identified and contacted.

Microchip I.D. is endorsed by many leading veterinarians. It's a permanent form of identification for a pet. It cannot fall off or be removed, as can a collar or even a tattoo. The problem is that several companies presently manufacture chips and there is as yet no standard "code." The various companies' "reading" devices can't yet interpret each other's microchips, so a veterinarian or animal control agency attempting to identify a dog with the "wrong" manufacturer's equipment would not be able to do so. If that chip was the dog's only I.D. he'd be out of luck. When this detail is worked out satisfactorily we may find wider use of electronic identification.

Even if you do have Fido marked with an electronic chip it's still a good idea to keep a metal or plastic I.D. tag attached to his collar at all times. If he happens to get lost and is found, anybody who can read will be able to phone the number engraved on his plain old-fashioned tag and return your dog to you immediately. Some day you may be really glad to hear your phone ring, with a call from your lost (and found!) buddy.

Tattoo I.D.

Tattooing is a practical and simple method of permanent identification for a dog. Many dogs will relax and lie still for petting and treats while the procedure is done. The tattoo is permanent, inexpensive, and not painful.

It is against federal law to use tattooed animals in research. That's another good reason to use this permanent I.D. Pet thieves and unscrupulous dealers are slightly hobbled by this law. Tattos were once usually done on the dog's ear flap, but horrid people have cut ears from stolen tattooed animals to disguise them for sale. (Some disguise!) Tattoos are now usually placed on the dog's inner thigh area.

There are several national tattoo registries. They record (for a small fee) your dog's tattoo number. If ever your dog is lost, then found, the registry will help reunite you with him.

OTHER EQUIPMENT

The main purpose of this chapter is to familiarize dog owners with the equipment necessary to train dogs by the methods in this book. There are many other pieces of equipment available that may or may not have anything to do with training. You could visit any well stocked pet supply store or open an animal specialty catalog to see an amazing array of dog equipment. You'll find everything from fringed bandannas to squeeky bananas, from hunting scents to french perfumes available for dogs these days.

It's fun to look at dog stuff; some items may be more useful to you than others. If cost was no object it might be fun to get carried away. There are just so many toys and treats and collars and dogbeds available... how would a person know which to select?

Safety Check
Safety is the main thing to keep in mind when choosing items for your dog. Check toys for flimsy construction or loose pieces that a dog might swallow and be sure toys are WAY too big for Fido to choke on. Examine the fastening hardware for strength on leashes, collars and harnesses. Make certain there are no rough places on buckles or straps to irritate your dog's skin.

Beds & Bedding
There are all kinds of dog beds on the market, from cots to four-poster canopy styles. They come in burlap or lambswool or fake fur or velvet. You can buy dog beds in fabrics to compliment your living room decor. You can even order a bed monogrammed with your dog's initials so he won't lose it when he goes to summer camp. Cushions

or beanbags, cuddlers or sleeping bags... or just bags of wood chips, different dogs prefer different sleeping accomodations.

Most dogs I've asked say they'd prefer the master's bed or couch to most any commercially made dog bed. Whether or not to allow a dog to sleep on people-furniture is an individual household decision. Many dogs do well sharing the master's furniture; others become posessive. In the latter case the dog's furniture-access rights should be immediately cancelled and a professional dog behavior specialist consulted.

Dog cushions and beds should be large enough and well-padded for comfort. Although cedar chips are frequently used as a flea-repellent stuffing for dog beds, cedar oil is somewhat toxic and the dust from the shavings is irritating. It seems to affect some dogs worse than others. Some dogs (and their human caretakers, too) are sensitive enough to cedar they may become ill or develop skin problems from exposure. If there is a flea problem in your area, a machine washable dog bed is a sensible sanitary alternative to a dusty sack of shavings. It does far more good to launder a dog's bed frequently than to simply repel the fleas from it.

The dog's resting area should be easily and thoroughly cleanable. This is true whether a dog sleeps on his own bed or shares the family's. A tightly woven bedspread makes a good washable cover for a couch or people-bed shared by a dog. The fabric should readily give up dog hair to the vacuum or washing machine. For health's sake, all dog beds and bedding should be machine washable and dryable.

Poop Scoop

The reality of life with Fido is there's a daily renewed supply of dog poop to pick up. Many dog owners use a garden shovel and a stick or a hoe to remove piles of feces from the yard. Really, there's a much less yucky way to get this ongoing job accomplished. Invest in a real poop scoop... it will change your life for the better!

The best scoopers are long-handled two piece devices. One handle terminates in a pan and the other in a flat hoe or a rake. On concrete the hoe works best. For use on grass or dirt, get one with a rake. When you buy a poop scooper be sure the scooping parts are sturdy and strongly fastened to the handles. These parts must withstand some action... and you sure won't like it if they fall off in the middle of a job.

Dog Food

So many brands and varieties of dog food are commercially available today that a buyer could be overwhelmed with choices. How can a person know the right brand to buy? A good rule of thumb is that if your dog is perfectly healthy and happy and beautiful, the dog food he's eating must suit him. If he's not healthy, happy, shiny and energetic, then a change in diet may be called for.

Ask some trusted dog folks to recommend good brands. Your veterinarian, groomer, breeder, pet supply dealer, trainer and best friend may all swear by different dog foods. Another information source would be the product companies themselves. (Most dog food bags carry a phone number for their product info division.) Listen to the recommendations of knowledgeable people, then do some checking yourself.

It's a good policy to avoid dog foods that contain dyes. They're unnecessary and have sometimes proven harmful to dogs. Likewise with many chemical preservatives; safer vitamin-based antioxidants have now begun to replace them in many dog foods.

Some dogs do poorly on certain common feed ingredients as soy, wheat, corn, or even beef. They may be allergic or sensitive. Some clues that can point to dietary intolerance are loose or very hard stools, flatulence (gassiness), weight loss, itching or poor coat. In some multiple dog households, each dog thrives on a different diet. When you find a dog food that works well for your dog, stay with it.

If you do find it necessary to change dog foods, most dogs do best if the change is made gradually. Begin by introducing just a few bites of the new food. This is especially important if your dog is one who tends to be sensitive to some food ingredients. If he does okay with that first taste, the next meal you could replace about one quarter of the old ration with the new. After a couple of days, increase the new and decrease the old again. It takes about five days to a week to change over from one food to another this way.

Treats & Goodies

There is a huge assortment of dog treats to choose from. Choose those containing wholesome ingredients, preferably no dyes or sugars and especially no chocolate. (Chocolate is extremely toxic to some dogs and not healthy for any.) Remember that all treats add calories to your dog's diet. Some dogs can afford that better than others.

Some treats (beef sticks, pig ears, etc.) may contain a significant amount of protein. We are accustomed to thinking of protein as a good thing, which it is, but excess protein will overtax a dog's kidneys and can cause or worsen health problems. Treats should be used sparingly and sensibly.

Many dog treats have red or yellow dyes mixed in to make them "look like" meat or cheese. The dogs I've known have never seemed concerned about what color their food was. That leads me to think the dyes are included in the biskits to fool the dog owner, not the dog. Hmmmm... I'm not fooled, is anyone else?

Dyes in foods are not necessary and many have been discovered (belatedly) to be cancer-causing. Let's just skip the dyed treats, for the future health of our dogs. Buy wisely, there ARE healthy dog snacks on the market.

Some people enjoy making homemade doggy treats from wholesome ingredients. There are recipe books available for making delicious doggy snacks. Raw carrots, apple slices or broccoli stems are surprisingly favorite treats for some dogs. Many will do tricks for a flake of unsweetened breakfast cereal. So many commercial treats sold for dogs contain sugars, chemical preservatives, unpronouncable ingredients and other unhealthy fare. Why buy those when healthier treats abound?

There are endless choices of products for dogs and dog owners. It can be fun to try many different tools, treats and toys. Be a sensible buyer; examine items you're puchasing for your dog as carefully as those you'd buy for yourself. There are all qualities of doggie items available. Safeguard your dog from inferior products... and enjoy the good ones!

Chapter 11

SCHOOL TIME FOR FIDO

Your dog will learn how to behave whether or not you intentionally involve yourself in his education. This would be great news for busy dogowners, except for the canine tendency to learn some fairly objectionable behaviors when not taught acceptable ones.

This situation is similar to the way human youngsters learn the ropes. If information is not provided by parents and teachers the "kids" pick up what they think they need to know on their own... or on the streetcorner.

Unguided children and unguided puppies both end up with bad habits. We who COULD have steered them toward greatness would certainly regret that.

Fido will learn new "tricks" either by being taught them intentionally or by simply observing the results of certain actions. Trial and error helps a dog figure out how to get what he wants, be it food, attention, or a means to escape from the yard. Your dog, whether you take an active role by training him or a passive role by not training him, will certainly learn SOMETHING... whether YOU like it or not!

ACTIVE TRAINING

Take an active role in your dog's education to minimize the bad habits he might adopt. Most dogs, like the rest of us, feel secure when they know what behavior is safe and useful in a particular situation. A first-time experience or unusual situation will cause a dog to seek out the information he needs to determine how to behave.

Puppies especially are always on the lookout for effective ways to interact with the environment. Left to his own devices Little Fido will learn to live by a self-taught set of pragmatic rules. Those "rules" may be quite the opposite of what you would have liked. A dog owner aware of a pup's natural quest for information can provide activities, toys, and situations that will HELP form acceptable behaviors.

An absence of intentional training amounts to "accidental" or "passive" training. Many dog owners simply do not realize the longterm bad effects this inadvertent "training" can have on their dogs.

A common illustration of the unfortunate "accidental training" phenomenon is the dog who barks excessively when left alone. It's quite normal for any young puppy to feel anxious when he first finds himself alone. In nature the natural thing for him to do would be cry until his mama rescued him. Any self-respecting mamadog would follow the sound of her pup's panicked wailing, find him, and lead him back to the safety of the den. The little pup's instinct to cry when lost or isolated is activated the first few times his human family leaves him.

The pup's built-in information tells him to howl and carry on until somebody comes along to save him. Often a penned or crated pup carries on loudly enough that someone returns and lets him out just to stop his noise. It's no wonder so many pups develop the habit of barking and howling when left alone.

He learns by that result that his noisy behavior got him what he desired... permission to rejoin the "family pack." A bad habit starts to form. Puppy-logic goes like this, "I bark, I bark, she comes, I'm free!" It takes only a few repetitions of this cause and effect scenario before little Fido has learned to make a terrible fuss whenever he's left alone.

An obvious improvement on the above hit and miss education would be for Fido's human family to take an active role in teaching him more acceptable behavior. Active training by an aware owner provides much better answers to a pup's questions about the world than what he would discover by chance.

Intent to teach and readiness to participate in Fido's search for information are vital if you're hoping to raise a companion animal with good manners. A confidence-inspiring introduction to "the rules" is useful before unacceptable behaviors can become habits. An active education by a caring teacher (that's you!) will make life with a dog easier and more pleasant for everyone.

Dogs love to please and, because they do, they also love to learn. When lessons are pleasant and positive, both dog and handler enjoy themselves. Education for a dog, as for a person, is a lifelong activity. The commands we teach our dogs are a language to communicate with them. They want to understand us. It's our responsibility to teach them with patience and kindness.

WHAT AGE TO START?

Whatever age your dog is, he can learn. As soon as you get a dog, begin teaching him the skills he needs to live happily in your household. Some people make the mistake of waiting until the new dog has "settled in" to begin training. This is a mistake. Right from the first moment Fido comes to live with you he'll be watching to see what's allowed and what isn't. The most important thing is to be consistent. Be sure YOU know what you want the rules to be before you try teaching them to your new dog. Be kind and patient, show him what your rules are. Don't expect him to learn them all at once though, no matter what his level of maturity.

Puppies
Little puppies learn especially fast because they've not yet formed strong habits. Puppies under four months of age learn new things faster than they will when they're older. At that age they're very curious and pay close attention to everything that attracts their attention. They are "clean slates," wide open to new experiences and ready to learn.

The keys to training a young puppy are to go slowly and to make it fun. Puppies lose heart in training if the lessons are too long or if the teacher's too stern. Make obedience training enjoyable and spontaneous, a game you and your little friend play together for fun. He'll love it and form good lifelong attitudes. Plus, you'll both have a great time!

Adult Dogs
Older dogs, contrary to the famous saying, <u>can</u> be taught "new tricks." An adult dog, like an adult person, can sometimes be rather set in his ways. A mature dog has formed habits and beliefs which will

take time to change. Dogs love to please. Your adult dog will try very hard if you're patient and consistent and make the lessons fun

An adult dog has already become accustomed to a certain way of life. Whether you've raised him from a pup or have only recently adopted him, if you decide to change a mature dog's habits it will take him a while to get used to the new ways. Bear with him, be patient. Remind him gently of the new "rules" when you need to. Be clear and uncomplicated... and always remember to praise your dog's cooperation. Help him know for sure when he's on the right track.

REWARDS

Fido will learn fastest when he enjoys the lesson. Set a positive tone, your dog will match your enthusiasm. Praise him and pet him, those rewards mean a lot to your dog and don't cost a cent. Be sure to give him plenty!

Food As A Motivator

Food (the "universal language") is a pleasant reward for Fido but must only be used sparingly. When tidbits are used to lure a dog into position he'll learn the command happily. Always be sure to remember to praise your dog too, even with a food reward. Treats should be very tiny, so the dog doesn't get more involved with the food than with the lesson. If treats are used excessively, your dog will become OBESE instead of OBEDIENT.

KIDS 'N' DOGS 'N' TRAINING

Children interested in training the family dog will usually be successful with the food reward method. This non-force method of teaching commands is more appropriate than strong arm tactics for use by junior trainers. Of course, first you, THE ADULT PACKLEADER, must teach the dog to be gentle and polite when he accepts tidbits.

An adult should be present, in case Fido decides to just grab the treat from Junior and be done with his training session. You must also teach Junior how to hold the food lure and how to give the command. Fido will "follow the food" just as well for a child as an adult. Children get a big kick out of being able to "make" Fido do his "tricks" for a treat. It's pleasant for the dog and gratifying for the child and doesn't pit one against the other in a battle of will or muscle.

Training Fido by physical force methods is dangerous for a child. The dog may resist Junior's efforts with some force of his own, perhaps biting. This is a natural reaction for a dog. It would be expected and accepted with other dogs... but it's a _very_ dangerous reaction around little people.

The food method of motivation does not require the trainer to "dominate" the dog. Most dogs consider children as peers (or possibly underlings) and don't think of them as "bosses" at all. Although Junior is not an authority figure to Fido, the dog is likely to obey without an argument just to get the food bit.

Be sure an adult is available to supervise whenever young children and dogs play together!

Dogs and children enjoy each other's company, but even when they've both been taught the "safety rules" they can sometimes get into trouble together. Newsworthy incidents involving injury of children by dogs occur each year. A large percentage of these mishaps involve a trusted family pet. Sometimes even "nice dogs" do inappropriate things. Sometimes nice kids do too, for that matter. Many dogs have been accidentally or intentionally injured by unsupervised children. Protect your little loved ones (two-legged AND four-legged) by exercising your status as packleader. Be there for them. It's really fun to watch the dogs and kids playing together... you may also be needed as a referee from time to time.

PRACTICE & PRACTICALITY

Before & After

Don't play exciting games with your dog just before or just after training sessions. The contrast between "play" and "work" will make it harder for him to concentrate on new commands. The lesson itself should be enjoyable and rewarding. YOUR attitude about training is important.

If you give Fido the idea that "schoolwork" is a boring chore and that "sports" are the only real fun, you'll deter him from reaching his fullest potential. If you and your dog spend quality time together "playing school," Fido will proudly do his best and you'll both enjoy training sessions more.

Attention Span

At first your dog's attention span may be quite short... probably only five to ten minutes. It may take a while at the beginning of each practice session to get Fido's attention focused. "Focus" will get easier as Fido learns HOW to learn. His attention span will lengthen quickly.

Praise and other rewards will also help a dog's attention span increase. Create interest by varying the lesson a little each time. Most dogs enjoy a certain amount of routine but they like adventure and don't like to be bored. Variety can add fun and liven things up.

Day-To-Day

After your dog has learned the basic commands he'll be a much more pleasant and reliable companion. You will, of course, need to keep him in practice. The best way is to use the command words in "conversation" with your dog every day. When you want him to do something, use one of the words he knows in a simple sentence. Put enough emphasis on that word so he realizes it's one he knows. It's exciting how rapidly dogs can learn to understand sentences laced with command words. As time goes on he'll be able to decipher more complex sentences.

Most of the basic command words are verbs, action words. You may have also taught your dog some nouns, the names of objects. Many dogs are also capable of learning adjectives, descriptive words like "big" or "new" or "squeeky." Be creative! Find ways to use what Fido has learned to make life more enjoyable and interesting for both of you.

Homework

Your "homework assignment" is to practice commands with your dog twice a day for about 10 to 15 minutes each session. Try to keep it fun. Don't over drill on any one command. Vary the lessons and don't practice for too long at a stint or Fido will get bored and frustrated. So will you. Praise your dog heartily for cooperating with you and enjoy how quickly he learns to understand your language.

Some days you may be too busy to manage two ten-minute practice sessions. Try to do one session for 15 to 20 minutes on those days, if your dog's attention span can handle it. Practice every day you possibly can. You must work consistently if you and Fido are to become a team. Skipping several days in a row will have a noticeable adverse effect on progress with lessons.

On the other hand, be willing to recognize when both you and your pal need a day off from schoolwork. Take a nice walk together on those days instead of "drilling" on the commands. Enjoy each other's company! If you use some imagination you'll find lots of ways to incorporate command words into enjoyable activities and everyday life. Really, that's what the training is for... REAL LIFE.

Have FUN with your happy and obedient dog!

THE "FORMAL" COMMANDS

Formalized obedience training consists mainly of teaching your dog useful words and gestures which help you to communicate with him. These words and signals are called "commands." Fido has no idea what the command words mean until he is taught to recognize them. Your job is to help him understand what you want him to do when he hears each command. You'll make it easier for your dog if you're consistent. Be patient with him and always remember to reward good behavior.

To enjoy a happy life in a human household a dog needs to recognize and obey some basic words and signals. The eight specific command words in this chapter will lay a good groundwork for that "vocabulary." Those commands are: Sit, Walk, Wait, Heel, Come, Down, Stay, and Stand.

To Give A Command

When you give a command say the dog's name first, then the command word. This way you'll have your dog's attention before you tell him what to do. ("Fido SIT.") Speak clearly in a normal friendly voice, there's no need to sound intimidating. Your dog will learn to obey whatever tone you use when training him. Speak in a pleasant voice but avoid "baby talk" when teaching commands. Your dog must be able to take your leadership seriously.

A friendly and confident sound to your voice will help Fido trust you and want to obey. A questioning or pleading tone does the opposite; it sounds submissive and the dog won't believe you really expect him to obey. You don't need a low or gruff voice to command your dog, just give him the impression you're confident about being his leader.

Say It Only Once!

Speak clearly when you give a command and DON'T REPEAT YOURSELF! Many handlers say the command over again when the dog doesn't obey the first time. This teaches Fido to wait until the "whole command" (including repetitions) has been spoken before he obeys. The "whole command" might sound like this: "Fido, can you SIT for me? SIT? SIT. Come on, SIT, SIT. Now SIT... SIT... I said SIT! Fido SIT!" and often ends with a tough military sounding voice, a snap of the fingers... and <u>finally</u> Fido SITS. This bad habit perpetuates the need to use a harsh tone and numerous repetitions of commands.

It's far better to give the command clearly <u>once</u>. Then, if the dog doesn't respond, do something to HELP him obey. That's how he'll learn to listen to the <u>first</u> command you give. Upon being made aware of this "multiple command syndrome," many handlers discover that they themselves have it. If this happens to you, do your best to change the habit as soon as possible. Repeating commands may be deeply ingrained in your lifetime behavior with dogs and may be difficult to change but you'll find it worth the effort.

The Words

Some handlers may wish to use different command words than the ones taught in this book... that's fine. Some people like to train their dogs in more than one language... that's fine and fun too. Some folks want their dogs to respond to whistle blasts or other non-verbal signals... no problem at all. Dogs are very adaptable creatures and will try hard to learn whatever you want them to. Whichever command "languages" you choose, your dog needs you to teach him consistently. He cannot learn without your help and patience. Help him learn to please you. He'll be happier and better adjusted when he knows exactly what you want him to do.

The better you understand your dog, the easier it will be for you to communicate with him in a way HE can understand. Dogs LOVE to please... so HAVE FUN helping Fido learn.

There is additional information in other parts of this book to help you teach Fido the command words. If you haven't already read the chapters "Dogs & Mankind," "Commands & Rewards," "Distractions & Magnets," "Crimes & Punishments," and "Raising A Proper Puppy," it will help to do so before you start teaching your dog the formal commands.

THE COMMAND: SIT

The SIT command can be used to stop a dog's movement and hold him still in a manageable position. It's also useful for teaching Fido not to jump on people, as he can't SIT and jump at the same time. He can also be trained to sit automatically at HEEL every time you stop, then wait for your command to proceed. The SIT command can be used in a variety of circumstances for safety, convenience and decorum.

The dog's position in the SIT is with his head up and his hindie squarely on the ground. Fido's own anatomical construction works in your favor when teaching this command. When a dog's chin is elevated a few inches above horizontal, he'll be more comfortable if he sits down. To help your dog achieve this, say "Fido SIT," and gently raise his chin. You could do this by focusing Fido's attention on a tidbit of food held slightly above his nose, or you could simply lift his chin up gently with your hand. In either case it will NOT be necessary to push down on Fido's rump.

The old-time "military style" dogtrainers taught handlers to use some very rough methods to force their dogs to SIT. They wrenched on choke-chain collars, pushed down hard on dogs' rumps, slapped the dogs at the base of the tail and did all manner of unpleasant and painful maneuvers to get poor Fido to SIT. There was little gentleness, compassion, or understanding involved. Unfortunately, even today an enormous number of trainers still use some of those same old unenlightened rough methods to teach commands. Let's work to change that! We know dogs can happily and more quickly learn with milder techniques.

Dogs love to please. SIT is a comfortable position for most dogs. With just a little encouragement Fido will readily learn this command. The following instructions describe how to teach SIT using a couple of pleasant, safe, gentle methods.

FOOD-TREAT METHOD FOR SIT

Dogs like food, so tidbits are a natural means of attracting Fido's attention and motivating him to learn. Be aware, though, that excessive reliance upon yummy treats is risky... it can turn Fido into a "foodaholic" or an incorrigible materialist.

The tidbits you use as lures and rewards to motivate your dog should be VERY small (1/4 in. x 1/4 in. is plenty) so Fido stays interested in the lesson without filling up on the treats. Too large a treat will actually distract a dog from learning. Be SURE to use praise and petting as rewards, even when you also "pay" your dog with tidbits.

What To Do

Hold a SMALL bit of some enticing food, such as dogtreat-jerky or unsweetened breakfast cereal, between your thumb and forefinger. Touch the tidbit to Fido's nose, then raise it up about TWO OR THREE inches (if it's too high the dog will jump or sit-up and beg.) Say "Fido SIT" as you raise the treat. Only lift it as much as necessary to get him to stretch his nose upwards.

As your dog raises his

head to keep track of the food he'll naturally lower his hindie to the floor to be more comfortable. He's SITTING! Praise him, "Good SIT!" and give him the treat and some nice petting. Be sure to hold the food bit ABOVE his nose, NOT UNDER it, when you give him the reward.

Give Fido the tidbit reward with one hand while you touch his neck and collar with the other. As he learns what to expect, then switch the order -- touch his neck first, THEN give him the food. This will help your dog learn not to dodge away when you reach for him. He'll form pleasant associations between the collar-touch and the food reward. Instead of worrying about being "captured" when he sees you reaching for him, he'll learn to expect the treat. It's a good habit to cultivate. On those occasions when you don't have a treat, your dog's basic optimism will make him cooperate anyway.

Praise & Petting

It is VITALLY IMPORTANT to pet and praise your dog for good behavior, even when a food reward is given. You will certainly want him to obey without needing tidbits to motivate him. You can "wean" Fido from the food reward by omitting it from time to time after he's become enthusiastic about obeying the command. Later, give him the tidbit only once in awhile so he won't be able to predict when he'll get it. Dogs are pretty optimistic, so each time he hears "Fido SIT!" he'll hurry to obey. He knows he's going to get <u>some</u> kind of reward and hopes maybe this will be the time the tidbit appears. You MUST praise him verbally and/or reward him with a kindly touch whenever he obeys your command. Otherwise he'll ONLY want to work for food-pay and may very well refuse to obey when there's no tidbit in sight.

HANDSIGNALS AS COMMANDS

A handsignal is a body language command. If you can focus your dog's attention on a food tidbit you can teach him to obey handsignals. The handsignals described in this book are pretty conventional; most trainers use similar ones. Each gesture-command is one smooth movement. This makes it easy for the dog to remember and is also the standard for obedience competitions. You'll only use one hand to give handsignals; you may use either hand.

The Handsignal for SIT

Start with your arms down at your sides. Turn the palm of one hand toward Fido. Bending that arm at the elbow, raise your hand in front of your body, briskly up toward your shoulder (same hand to same shoulder). You don't have to actually touch your shoulder, just be sure to use enough upward movement for your dog to easily recognize it as a signal.

This hand motion is similar to the way you'd raise the tidbit lure when teaching Fido to SIT. In fact, if your dog understands he's to sit (not jump) for the treat, he has already almost learned this handsignal.

When teaching the handsignal, say "Fido SIT" as you raise your hand, palm upward. After he learns to respond to the word-plus-hand command, try using just the handsignal. Your dog will learn to obey either a verbal or silent command to SIT. Remember always to reward his cooperation.

NON-FOOD METHOD TO TEACH SIT

You may prefer to teach the SIT command without using food rewards. Or there may come a time when your already trained dog, who should know better, refuses to act on the familiar SIT command. Don't worry, there are gentle ways to help Fido place his body into the SITTING position. Dark-ages dog trainers "had to" hit their dogs or jerk and slam them around to teach this easy command... YOU WON'T. Dogs of different ages and personalities require different methods to help them learn to SIT, but roughness is not necessary.

When training, always use the LEAST FORCEFUL METHOD possible for any individual dog. Dogs require different degrees of physicality in training. Excessive force will cause Fido to resist the lessons out of either fear or a struggle for dominance. Gentler methods give your dog no reason to fear or to fight you and are the kindest, most effective way to teach.

What To Do

Young Puppies. If you simply tilt a pup's chin slightly upwards he will usually sit. Or you might try raising your hand a little above the pup's head. As he watches your movement his chin will be elevated and he'll probably sit.

To teach your pup to SIT on command... say "Fido SIT" then raise his chin gently and his bottom will lower itself. Praise heartily "Good SIT!" while you steady him in that position and soothingly stroke his chest for a moment. DO NOT continue to hold his chin up after he sits, that would make him uncomfortable. Most pups and dogs really enjoy having the center of their chest gently scratched. Many will remain sitting as long as someone will pet that spot.

If Little Fido doesn't sit when you raise his chin, cup your other hand gently behind his back legs under his bottom. Seat him into your hand, then lower his hindie carefully to the ground. These are good and kindly ways to help your puppy understand what to do when you tell him "SIT."

Most Dogs: Even if Fido's no longer a puppy you may still be able to train him by the ultra-gentle "young puppy method" described above. Try that first. Sensitive dogs of all ages respond well to the chin-lift method. Another gentle way to sit a dog is to slide your hand over his tail and down along behind the back of his rear legs. Some dogs will sit if you merely touch them beside the base of the tail. Always try the gentlest methods first.

Boisterous or Resistant Dogs: Some dogs have been denied the advantages of early training. They may have become too strong and self-willed to learn SIT with just the gentle chin-lift method. Some "skateboarder" pups and older dogs can be mighty boisterous or set in their ways. They may need a bit stronger method to teach them how to SIT without using a food lure. You may sometimes need to be a bit more "physical" with Rowdy Fido, but there's no necessity to be rough or intimidating.

The "Jelly Spot"

NEVER PUSH DOWN ON A DOG'S BACK when teaching SIT or any other command. It is painful for the dog and permanent injuries could result. Long ago, trainers routinely taught SIT by pushing down hard on the dog's rump. Some dogs were injured in that training process by the rough force applied to the hips or spine. Unbeknownst to those trainers, there was a way. They could have been using MUCH LESS FORCE and getting a BETTER SIT, too. If only they'd known about Fido's "Jelly Spot."

The "Jelly Spot" is located just forward of the dog's hipbones.

There are a pair of these sensitive spots, one on either side. Light pressure there makes most dogs' hind legs "turn to jelly." This makes it easy to gently guide the hindie to the ground without using downward force.

Light pressure on the Jelly Spots will make most dogs immediately SIT. It will be helpful to lift Fido's chin slightly as you squeeze the Jelly Spot. That will give his body two messages that both tell him to SIT for his own comfort.

"Jelly Spot"

*

What To Do

To teach your boisterous dog to SIT on command, say "Fido SIT." then lift his chin wth your right hand and squeeze the Jelly Spots with your left. Some dogs are quite sensitive there, others may be tougher. Use only as much pressure as you re-ally need. It should take less than one second of pressure for Fido to begin to SIT. If it takes longer, you're prob-ably not pressing right on the "Jelly Spot."

As soon as your dog's legs start to yield, immediately STOP SQUEEZING. Quickly but gently guide his hindie to the ground. Continue to elevate his chin until his bottom actually touches the ground, then immediately release his chin. Your dog will be SITTING, so praise him and soothingly scratch the center of his chest while he SITS there. Don't worry if he gets up right away, the STAY command will be taught later.

If your dog is headstrong and hard-bodied, you might need to be more convincing when teaching him to SIT. Instead of just lifting his chin, give an upward-and-backward pull on his collar as you squeeze the Jelly Spot with your other hand. It may help to slightly unbalance a rambunctios dog by pulling his haunches toward you as you squeeze the Jelly Spots and lower his hindie to the ground. That will usually SIT the most difficult dog. Hold this type of dog in the SIT position for a few seconds so you're able to praise him for his "obedience" before he pops back up again.

Plan B...

If you apply pressure to the Jelly Spot and your dog doesn't yield, you may have your fingers on the wrong spots. Locate the forward point of the hipbones and touch there, then roll your fingers slightly forward. That's where the spot should be. If you just can't find it or your dog reacts poorly, use one of the other methods in the book. Every dog is unique. Don't keep trying something that doesn't work in your particular dog's case.

If you find using the squeeze-method to teach Fido to SIT is too "physical" for you or that your dog just doesn't respond well to it, give the food-lure method a try. You may find that even your lovable rowdy hard-head responds well to tidbit motivation. It won't "spoil" him to lure him toward correct behaviors with yummies at first. Just use the treats wisely and "wean" your dog from them after he's learned what "SIT" means.

Some dogs learn best with a tidbit lure, some learn best by being helped into position, and still others learn fastest when methods are combined. See what works best for you and your dog. NEVER use more force than absolutely necessary, and ALWAYS remember to reward your dog with praise and petting, even when you also give him a food reward.

Consistency and reward are the keys to teaching any command to any dog, so be patient. Fido will willingly obey, once he understands what he is supposed to do.

What NOT To Do

◆ NEVER HIT OR SLAP you dog's rump of tail (or anyplace else) to teach him to SIT! That technique is left over from the "dark ages" of dog training. It's an insensitive and bully-like tactic which merely demonstrates a handler's lack of ability to communicate with the dog. Dogs love to please if they know how. Punishment is a very inappropriate way to teach a new command.

◆   NEVER press down on your dog's back! It may harm him if you do. Quickly and lightly squeeze the Jelly Spots instead.

◆   DON'T JUMP to the conclusion that Fido is "just being stubborn" if he's slow to respond to SIT. Some dogs have problems with their hips or "knees" (stifles) and it may be difficult or painful for them to sit or to get up again. Give your dog the benefit of the doubt. Be observant: if you see any clues that suggest pain or weakness, take your little fur-friend to see his nice doctor right away.

If your dog is slow to sit or seems to have trouble getting up, or if he winces when you touch his back or hips, these are reasons to suspect anatomical problems. Your veterinarian is the best person to advise you on this matter. She can diagnose or rule out physical causes that could be making it painful for your dog to obey. Some problems are treatable; many dogs can be helped medically or surgically. Talk to your vet.

THE COMMAND: **WALK**

The WALK command teaches your dog to move along politely on a loose leash. This command allows Fido to be ahead or behind you or to either side... but he MUST NOT PULL THE LEASH TAUT. This command is handy for exercise or potty outings. Fido will learn not to strain at the leash and will enjoy a six-foot radius of "freedom" around you. It will also be more pleasant for you to walk your dog without having a muscle contest with him.

What To Do

Hold the leash in your right hand with the "handle loop" over your thumb. Close your hand securely on the lead and hold your hand near your body at about hip or waist level. In a happy voice, command "Fido WALK"... then step out briskly. Speak the command clearly so Fido learns to recognize the new word. Don't wait for him to go first; you're the leader, remember?

Walk as if you have a destination in mind. Don't dawdle along or your dog won't be very interested in going with you. Turn frequently, surprise him with sudden changes of direction. Don't warn or wait for him when you turn... just GO. Turn abruptly whenever Fido gets distraced from you. He'll pay better attention as he realizes that he can't predict you movements unless he watches you closely.

When your dog WALKS along with you properly, praise him. Be sure to include the command word in a praise phrase ("Good WALK!") Your dog will learn the new "vocabulary" most quickly when you praise him this way.

Holding the Leash for WALK

Special Cases

Baby Puppy or Shy Dog: At first, gently attach the lead to your dog's collar. Tell him he's a good boy and just stand there with him. If he walks around or tries to get away, move right along with him. DON'T FIGHT HIM or try to control him at this point or he might panic. Just act as if the whole thing is "no big deal." Your display of calm assurance will help Fido relax and accept the new situation.

Once your "shy" dog accepts the leash you can begin teaching him the WALK command. Pat your dog, then command him in a friendly happy tone, "Fido WALK." Turn away from the dog and pat your leg to encourage him to come along with you as you walk away.

If he doesn't follow right away, stop, but keep your back turned to him. Tug-and-release the leash lightly a couple of times, like ringing a jingle-bell, and make a little "clucking" or "kissing" sound to attract his attention. A shy dog may feel less threatened if you bend forward slightly when you're teaching this command. Stay relaxed and be sure to use a HAPPY, encouraging tone of voice.

A young or shy dog may sometimes be enticed to follow on leash if he's offered a yummy tidbit. Give him a tiny taste before you start to walk, then another when he's gone a few steps with you. Don't overuse the tidbit lure! Discontinue food incentives for WALK as soon as your dog no longer fears the leash. The idea is for him to follow YOU, not just the food.

The Boisterous Dog: Hold your end of the leash close to your body with both hands. This rowdy ball-of-fire may try to take you for a flying ride! If your dog goes racing out to the end of the lead when you start to walk, brace yourself, turn in the opposite direction, and stride briskly away. Turn frequently to keep his attention.

After Rowdy Fido's main resistance to WALK is over, you'll only need to give the lead a light corrective tug to remind your dog to pay attention. A quick tug-and-release JUST BEFORE he reaches the end of the lead works better than a harder jerk after he's already started pulling. This quick contrast between loose and tight lead will refocus the dog on the handler. It sets a limit and reminds the dog to stay close. If you cannot get Fido's attention with a quick tug or two, do an immediate sudden turn.

Your abrupt change will turn Fido around in mid-dash and cause him to move in your direction. Praise him for this. Say "Good WALK!" even if your sudden turn gave him a surprise. You'll probably have to repeat this sudden turn several times in a row before Fido realizes that he needs to stick with you more closely.

The WALK command gives Fido plenty of freedom to sniff out the neighborhood dog messages, do his potty, and even say "Hi" to friends you meet along the way. The only rule is that Fido must NOT PULL on the leash while he walks with you. Not even a little bit. The same rule applies to the handler: You must NOT keep the leash tight while walking with Fido. Not even a little bit. If either you or your dog maintains ANY steady tension on the leash, no matter how light, the result will be a dog who pulls.

Be sure to make your WALK corrections crisply and release your pull immediately. Do not drag or draw with steady pressure on the lead or Fido will respond with a steady pull of his own. For minor corrections, use a quick, light tug-and-release done with a brisk snap of the wrist. If Fido doesn't get the message when you tug once, either turn away suddenly or use two or three brisk tug-and-release corrections in rapid succession to recapture his attention.

ALWAYS PRAISE AFTER CORRECTIONS. If a correction is made properly, your dog will end up obeying the original command. Praise him for being good, even if you had to gently "make him do it." This will help him understand what's expected and how he can please you.

After your dog figures out the benefits of walking near you on a loose leash, you'll both be able to enjoy long strolls around the block and quick trips out to pick up the mail. The WALK command will teach your dog to become more attentive and help ready him for the more formal HEEL command.

THE COMMAND: **WAIT**

The WAIT command stops your dog from proceeding until you give him permission. While you're walking your dog, use the WAIT command any time you want him to stop. Have him WAIT until you give a command to move again. WAIT allows you to safely control your dog when you come to a busy corner, pause to chat with a friend, or stop to tie your shoe.

WAIT can also be used to keep your dog from bolting through an open door or gate and from entering or leaving a car without permission. Dogs have been lost forever when a gate or door was left ajar for just a moment. WAIT keeps Fido in... or out, awaiting your release command, until you determine it's safe for him to go on.

The WAIT command does NOT require the dog to hold perfectly still in a certain position, but he MUST NOT walk away until you give the release. When you need your dog to hold a specific position, STAY would be the command to use instead of WAIT.

What To Do

The easiest way to teach WAIT is to work the command into your WALK practice sessions. As you walk your dog along on the loose six foot leash, suddenly freeze and say "WAIT!" in a crisp, urgent-sounding, authoritative voice.

Your dog may be startled by your sudden "statue" posture and warning tone. He will probably respond by stopping instantly and looking around for whatever "danger" his packleader (you) might have sensed. This is a natural response.

When he stops with you, praise him proudly, "Good WAIT!" and clap your hands a few times to let him know everything's just wonderful. Then tell him "Okay Fido, WALK" and start out again in a relaxed manner. Go about ten steps or so and repeat the WAIT exercise (urgent voice, freeze). Always praise your dog for stopping when he hears the command "WAIT."

WAIT At Doors

To introduce WAIT-At-Doors, put Fido on his leash, tell him "WALK" and approach the door of your choice. It could be a house door or a gate to the yard. Take your dog up to the door. Put your hand on the doorknob or latch and tell Fido to "WAIT." Then start to open the door.

Open it just a little at first. You'll probably have to stop Fido from rushing immediately through the opening. When he starts to barge past you, give a quick pull on the leash to stop him, then shut the door quickly before he can get out. Look sternly at your dog and repeat "WAIT!" Then start to open the door again and give him another chance.

If you stand by the door in just the right place you may be able to block the opening with your knee (or ankle for pups and toy breeds.) This strengthens the idea of a barrier when first teaching this command. Be prepared to block Fido's escape if necessary (which it probably will be.) Praise him if he WAITS correctly, even if you had to stop him. The praise will help your dog understand the concept of what WAIT means.

As Fido begins to realize he must not barge through, increase the door's opening to a width through which he could pass, but keep him WAITING. When he can withstand that much temptation, open the door all the way and still make him WAIT. If he obeys, give him the release command and let him go through the door. Praise him!

It may take several repetitions before your dog understands the new WAIT-At-Doors rule. It will be easier if you've already taught him to WAIT when you stop during WALK command practice.

Always use the WAIT command whenever you open a door or gate. Fido will soon develop the safe habit of waiting for permission before going through an opening. That way, when the neighbor child comes to visit and inadvertently leaves the gate ajar your good dog will know to stay in the yard... even though he COULD escape. You'll be glad he learned the WAIT-At-Doors exercise!

THE RELEASE COMMAND PHRASE

To tell your dog he does not have to WAIT any longer, say "Okay Fido, GO AHEAD" and motion with your hand by sweeping it toward the door invitingly. This is the Release Command and it's very important. Use the whole phrase! Don't just say "Okay" and let him go, give him the "GO AHEAD" command as well. If you use "Okay" by itself as the release command your dog may accidentally release himself sometime if he hears that word spoken nearby.

Say the Release Command phrase in a happy voice so Fido will know he's not in trouble. Some dogs try so hard to do the right thing that you may at first have to give the release command a couple of times before they're certain you really mean it. If your dog is unsure, tell him, "Okay Fido, Good GO AHEAD." Clap your hands playfully to let him know it's okay to relax.

THE COMMAND: HEEL

The HEEL command puts your dog close to your left leg, facing the same direction you are. HEEL requires Fido to be in that spot whether you are moving or standing still. He should be close but not touching you. HEEL keeps Fido less than a foot away with his collar next to your leg.

This command is taught on a loose leash. It's similar to WALK, but much closer and always at your left side. HEEL allows more precise "formal" control of your dog than the more relaxed WALK command. It also makes eye contact easy between you and Fido.

Which Side Are You On?

Why is HEEL always taught with the dog to the handler's left? Mainly because that's historically been the rule. It is also the rule for dogs today to HEEL at the handler's left in obedience competition. In Olden Days it was commonplace to walk with one's "dogge" on the left and one's "steede" on the right. No horse, you say? Well, how about walking with your dog on the left so your right hand is free to manage your sword? No sword either? Or perhaps you're left handed? No worry, it'll work out okay.

There's a safety feature in left-hand HEELING, at least in countries where cars are driven on the right. If Fido is HEELING correctly by your left he'll be farther away from oncoming vehicles.

Although it's traditional to have the dog HEEL on the left, a handler may have reasons to train a dog to walk on the right. Some folks need their dogs to be able to switch sides on command. A dog can readily learn to do this. Fido may be taught a different command word, with a handsignal to match, for each side.

How To Hold the Leash for HEEL

Hold the leash in your right hand with the loop over your thumb.

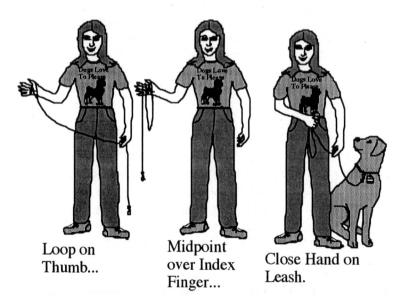

Loop on Thumb...   Midpoint over Index Finger...   Close Hand on Leash.

Holding the Leash for HEEL

Pick up the leash near its midpoint and place this "half-way bend" over your right index finger as shown in the illustration. Then close your hand on the shortened leash.

This one handed hold on the lead leaves your left hand free to adjust the leash and give supporting strength during corrections. You'll also use your left hand to pet your dog and encourage him to remain close.

The leash must be loose enough that the clip **hangs down** from the ring on the dog's collar. If the clip is lifted up, the lead is being held too short. A loose lead is essential when teaching proper HEELING. The dog must not get the <u>mistaken</u> idea that the leash is to be tight. You don't want your dog to get the habit of pulling against you.

Adjust your leash length when HEELING by changing the length of the "half way" loop over your right index finger. Close your fist on this fold of the lead, once adjusted, to keep the strap from slipping through your fingers if Fido suddenly pulls.

Teaching HEEL

Start off with the WALK command for a few minutes to get your dog focused. Then say "Fido HEEL" and do an About-Turn to your right. (Turns are described in the next section.) Pat your leg to encourage Fido to move in close. As he comes up to your hand to get some of that inviting patting, keep moving. Shorten your leash a bit (keep it loose, though) and reward your dog with petting and verbal praise. Tell him he's "Good to HEEL!"

If Fido lags behind instead of HEELING properly, clap your hands or pat your leg to encourage him to hurry up. Don't try to drag him along. Friendly encouragement works much better. Pet him when he's in the correct HEEL position.

◆ It's VERY IMPORTANT to keep your leash LOOSE, except for the instant it takes to correct your dog's speed or direction. The "surprise" capability of a loose lead makes milder leash corrections effective. On a tight leash a dog tries to out-pull his handler rather than yield. A quick tug-and-release or About Turn gives a dog nothing to resist or rebel against and makes it easier to teach him.

TWO "GOOD TURNS" for HEELING

There are two types of turns you'll need to know to teach your dog to HEEL on a loose leash. These two "good turns" are the "About Turn" and the "Left About Turn."

The ABOUT TURN

The About Turn is a 180-degree turn to the right (away from the dog when at HEEL.) This turn is useful as a directional change and also as a training aid for both the WALK and HEEL commands.

What To Do

While you're walking along with your dog, suddenly turn 180-degrees about-face and head off in the opposite direction. A pivoting movement on the balls of your feet will help you make this turn smoothly. Don't command or warn your dog when you turn. Fido's job is to pay attention. If he lags behind when you turn, the lead will quickly tighten, causing a sudden corrective pull. That will automatically turn your dog around and head him in your direction. PRAISE HIM for being with you!

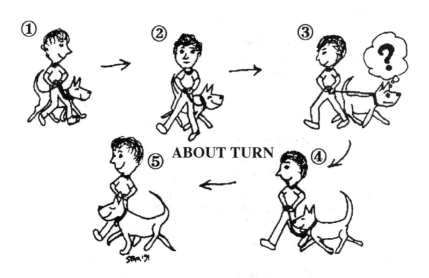

ABOUT TURN

Fido will be surprised to find his direction changed so suddenly, but your praise will let him know he's on the right track and you're pleased with him. After a few good About Turns your dog will figure out that he must pay close attention to keep up, avoid sudden corrections, and earn your enthusiastic approval.

The About Turn is especially valuable as a training aid when a dog lunges or rushes on ahead. It also helps when he's distracted by magnets. Fido HAS to focus on the handler and hurry along to make the About Turn. If he doesn't, he'll receive an automatic leash correction when the handler suddenly changes directions. If the outside magnets are VERY strong, it may sometimes be necessary to do several turns in rapid succession to recapture a dog's wandering attention.

What NOT To Do

◆   DO NOT JERK THE LEASH when doing an About Turn! If you warn your dog with a tug before turning, he'll get the wrong idea. He'll think <u>you</u> are supposed to keep him posted of your moves at all times. That's the opposite of what you're trying to teach him, which is that it's <u>his</u> responsibility to keep an eye on <u>you</u>!

Any time your dog is watching he'll have plenty of time to make the turn with you. He won't get a leash pull if he chooses to pay attention. When a handler jerks the lead as he turns it doesn't give the dog any time to make the right decision. That's not really fair.

◆   DO NOT COMMAND OR WARN before doing an About Turn. This is for the same reason as above: your <u>dog</u> must watch <u>you</u>. If you warn him with his name or a command (or say "ahem") he will not have to stay alert to your body movements.

When you turn, don't warn or- nag. Just hold your leash firmly, turn and go. The leash will tighten automatically if your dog isn't paying attention. You won't need to pull or tug or jerk at all. Let the leash do the "dirty work."

Your dog will start to understand that if he pays attention and turns with you there will be no leash pull but there WILL be praise and congratulations. He'll be proud of his ability to turn quickly with you. This is the perfect background to lay for future off-leash close HEELING work.

Always remember to praise good About Turns. This is true

even when you are working without any verbal command to turn. The dog learns to obey your body cue as a command. He MUST be praised for that!

The LEFT ABOUT TURN

The Left About Turn is a helpful training maneuver when the dog edges ahead just a little instead of HEELING correctly at the handler's side. In the Left About Turn the dog is required to slow down and move out of the handler's way. The handler turns sharply in front of the dog and the dog must yield.

The Left About Turn is 180-degrees to the left instead of the right. You will step in front of your dog, directly in his path, as you make this turn. He must move out of your way and turn with you. It promotes cooperation and it's a rather nice looking step when done smoothly.

This turn is especially good for use with dogs who forge slightly ahead of the handler. The sudden turn causes them to back up slightly... into the proper HEEL position by the handler's left leg. This teaches the dog to stay back in the correct spot and keeps him out from under foot.

The Left About Turn is great while HEELING, but it doesn't work well with the WALK command. The longer leash for WALK drags and tangles on Left About Turns. Plus, because the dog is allowed free range ahead, up to the leash limit with WALK, he can't see the handler make the turn to the left. He won't be able to get out of the way and both dog and handler will end up tangled or tripping over the lead. Left About Turn is really only useful during HEELING.

CAUTION: Sensitive dogs try so hard to be in the proper position for the Left About Turn they may hang back too far behind the handler. This is not the correct HEEL position, so it must be gently corrected. Don't try to pull your dog up to you. Instead clap your hands or pet and encourage him. If you pull on the leash he'll only want to hang back more.

The Left About Turn should be used sparingly with dogs of a sensitive temperament. Also, be sure to praise happily the <u>instant</u> your dog makes a good turn with you. Otherwise a sensitive dog may develop a habit of lagging, anticipating the turn too soon, trying TOO hard to please you with a crisp Left About Turn.

What To Do

Instead of turning clockwise (to the right) as in the About Turn, you and your dog will turn counter-clockwise (to the left.) The Left About Turn requires Fido to slow his pace and move out of your path when you cross in front of him as you turn to your left.

Be careful to avoid treading on your dog's toes as you turn! This is especially important with puppies and toy breeds because they're "right in the way" and also quite fragile. Keep your feet close to the ground when you make your Left About Turn. This will help protect tiny toes from being scrunched.

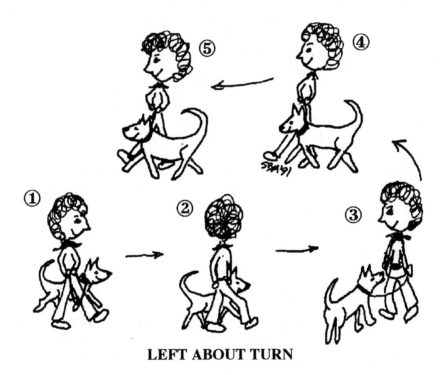

LEFT ABOUT TURN

Shorten your leash a bit as you turn. This will help guide your dog out of your path and keep him from tripping you. Loosen your leash again the instant you've made the turn.

It's very important to praise your dog immediately after a Left About Turn. It's startling for a dog when you step out in front of him as you turn. Fido was expecting to occupy that space himself and may worry that he's done something wrong. When he hears your praise he'll stop worrying because he'll know you're pleased with him. Praise helps Fido really <u>want</u> to pay attention.

If your dog is a big rowdy galoot, you may have to lean into his shoulder a bit as you turn if he doesn't move out of your path. Don't crash into him, just crowd him over. You may need to lean rather hard into some of the bigger guys. Use only enough contact to give your dog the idea he needs to move out of the way and adjust his HEEL position to you.

Using The "TWO GOOD TURNS"

Take plenty of opportunities to use both the About Turn and the Left About Turn. These "two good turns" will be very helpful for you whenever Fido is distracted by strong magnets. Either turn will quickly refocus your dog's attention back to you.

Use the About Turn when Fido goes racing out ahead when you're working on WALK or HEEL. Suddenly do an About Turn and stride briskly away. Fido has to turn too, because the leash will tighten automatically as you walk away. Praise when he's with you again.

Use the Left About Turn when Fido forges slightly ahead of you when he's supposed to be HEELING. Your abrupt left turn into his path of movement will refocus him on the proper HEEL position. He will learn to make adjustments in his speed, respecting your leadership.

What NOT To Do

◆   DON'T JERK THE LEASH when you command HEEL. It's common to see handlers give a command and simultaneously yank on the leash. This is very unfair to the dog. Before Fido could <u>possibly</u> have time to respond to the word, his handler has punished him. In fact, this punishes the dog for just <u>hearing</u> the command. This is certainly not very logical training. Far too many people develop this sloppy and insensitive habit without even realizing.

◆   DON'T DRAG YOUR DOG. It won't teach him to HEEL. In fact, it will teach him to pull! Encouragement works much better.

◆   DON'T LET YOUR DOG DRAG YOU. It's not much fun to take

a dog places if he tries to tow the handler along behind. Don't let him do it to you. A quick tug-and-release or About Turn works well.

♦ DON'T USE FOOD REWARDS FOR HEEL. If you do, Fido may tend to walk sort of sideways in front of you so he can see the "cookie" better. He needs to focus on your movement, not a treat. He's supposed to pay attention to you when you turn. Praise and petting work well for WALK and HEEL, so omit the food lures when teaching or practicing these commands.

HEELING with your dog is a bit like dancing. Your dog is your dance partner and he's supposed to follow your lead. The more closely he watches you the better he'll respond to your cues and commands and the better you'll dance together. A dog who HEELS politely is a delight to take anywhere. He will bring compliments upon himself and his master wherever they go.

The "AUTOMATIC SIT" With HEEL

After your dog understands the HEEL and SIT commands you can combine them to teach him to SIT automatically when you stop. This is a handy thing for him to do, as it keeps him safer around traffic and distractions. The Automatic Sit keeps the dog's attention focused on his handler, even when not moving.

What To Do

Stop abruptly while you are HEELING and command your dog to SIT. Your abrupt halt will grab Fido's attention if you've already trained him to WAIT on command. Your quick SIT command will tell him what he's supposed to do.

Give a quick, light tug-and-release as you halt, to prevent Fido from sailing on past you. It will become a cue for him to SIT immediately. Don't yank, just teach that the light tug means "SIT." Just as you don't need to shout a command word, you don't need to overdo physical "body commands" either.

Be sure to RELEASE tension on the lead as soon as your dog SITS. The release of tension is part of the reward Fido gets for his cooperation. If the lead is kept tight after the dog obeys, he may rightfully become confused.

After working on this for awhile, to make the SIT response automatic, start <u>omitting</u> the command. Pause for just ONE SECOND after you halt, to give your dog a chance to SIT without being told. Praise him enthusiastically if he does!

If he doesn't get the idea right away, he might just think he's supposed to wait for you to give the command. Help him understand he's to do it without a verbal command. Just cue him with your lead and help him SIT, if necessary. Praise him "Good SIT!" as if he'd done it all on his own. Soon he will!

Keep trying. The keys to success with the Automatic Sit are the abruptness of your halt and the quality and timing of your praise. If you'll help your dog get the idea, soon he'll understand what you want. He will SIT immediately each time you halt, without a word from you.

THE COMMAND: **COME**

Every dog owner knows how important it is for Fido to COME right away when he's called. Slow response or no response to "COME" is dangerous, annoying, and may result in harm or hardship for both dog and owner. Quick response to this command may save a dog's life. A dog who can be trusted to COME when called can be safely included in many more activities and taken for outings in marvelous places. He can really enjoy his life as your faithful companion and friend.

It seems when it's most important for a dog to respond to the command COME, he is usually headed <u>away</u>. With the dog's back toward us it can be really difficult to redirect his attention. For this reason it's useful to teach a dog to COME by calling when his back is turned. When he learns the command this way he'll be accustomed to turning away from interesting distractions when he hears your call.

Puppies under four months of age are usually not very bold on their own. Most don't feel comfortable exploring alone yet and prefer to stay close to someone with a bit of authority. Young puppies respond very quickly to this fun lesson, even off leash.

Older pups and adult dogs are more self-directed than little puppies and will learn the COME lesson best when on leash. The leash gives a "handle" so the trainer may be sure Fido won't take off instead of COMING when called.

If your dog has shown any inclination to ignore your call, be sure to use the leash or long line when teaching this command. Some dogs, regardless of breed or age, are just more independent than others. It's not safe to work them off lead because they might not obey. Try never to give your dog an opportunity to disobey the important COME command. A habit formed early will last a lifetime. Make sure all Fido's habits are good ones!

What To Do

Start out with your dog on the WALK command. When he gets a little way ahead of you and isn't paying attention, suddenly call him in a happy voice, "Fido COME!" Be sure you say his name before the command to let him know you're talking to him.

Back away from your dog about six or ten steps. You need not run, but move briskly, in a way that inspires the dog's chase reaction. Make it fun! Use a happy voice and move with energy. Most dogs will want to run toward you if you back away; it's a natural response.

While walking forward, suddenly call your dog and back up briskly without turning. The DOG TURNS and COMES.

Because your dog will be on a leash for this lesson he'll have to move toward you as you back away. If he doesn't turn around and COME right away when you call, he'll get a "boink" from the leash as you back up. Keep backing up until Fido is coming towards you. That will hurry him along.

When your dog gets close, suddenly stop and let him "catch" you. Make a big happy fuss over him when he does. Make nice happy eye contact, pet him, and praise him enthusiastically. "Good COME!"

Stand erect, but bend your knees just a little when you stop. Fido may accidentally crash into your legs when you come abruptly to a halt. He will probably come to a sliding stop and sit at your feet. You may encourage this by saying, in a firm-yet-happy voice, "SIT!" just before he piles into you. Help your dog sit facing you as you pet him and praise him for COMING. "Good COME and SIT!"

This quick SIT, facing you, is a nice touch for two good reasons. A SITTING dog is holding still... and a SITTING dog is not <u>jumping</u> on you.

Pet your dog and praise him lavishly when he COMES to you, whether he SITS or not. You can help him SIT as you're petting him for his wonderful response to the all-important COME command.

Remember:

♦ When you call Fido, BACK UP WITHOUT TURNING AROUND. The dog is supposed to turn around, not the handler.

♦ Say your dog's name FIRST, before the command to COME.

♦ Use a happy, friendly voice.

♦ Praise and pet your dog enthusiastically when he COMES.

COME-WHEN-CALLED WITH FOOD REWARDS

Many dogs don't like to COME when called if they're "busy" playing. These dogs have figured out how often the command "COME" actually translates to "THE FUN IS OVER." To prevent your dog from getting that common bad impression, call him once in awhile for no other reason than just to give him a special reward.

A toy might work here as a reward, but nearly every dog's <u>favorite</u> treat is some yummy tidbit. It's important when teaching your dog to COME away from play to use a reward that he thinks is really great... even irresistible. The more he enjoys the special reward, the more positive association your dog will form to the COME command.

Try this first when your dog is only mildly interested in some other pleasant activity he's been doing for a while (chewing on a toy or lounging in the yard.) Stand near him when you command the first time, make it easy for him to obey. When he does, reward him with the special treat. After a few repetitions of the command/reward sequence, Fido will develop enthusiasm for this new "game." Then you'll be able to call him away from such strong magnets as playing with another dog.

What To Do

Call your dog to you. "Fido COME!" Make yourself very interesting; back away, hop up and down, run around, dance in a circle... whatever it takes to strengthen your magnet and capture your dog's attention. When he COMES, pet him, praise him using an enthusiastic praise phrase ("Good to COME!!!") and give him the tasty treat.

Then let Fido go back to his play. In fact, TELL him to go play again. The idea is to let him know that obedience to the command "COME" has far more benefits than drawbacks. He won't have to worry that he'll miss out on anything. When he hears you call him, he'll have an optimistic attitude about the command and will COME to you quickly.

A food tidbit is a nice reward for COME. You can also use the yummy to encourage Fido to SIT when he gets to you. If you've already trained your dog to SIT for a tidbit lure, it will be easy to teach him to COME and SIT.

Remember, of course, to reward your dog with happy praise and petting, even when you also use a food lure. You'll need to "wean" him from the lure eventually, so be sure to "pay" him with pleasant voice and touch right from the very first lesson.

Beware Of Food Addiction!

Dogs can become "addicted" to food rewards all too easily. If this happens to your dog, he'll not want to COME to you unless he knows you're holding snacks. He may decide the only reason to obey is for food. This would be a bad situation indeed; your dog would only be obedient when hungry. Don't let your dog develop this addiction in the first place.

Never make the mistake of waving the food treat around so Fido sees it when you call him. He will quickly realize that you always show it if you have one. When you don't have a treat and you call your dog you won't have anything to wave around in promise... so he probably won't come to you. Frustrated dog owners sometimes feel that if they show the dog a big enough piece of sirloin he'll be bound to come when called. The trouble is, top sirloin becomes the "currency" and the dog soon won't work for anything less. If you don't have any with you, well... you'll just be out of luck.

Instead of waving around a big piece of food when you call your dog, keep your tidbit hidden in a pocket. Only make the yummy appear after your dog has COME to you. Ta-daaaa!!! "What a good dog to COME!" Fido will love it. His natural curiosity and optimism will make him run to you full speed when you call.

Tiny Tidbits Best

Use food rewards and lures sparingly and sensibly. Break tidbits into very tiny pieces. Just a taste one-quarter inch square is plenty, even for a big dog. Small treats are more effective than bigger ones because the treat seems more rare, exotic, and "expensive." He'll be more interested in giving you what you want (COME & SIT) in order to get what he wants (the tasty treat.)

Small tidbits have other benefits as well. The dog doesn't tend to carry away the tiny crumb and guard it. Also, the small tidbit is more of a "magic flavor dot" than an item of food. Small treats don't fill up a dog's belly, either, so he'll stay interested in the lesson longer. Best of all, with the treats being so small, rather than becoming dependent upon them the dog becomes optimistic about them. Instead of checking the breeze to smell if you're holding treats before he decides to COME on command, your dog will race to you in joyous optimism.

As always, remember to use praise and touch rewards along with any foodies you give.

Weaning and "The Lottery"

At first, give Fido a tidbit every time you call him. When he has been responsing well for a while, change to giving the tidbit only every second or third time. Dogs are optimistic creatures, so even when there isn't a food treat, Fido will hope there is and rush to find out. This phenomenon is similar to our own species' eager purchase of Lottery tickets. Sales are most brisk when no prize has been awarded for awhile. Optimists take the chance, even when they know the odds against winning the Big Prize are monumental.

Food lures and treats work well to enhance most dogs' desire to cooperate. It's best, of course, if a dog's main motivation is to please his packleader. To keep a dog from deciding to work ONLY for food, it's important to "wean" from treat motivation after he learns to respond well to a command. This is not to say he'll never get a treat again, just that tidbits will be given at unpredictable intervals rather than every single time he obeys.

Always pet and praise your dog for COMING to you. Once in while surprise him with a tidbit too. He will COME when you call because he wants to please you AND because this might be the time he wins the Yummy Lottery!

PREVENT PROBLEMS

The food lure and backing away method of teaching COME is fun for Fido. It's action-packed, rewarding, and full of surprises. You might, at any time, suddenly back up and call him. Your dog never knows when you'll do it, so he learns to stay alert and COME to you quickly. He knows you'll be pleased when he COMES to your call and will reward him well. He also learns that, if he acts a bit stubborn once in awhile, you can correct him with a quick tug on his leash.

The "Artful Dodger"

Many dogs try to dodge away when anyone reaches for their collar. This is frustrating for dog owners, because it makes a dog very hard to "capture" once he develops this habit. You can teach your dog not to do this evasive trick by using a food lure to teach him to hold still while you take hold of his collar.

Call your dog to COME to you. When he does, have him SIT facing you before you give him the tidbit. While you're awarding him the taste treat, touch his collar with your other hand. If Fido's attention is focused on the treat (and it probably will be) he'll barely notice your hand. Scratch his neck lightly with your fingers through his collar. Hold his collar. Pretty soon it will be no big deal to the dog to have his collar touched.

When he can accept the treat-plus-collar-touch, switch the order. Reach for the collar first, then give the treat after you're pleasantly scratching his neck. He'll learn to associate the reaching and touching hand with the pleasant scratching and the yummy treat.

When a dog has learned this he won't resist a reaching hand or a touch on his neck or collar. This will make him a much safer and more reliable companion.

A Word Of Warning

NEVER CALL YOUR DOG TO YOU TO PUNISH HIM! He will think you're punishing his obedience to the COME command. Your dog may be afraid to COME to you the next time you call.

If you must discipline your dog, go to him... don't call him to you. Why should Fido COME to you if he thinks you might randomly punish him when he gets there? Think about his point of view, it makes perfect sense.

Try to make sure COME is a command your dog trusts and enjoys. It's one of the most important words he needs to know! Encourage Fido with your voice, clap your hands or pat your leg. Pet him and praise him. Sometimes give him a little foodie-treat. Happy praise and other nice rewards will give your dog the idea that COMING quickly to you when you call is very worthwhile.

The LONG-LINE for COME

After Fido will reliably COME to you on a leash, you can start working with him on a light long-line. The idea of the long-line is to teach Fido you can control him from a greater distance than allowed by the six foot training lead.

Your Long-Line

An excellent long-line can be made from a length of light, soft, round-braided nylon cord. Nylon cord is very strong and durable, so you won't need to worry about your dog breaking it AS LONG AS YOU NEVER LET HIM CHEW ON IT! Depending on the size of your dog the long-line cord should be from one-eighth to one-quarter inch thick. The line should be thirty to fifty feet long.

Tie a thumb loop in one end of the cord. Hold that end the same way you would a leash. Tie the other end of the longline securely to your dog's collar on the same ring you'd fasten the leash.

Don't tie a leash clip to the dog's end of the line; it would jingle and weigh enough to remind Fido he has a "leash" on. That would spoil the surprise effect of the light long-line. The idea is to give your dog the impression you can ALWAYS reach him, even at a distance.

What To Do

Take your dog to a big open space where nothing can tangle or catch on the long-line. When you start out, attach both the leash and the long-line to your dog's collar. Practice WALK, holding the leash for awhile, letting the long-line drag along the ground while Fido gets used to it. Every so often call your dog to COME to you from just a leash length away. Reward him when he obeys, just as you normally would.

After a few minutes of on-leash work, pick up the thumb loop tied in the dragging end of the long-line, then take Fido's leash off. Tell him "Okay, GO AHEAD" and let him relax and run around a little.

Before Fido reaches the end of the long-line, call him to you and take a few quick steps away. If he COMES right away the line will not tighten or correct him. Reward his good behavior and make a pleasant fuss over him.

If Fido runs further away instead of COMING to you, the long-line will tighten unexpectedly when he suddenly reaches the end. That will give your dog a elastic-like pull on his collar which will turn him around to face you. With his direction corrected in this way, you can call your dog again and run a few steps away. This gives him a fresh opportunity to do the right thing. Praise your dog then, when he COMES to you, even though he HADN'T initially planned to obey.

It's best to call your dog BEFORE he reaches the end of the long-line. That way he won't know exactly how long your "reach" is. If, when you call, you turn and run away from your dog with the line attached, he'll get a surprising "boink" if he's not paying attention. When he reaches the limiting end of the long-line, the slight stretch will turn him around in mid-dash and hasten him in your direction.

Preparing For Off-Leash Work

After practicing for awhile, drop the end of the long-line and call your dog. Be sure to stay near the end of the cord so you'll be able to step on it quickly if Fido decides to make a break for it.

Never try to grab the long-line with your bare hand if your dog is running! The friction as it slides through your fingers can give you a nasty "rope burn." Always step on the long-line to stop the dog or slow him down before you try to grab hold of the slippery thin nylon cord.

Continue to increase both distance and distractions as you prepare Fido for off-lead work. If you have a fenced yard or access to a safely enclosed outdoor area like a tennis court, go ahead and test your dog's obedience to the COME command. Let Fido sniff around and exercise himself for a few minutes, then call him. Use the same tone of voice you'd normally use to call him; you've taught him to respond to that. He'll be most likely to COME to you now if the command tone is the same as he's learned.

Correct your dog if he doesn't quickly obey the command. Help him learn to please you. Make it easy for him to succeed and impossible for him to disobey. ALWAYS praise Fido when he COMES to your call... even if you have to help him. Pet him, touch his collar, scratch his neck. Give him a food reward once in awhile to keep his interest high.

Make new lessons and all practice sessions fun, but remember that "COME" is a very serious command. Your dog will soon learn that it's a GOOD idea to COME when he's called. He'll learn you can control him at varying distances. That makes you a little bit more "magical" than before.

When Fido reliably COMES to your call he can be safely included in much more family fun!

FINISH (TO HEEL FROM IN FRONT)

You can teach your dog a little extra step once he COMES to your call and SITS facing you. Fido will learn to go from his SIT in front of you into the HEEL position at your left side. In everyday life it's often convenient to send your dog to HEEL after he COMES to you. In obedience trials this is required. It's called the "FINISH" exercise.

There are several different ways to teach the two accepted methods for FINISH to HEEL. In one FINISH the dog goes from right to left <u>behind</u> the handler to the HEEL position. The other, the "swing" FINISH, moves the dog in a quick small circle at the handler's left, into HEEL. These two methods accomplish the same purpose and either is acceptable in the show ring.

What Happens In The FINISH Exercise

The verbal command "HEEL" is normally used to cue a dog for the FINISH exercise, because the dog is expected to go to the HEEL position. Most trainers use that command for this exercise. Whether you are moving or standing still, "HEEL" means the same thing. The dog is to remain close to your left side, facing the same direction you are. Really, as with any command, the word you use is up to you. The important things to remember are to use the command consistently and always reward your dog when he obeys.

Different Methods

Three methods for teaching the FINISH are included here because different obedience instructors use different methods. Over the years I've used all three methods described in this book and taught them at different times to my students. After working with each of the methods on many different types of dogs (and handlers), my personal preference is Method #1, the simplest.

When first teaching any of the FINISH methods in this book, the handler will move several steps. In Method #1 the handler merely moves forward a few feet. Method #2 involves walking backwards a few steps, then forward again to the original position. Method #3 is the most complicated; the leash is passed from right hand to left behind the handler's back while she walks backwards a couple of steps and then forwards again.

The handler's movement in these methods communicates to the dog he must get up from his SIT in front and go to the HEEL position.

With all three methods the handler will start by moving several steps and gradually reduce the amount of movement as the dog becomes more proficient. After Fido understands the exercise, the handler will not move at all. The dog will get up and FINISH to HEEL on command with either voice or handsignal.

Foodies Or Force?

Way back in the "dark ages" of dog training, FINISH was taught by hauling the dog (using lead and choke collar) from an obedient SIT in front of the handler, around behind and into the HEEL position. UGH! No wonder many dogs seemed unenthusiastic about this exercise. Nowadays we know better. Dogs will happily learn to go to HEEL by following the trainer's movement and a tiny tidbit treat. (Such an amazing discovery, eh?)

FINISH to HEEL does not require force in training. Your dog can learn the exercise easily with gentleness and fun. He will learn to obey this command with joy. If you compete in obedience trials this may be very good news. A dog with a happy, snappy FINISH may not actually earn any extra points, but he will put the judge in a good mood.

Dog's Movement in FINISH Methods #1 and #2
Circle to the Left of Handler

FINISH to HEEL -- METHOD #1

With this FINISH method the handler moves forward and the dog swings left in a small circle into HEEL position.

What To Do (Method #1)

a) Hold a food treat AND the leash in your left hand. Show Fido the treat to capture his interest.

b) Say "Fido HEEL" and, starting with your left foot, walk forward a few steps.

c) As Fido stands up to follow you, encourage him (with the tidbit) to move in a small circle (counter-clockwise) at your left side.

d) Help Fido into the proper HEEL position.

e) Hold the treat (in your left hand) above your dog's nose to SIT him.

g) Reward your dog with the tidbit and an enthusiastic "Good HEEL!" Praise and pet him and let him know how great he is.

FINISH to HEEL -- METHOD #2

This FINISH method, like the previous one, moves the dog in a small circle to HEEL at the handler's left side. The handler moves first backward, <u>then</u> forward, in this method. The dog swings left into HEEL position.

What To Do (Method #2)

a) Hold a food treat AND the leash in your left hand; show Fido the treat to capture his interest.

b) Say "Fido HEEL" and, starting with your left foot, walk <u>backwards</u> a few steps.

c) As your dog gets up to follow you, encourage him with the tidbit to turn a small circle at your side so he's facing the same direction you are.

d) Then walk a few steps forward and stop with your feet together.

e) Help Fido SIT in the HEEL position at your left side. (If you hold the treat up above his nose when you stop he'll probably SIT.)

f) Reward with the tidbit and enthusiastic praise and petting. "Good HEEL!"

FINISH to HEEL -- METHOD # 3

In this method the dog passes BEHIND the handler from right to left, ending up at the handler's left side in HEEL position.

What To Do (Method #3)

a) Hold a food treat and the leash in your <u>right</u> hand.

b) Show your dog the treat and say "Fido HEEL." Then starting with your right foot, take a couple of steps backward.

c) As Fido stands up to follow you, move him to your <u>right</u>.

d) Take a step forward and pass the leash and the treat (and the dog) <u>behind</u> your back from right to left.

e) Bring Fido up to your left side into HEEL position.

f) Hold the treat in your left hand, above his nose, to encourage your dog to SIT.

g) Reward your dog with the tidbit, petting, and "Good HEEL" praise.

Which FINISH Method Should You Choose?

The first two methods described above are less complicated for handlers than the third, as the handler is not required to change hands with the leash. These two swing-left methods also allow the handler to keep the dog in sight during the exercise. This can be advantageous with an easily distracted dog.

The third method (passing behind the handler), although more complicated, does have an advantage. The dog can FINISH using less turn-around space. This is a consideration when working in close quarters with a large dog. This method does have the drawback, though, of putting the dog momentarily out of sight as he passes behind the handler.

Really it's a matter of personal preference which FINISH method you choose. Some dogs and handlers work better with one method, some another. You could experiment with each to feel which one best suits you and your dog. Whichever method you decide upon, stick with that one until Fido has mastered it. Some dogs are capable of learning both the swing FINISH and the other. If you'd like to teach both types of FINISH to your dog, wait until he knows one of them well, then introduce the second.

THE COMMAND: **DOWN**

The DOWN command (also known as "Lie Down") makes it easy for you to keep Fido quiet, comfortable, and controlled for fairly long periods of time. This command can be handy on social occasions or when you just want your dog to mellow out for awhile around home.

In dog society, when a pack member is dominated by a higher ranking individual he admits his inferior rank by lowering his head or lying down. Extreme submission is represented posturally by the underdog voluntarily rolling over on his back. This exposes his vulnerable belly to the top dog. Because of this instinctive association between submission and lying down, some dogs are uncomfortable at first with the DOWN command. It's important to be aware of this natural reaction and use non-threatening techniques to teach this command.

Back In The "Bad Old Days"

The old methods of teaching the DOWN command used forceful and humiliating tactics. Dogs were jerked off their feet, slammed chin-first into the floor, slapped on the most sensitive part of the nose, and otherwise bullied into lying down. It's no wonder the DOWN command caused resistance and behavior problems in so many dogs!

Dominant dogs resent being roughly forced into the DOWN position. The old bullying methods often caused dogs to resist this command. Submissive dogs, on the other hand, were emotionally overwhelmed by the old "force" methods. They would cower or roll over when given the DOWN command.

The fears and resentments created in dogs by "force" methods can result in long-lasting attitude and behavior problems. These problems may include aggression toward the handler. These reactions do not occur when force is avoided. Gentle understanding should be used when teaching this or any command.

The FOOD TREAT Method for Teaching DOWN

Most dogs can be encouraged to cooperate when a food lure is used to introduce the DOWN command. A dog may not even realize at first that he's learning a command as he follows the tidbit to the ground. That fine... soon enough he'll leap into the DOWN position on command if trained by this pleasant method.

What To Do
It's easiest to coax a dog to DOWN if you start with him in a sitting position.

a) First show Fido a tidbit, let him smell it, then raise it up slightly to have him SIT. Give him the treat and praise him "Good SIT!"

b) Now immediately show him a new tidbit, then slowly lower the "bait" to the floor. (Don't give a command yet, just let him follow the treat down.)

c) Hold the treat on the floor, right where Fido's nose will be when he does lie down. Many dogs (especially pups) will eagerly follow the yummy as you lower it and will DOWN immediately.

If your dog does this, praise him "Good DOWN!" and give him the treat. He will associate the "DOWN" command with the praise phrase and treat reward. Fido will happily obey the command without developing a stubborn or resistant attitude.

When you give the treat, keep your food-hand on the floor. That helps assure that your dog will remain in the DOWN position for a moment while you reward him for his cooperation.

The Tunnel Trick
If your dog doesn't lie down right away when you introduce this new exercise, there is a neat trick to try. Hide the tidbit lure inside the little "tunnel" of your mostly closed hand. Fido may try to stick his

nose inside the "tunnel," so brace your hand to hold it still.

He may also paw or "dig" at your hand for the food; don't worry, that generally means he's about to lie down.

Say "Good DOWN!" when he finally does. Open the "tunnel" and give Fido the treat with your hand resting on the floor.

Preventing Bad Attitudes

Wait until Fido catches on to the down-for-food position before you start giving him the verbal command. Just let him follow the tidbit to the ground a few times and be rewarded with the treat and the praise phrase "Good DOWN!" It will only take two or three successes for your dog to get the right idea, so wait to place a "name" on this new "game" until your dog enjoys playing it with you.

Don't confuse your dog by repeating "DOWN... DOWN... DOWN..." while he's still trying to figure out how to get the tidbit from your hand. It's better for Fido to hear the new command word only as part of the praise phrase at first so he'll learn to associate it with the pleasant reward.

After your dog catches on to following the treat, then you can start using the command. Say "Fido DOWN" as you lower your hand (with the tidbit) toward the ground. This also begins to teach your dog the handsignal for this command. Soon he'll respond to either the verbal command or handsignal for DOWN.

The HANDSIGNAL For DOWN

While Fido is learning the word "DOWN," following the tidbit in your hand to the ground, he'll also be learning the handsignal. He will connect the downward sweep of your hand with the tasty reward and will lie down when he sees you move your hand in that manner.

A handsignal should be simple, smooth, and distinct from other gestures. The movement must be easy to see from a distance.

Handsignals are most readily understood when the gesture naturally indicates the body movement we wish the dog to make. Some people use a raised hand as a signal for DOWN, holding their hand up in the air until the dog has obeyed. I prefer a DOWNSWEEPING gesture because it's a more natural signal for the dog to move downwards.

You may use either hand for the signal. Just be sure to give the signal the same way each time. Don't confuse your dog.

If you intend to compete in obedience trials it's vital that whatever handsignal you use is <u>one</u> smooth motion. You'd be disqualified if you repeated a verbal command and the same rule is true for handsignal commands. A handler who gives repeated signals is penalized with disqualification. The rules for obedience competition are very specific. Study the official trial regulations and keep them in mind if you're training your dog for competition.

What To Do

Raise your open right hand and say "Fido DOWN." Then lower your hand, palm downwards, in a dramatic sweep. If you're using a tidbit, hold it between your thumb and forefinger and extend the other three fingers for the "open hand" signal.

Wean your dog from the food lure as soon as he understands the handsignal. Switch from using the treat as a lure to using it as a reward after proper response to the DOWN command. Just give the command and use the handsignal empty-handed. Keep the treat in your pocket so Fido can't see it. Delay the food reward until after the praise phrase.

What NOT To Do
♦ <u>DON'T</u> "pretend" to have a tidbit

by holding your hand as if you were hiding something. Your dog will think you're deceitful and will lose interest in this "trick."

Changing An Existing Negative Attitude

If your dog has already developed a negative attitude toward the DOWN command you can help him learn to overcome it. Bad attitudes about this exercise are most often the result of earlier "force training."

Sometimes just the sound of the "D" word (DOWN) is enough to upset a dog. They may whine and try to avoid being touched. Some may even growl or snap when reached for after they've heard this command. A dog with an attitude that bad can often still be helped if a new command word is chosen. The old word has a bad meaning to the dog, so just give him a new one. That will allow a fresh start with this exercise without any unwanted attitude baggage about the word.

In any case, omit the command word until <u>after</u> the dog has willingly followed a treat to the DOWN position. Resist the urge to say the command until the position itself is easy and non-threatening to Fido's self-image. This method will make "DOWN" more pleasant for him and easier for both of you. Fido won't be worrying about whether it's submissive to obey the command. He'll just lie down because he's following the yummy.

When your dog follows the treat well, begin to use a praise phrase when he lies down. Include the command word you'll use for this exercise. When he's heard the word in the praise phrase a few times, say the command in a friendly voice <u>as</u> you lower the tidbit to the floor. Do that a few times, then switch to commanding <u>first</u>, then lowering the treat. Soon your dog will hear the command word and lie down without a fuss.

Be sure to wean your dog from the food lure as you would with any command. Fido will still hope for the treat every time but will be delighted to receive it once in awhile. ALWAYS praise when the dog cooperates, whether or not you give him a tidbit as a reward. He needs these other rewards (praise, petting) as well.

Make learning the DOWN command as much fun for the

dog as you possibly can. Make it like a clever circus trick. Give plenty of praise and be patient. Soon this commanded position will become easy and non-threatening for your dog. This will be so even if an unfortunate introduction to this exercise had soured the dog's attitude.

The GENTLE NON-FOOD Method to Teach DOWN

Eventually all dogs must be able to obey the DOWN command without treats. There are also some dogs who (hard as it may be to believe) are simply not motivated by food treats. You may have some reason not to use food lures or rewards in training your particular dog. No problem! It's not necessary to teach DOWN using food. There are gentle alternatives that don't involve yummies.

Some dogs have no "issues" about the submissiveness of the DOWN position and will be quite happy to go along with whatever you might suggest. (These dogs are easy to teach any command!) Some other dogs are more self-willed and resist new lessons. The following section includes techniques which can be tailored to the individual.

What To Do

It's easiest to begin this lesson after you've worked your dog for awhile on other commands he already knows. If you try this lesson after your dog's first initial burst of energy has passed he'll be more likely to go along with it.

With the dog already SITTING, give the handsignal for DOWN, but <u>don't</u> say the command. Pat the ground invitingly in front of your dog, as if there was a nice soft comfy cushion there for him. Many dogs will coooperate right away by lying down on the "invisible cushion."

Praise your dog "Good DOWN" crooningly rather than with excitement. Stroke him slowly on his chest while he remains for moment in the DOWN position. Petting the dog's chest will help keep him in the DOWN. Head petting is more likely to "pop" him right back up again.

Don't make the mistake of giving belly rubs to your dog to reward him for obeying the DOWN command. If you do he may <u>always</u> try to flop over into that undignified (albeit cute) position. You won't need to lift him or straighten him back up if he already has this silly habit... it's hard to do that once a dog gets rolling around, anyway. Instead, simply ignore your upside-down wiggly dog. Don't scratch his belly no matter how "inviting" he tries to make it look. Pretend not to notice; don't look. If he gets no reaction he'll become bored with his own antics and stop. (You can give him his belly rubs at more appropriate cuddling times.) Voice praise him for DOWN, but don't reach to pet him or he'll be likely to get goofy again.

What To Do When Fido Will <u>Not</u> DOWN

Once your dog has learned to obey the DOWN command, he'll usually do it as soon as you tell him to. There may be times, though, when he'll choose to ignore or disobey. Dogs DO have minds of their own! When this happens you will need to correct your dog. Be firm but gentle with corrections. You don't need to scare Fido or start a war over a little normal willfull-ness.

If your dog will not go DOWN when you command, gently lift both his front legs (from the side, <u>not</u> the front) and "stretch" his front end forward while his back end stays put.

Don't grab his feet or pull his legs. That's rough and scarey and causes a dog to fight for control of his body.

Instead, reach under both front legs from the side and gently grasp the farthest foreleg just above the dog's "wrist." Lift both his forelegs, supporting their weight on your forearm. Without yanking or twisting, gently stretch your dog forward into the DOWN position.

For added control of Fido's front end, hold his collar in your left hand while you gently lift both his forelegs with your right. Rest your left arm on your dog's shoulders. Don't lean on him, but guide him into the DOWN position. A good hold on the collar will help if your dog is large or rambunctious.

CAUTION: DO NOT PRESS DOWN ON YOUR DOG'S BACK.

Downward pressure on a dog's spine can hurt, cause him to fear the DOWN command, and may injure him severely. Any downward pressure, no matter how light, should be on the shoulders ONLY.

CAUTION: ALWAYS USE THE LIGHTEST CORRECTION that will work for your particular dog.

Overcorrection for the DOWN command can cause a dog to feel extremely threatened. It may even provoke him to self-protective violence against his own master. Don't damage your relationship with your dog by being rough.

AND... ALWAYS PRAISE GOOD BEHAVIOR!

THE COMMAND: STAY

The STAY command requires Fido to hold a specific position (sitting, down, or standing) until commanded otherwise. There are many situations in everyday life perfect for the use of STAY, so you'll find plenty of opportunities to practice this important command. STAY allows you to settle your dog and safely leave him in one location while you are busy nearby in another.

What To Do

First teach Fido to SIT. This is an easy position to start from when adding STAY to your dog's command vocabulary. When he has learned the SIT-STAY exercise you can also teach him DOWN-STAY and STAND-STAY.

Arrange your dog so he's sitting at HEEL on your left. Gather up the lead fairly short but not taut. The clip on the leash should hang down by its own weight from the dog's collar. Be ready to give a quick upward pull on the lead if your dog starts to move from the SIT position. The purpose of holding the lead short is <u>not</u> to actually <u>hold</u> him in position, but to stop him instantly if he tries to leave his spot.

Tell your dog "STAY." Do not use his name with the STAY command or he'll probably want to get up and follow you. When you say the command also give the handsignal for STAY.

The HANDSIGNAL For STAY

Bring your open right hand in front of the dog's eyes (NOT his nose.) Hold your fingers straight and your palm toward the dog. The signal is similar to the hand gesture a traffic officer would use to stop a line of cars.

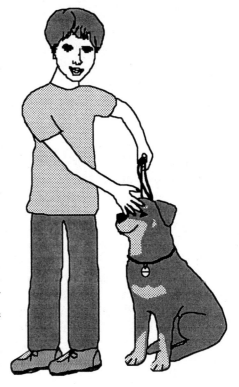

Hold your hand in front of Fido's face for only one or two seconds, then take your hand away. If you leave it there too long Fido will tend to follow when you move it away. He may think he only has to stay there as long as your hand remains in front of his eyes. Really, the handsignal is only to command the dog what to do, NOT to hold him there afterwards.

Leaving The Dog

After you have commanded Fido to STAY with both voice and handsignal, pivot out in front of him. Don't go anywhere yet, just stand toe-to-toe with him. Wait there for about five or ten seconds, holding the lead loose but ready above his head. Then pivot back into HEEL position and praise your dog, "Good STAY!"

When your dog can hold a STAY for ten seconds with you standing right in front of him, begin to increase your distance. Don't try to progress too rapidly with this command (as many handlers are tempted to do.) Slow and steady progress is best. You'll want your dog, for his own safety and your peace of mind, to be rock solid on this command.

Returning To The Dog

Accustom your dog to movement around him while practicing STAY. A good way to start this is to return to your dog after the STAY by walking around behind him, stopping in the HEEL position.

At first you may need to keep your hand on Fido's cheek or head as you walk behind him, to steady him and keep him from getting up and following you. Your touch will reassure the dog you're not really going anywhere. Soon he'll understand you want him to STAY until you return to the HEEL spot. In obedience competition handlers are required to return to their dogs this way, passing behind them and then to HEEL.

If He Moves

To do the STAY properly your dog must remain <u>exactly</u> where you left him. If he moves from that spot, put him right back as if it was marked with an "X." Don't let him move even a few inches from his "X" or soon he'll be moving feet... then yards.

Reposition Fido on his STAY spot the instant he starts to move. Repeat the STAY command with both voice and handsignal. Then step out in front of your dog again and face him. If he moves off the spot, pull up on his leash quickly (three rapid tugs will work well if he ignores just one.) Put your dog back on the same spot again and tell him "STAY." After several repetitions he'll start to get the idea. Be patient. When he's held his position for five to ten seconds, return to him (to the HEEL spot) and praise him, "Good STAY!"

Increase Difficulty

As Fido's ability to STAY improves, try increasing both time and distance factors. Do this gradually, a few seconds and a few feet at a time. Practice on leash until your dog is quite reliable. Try to help him succeed. Prevent him from making mistakes. If a loose dog breaks his STAY and runs off, he's learned a very bad lesson.

Use your long-line to practice STAY at an increased distance without sacrificing your ability to manage your dog. This control is especially important if your dog has already started to form the dangerous habit of running off.

And, of course, ALWAYS PRAISE your dog whenever he tries to please you!

RELEASE From The STAY

Fido needs to learn to hold his STAY position until you release him from it. You'll need to teach your dog the release phrase, "Okay Fido, HEEL." This phrase is used after a STAY instead of just turning the dog loose. Fido will learn to hold his position more securely this way and will be less likely to break the important STAY command.

What To Do

After returning to your dog's side, praise him for his good STAY. Then tell him "Okay Fido, HEEL" and take two or three steps forward with him at your left. Have him SIT when you stop. Now the STAY command is formally over. Praise your dog again.

Don't just say "Okay" and then let him dash away. That's a dangerous thing to do because we use that word so casually in conversation. A dog might hear the word "Okay" spoken nearby and optimistically (and mistakenly!) think it was meant to release him from a STAY. He might bound blithely out into traffic. So be sure to use the whole release phrase after a STAY. "Okay Fido, HEEL" tells him clearly that the STAY is over, but it gives him one more "trick" to do before his job is done. This will help keep him more attentive to you... and keep him safer.

Training Tip

DO NOT teach your dog to COME from a STAY until he's fairly advanced in his basic obedience training. It's long been a common practice at basic obedience classes to teach the dogs to STAY and then call them. This is done mainly to practice for the "RECALL" exercise in obedience competition. The Recall exercise requires the dog to SIT-STAY, then to COME and SIT in front, then FINISH to HEEL on command.

STAY and COME are opposites. To teach them together to beginner-dogs as one exercise can be rather confusing for them. You could imagine how difficult this could be for someone learning a new language, as your dog is. Both STAY and COME are extremely important commands and, for safety's sake, must be individually understood by your dog. While you're teaching him what these words mean, try to keep things as clear and simple as you can.

After you're sure Fido understands both STAY and COME individually, then you could start to put them together for the "RE-CALL" exercise. Go ahead and teach your dog the RECALL, even if you never plan to enter competiton. It's fun and challenging. Don't teach it too soon though, and don't practice it more than twice in a row. If you do, Fido may start to anticipate the COME command and become unreliable on STAY.

Another Caution

Don't tell your dog to "STAY" when you say goodbye to him in the morning as you set off for work or school. If he actually obeyed that STAY command he would have to remain in that <u>exact</u> spot all day long, until you came home in the evening and released him. That's a bit unreasonable to expect of him and it's probably not what you really meant.

Instead of using the command word, "STAY," when you leave say something a little less formal, like "Stay Home" or "Wait for Me" or "Watch the House." Fido will feel like he has a job to do that way. He won't have to wonder if it's okay to move while you're gone. Don't ask him to do the impossible! This may seem funny, but it's serious to a dog. Dogs are rather literal-minded folk. The commands you give your dog must have consistent definitions if he is to understand and reliably obey.

THE COMMAND: STAND

This command may be used any time you'd like your dog to stand still for a bit. The "Stand for Examination" exercise is associated in most people's minds with its use in dog shows. It's also a very handy command for everyday life, even if you don't enter competition.

STAND is great while you towel dry your dog after a bath or coming in from the rain. Your dog's groomer will appreciate this command too; it's a lot simpler and safer to bathe and brush a dog when he'll STAND still. Veterinary diagnosis and treatment will also be easier if your dog has been taught this command.

You may have already taught your dog to SIT and to STAY. Both those words begin with the "S" sound. Now you are about to teach him another "S" word, "STAND." These three command words sound

enough alike that you'll need to pay attention to saying them clearly to your dog. Repeat the new word "STAND" in context with praise when you teach it. Be sure to practice this command in everyday life often enough that Fido will remember what it means. (If you live in a rainy climate you'll get <u>plenty</u> of opportunity to practice STAND.)

What To Do

Start with a few minutes of HEELING practice. Halt and have your dog SIT, as usual, when he stops with you. Praise him for his "Automatic SIT" so he knows he did the right thing.

Now tell Fido to HEEL again and take a few steps forward to get him up and moving.

As soon as your dog is HEELING, turn to your left (facing your dog's right side) and stop. As you turn and stop say "Fido STAND."

Gently support your dog's tummy with your left hand to prevent him from SITTING. Hold your right hand on his chest lightly to keep him from walking forward.

Stroke your dog's tummy and chest gently and very slowly. Vigorous petting is too stimulating and would make Fido want to wiggle around. Praise him calmly, "Goooood STAND."

When you turn toward your dog as you stop for STAND, that will give him a quite different body cue than the abrupt forward-facing halt for the Automatic Sit. Turn to face your dog's side and gently support and stroke him to help him learn what "STAND" means.

If you plan to show your dog in both obedience and conformation competitions, this side-turn cue for STAND will be very helpful. The two different types of stop (for Automatic Sit or for STAND) use distinctly dissimilar body movements by the handler. Fido learns the straight-facing stop means "SIT" and the side-turn stop means "STAND." This helps protect your dog from confusion about which behaviors are expected in the two types of competition.

STAND-STAY

When Fido has learned the concept of STAND, you may give the STAY handsignal and tell him "Good STAND... STAY." Stand by him for a moment, then praise him calmly.

After your dog has held the STAND-STAY for about five seconds, give him the release command. Say "Okay Fido, HEEL" and take two or three steps forward. Then halt abruptly, facing forwar. This is the cue for the Automatic Sit. If your dog does not SIT automatically, gently help him into position, then praise him warmly.

◆ DO NOT PULL ON THE LEAD OR COLLAR when working on STAND. If you raise the dog's head, he may interpret it as a cue to SIT. Try not to confuse your dog about these similar sounding commands.

Gentle Patience Is the Key
Be especially patient and gentle with your dog when teaching the STAND command. After all, you've probably just spent a good number of practice sessions working on the Automatic Sit. Your dog

knows how pleased you've been when he SITS quickly without command when you halt. He might be confused at first with this apparent change in the rules (STAND instead of SIT) and may be uncertain of what's expected.

Help him understand and encourage him with this new command. Be patient, speak clearly, and gently correct Fido's body position as needed. Your dog may be genuinely surprised that you actually want him to STAND instead of SITTING automatically. As he becomes familiar with this command and recognizes the different body cues he'll figure it out. Be sure to praise appropriate responses.

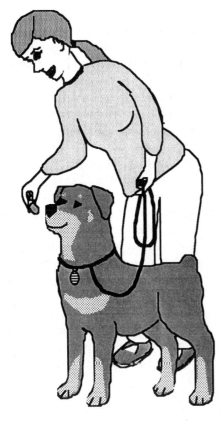

Using A FOOD TREAT To Teach STAND

You can use a tidbit as a lure when teaching your dog to STAND, but be careful how high you hold it. If you hold the treat too high, Fido may think you want him to SIT. If you hold it too low, he may think it's a signal to DOWN. Hold the tidbit on the same level as the dog's nose to encourage him to remain standing.

What To Do

Hold the treat in your right hand. Put it in front of your dog's nose as you turn toward his side and stop. Command "Fido STAND." If he remains STANDING, give him the treat and praise him, "Good STAND."

If, instead of STAND-ING, your dog SITS when you stop, simply start over again. Don't try to lift him up, that would make him uncomfortable. Just hold the treat in front of his nose and then move it ahead of him so he'll follow it forward. As he STANDS, praise him. Remember to use the "STAND" command in the praise phrase.

Feed him the tidbit while you praise him "Gooooood STAND." It may help at first to gently support Fido's tummy so he'll know you don't want him to SIT. Be very gentle! Dog tummies are soft and sensitive, just like our own.

Be sure your dog is actually STANDING when you give him the tidbit and praise. He'd surely get confused if he was SITTING while you praised him "Good STAND!" Help your dog as much as you can while he's trying to figure out what you want him to do.

For A Solid Stand

As your dog gets more solid on the STAND-STAY you can first increase the <u>time</u> he's required to hold the position, then increase the distance. You can also start introducing distractions to challenge your dog's attention.

Ask a friend to help you teach your dog to hold a STAND-STAY while examined. Begin by having the helper just walk past your dog on his STAND-STAY. Then have him stop and gently touch Fido's head and back. Increase the amount of contact until your helper can examine Fido all over.

If your dog moves out of position during the "exam," gently and patiently place him back where he was. Re-command him to STAND and STAY, then try again. If he moves a couple of times in a row, the distraction is probably just a little too strong for him yet. Decrease the amount of touching to where he's able to hold still again. End the lesson on a successful note so your dog feels he's done right. Praise him warmly whenever he cooperates.

Don't over-practice this command. Like any other, this command can become boring for your dog if practiced for too long at a stint. Keep lessons varied and interesting for best results. Start work on this command on leash, then later graduate to the off lead STAND-STAY.

PRACTICE WHAT YOU TEACH

Practice the lessons in this chapter consistently. While you are teaching the commands, practice with your dog for ten to fifteen minutes twice each day. Even after your dog knows all the basics it will be important to keep them fresh in his mind. Your dog will feel more confident and happy about obedience lessons if he gets regular practice. Training sessions are high quality time together for you and your dog. Fido will enjoy knowing you're pleased with him when he obeys. Of course, you'll enjoy your buddy more that way too.

Don't over-drill your dog on commands. Twice daily practice, ten or fifteen minutes each session should be plenty if you train regularly. Make practice fun for your dog with lots of praise and petting and an occasional treat or toy as rewards.

Use the commands in everyday living situations, not just when practicing "drill." All the commands are useful when you need your dog to understand what you want him to do. Remember, you've taught him a working vocabulary of command words. Use them! Your dog will feel smart and proud he's able to understand you.

Reward your dog for good behavior. Gently correct his mistakes. Be patient and positive, training is <u>fun</u> work. You'll be amazed to find out how fast your dog will learn when he enjoys the lessons. Appreciate how hard he works to understand and please you.

Trained Dogs Are Happier!

Trained dogs are happier. They can go more places and do more interesting things with their human families. When dogs have good manners and know some useful commands they make lots of friends for themselves (and their handlers!) Dogs love to please... we just have to teach them how in ways they can understand.

Chapter 12

AT HOME & AWAY

Your dog's manners at home will be very much improved when he's had a good education. He'll be gentler, quieter, more respectful, and more fun. You're probably already enjoying some improvements in Fido's behavior if you've started teaching him how to please you. Friends may also have noticed how much nicer your dog is to be around lately. Fido's new and improved behavior will help make him a truly cherished member of your family. Great! There may still be a few things to work on, though, to make your relationship with your dog the very best it can be.

FIDO AT HOME

Years ago it was safer for dogs to run free. People spent more time close to home and many folks worked outdoors all day on the family farm. Times have changed; things are very different now. Most people work away from home and even the children are off at school and other organized activities all week long. More people now live in apartments or homes on small suburban lots instead of vast acreages. What once was open countryside is now criss-crossed with high speed roads. With todays's leash laws and dangerously fast traffic, it's a matter of growing importance to keep Fido safe at home.

Just telling your dog to stay home in the yard while you're away will not reliably keep him there. Some dogs do lounge on the porch the whole time their masters are gone... but most would rather go off in search of adventure. This brings up the question of HOW to make sure Fido doesn't get himself into trouble when he's left at home alone.

Boundary Training

It would be nice if we could just show Fido the property line, tell him not to cross it, and be sure he'd remember to stay in the yard. Well, boundary training your dog is a good idea but it's certainly <u>NOT</u> 100% sure. In fact, depending upon the individual dog's maturity and the strength of the magnets outside his yard, boundary training may not be very sure at all.

Have you ever been driving down the road and suddenly seen a ball roll out into the street? Was it followed closely by a child who forgot to check for cars before dashing out after the ball? Probably! How many times do you suppose his parents had warned him to "look both ways?" How old was that child? Now, how old is your dog? Get the point?

We cannot expect our dogs to always remember a lesson sometimes human children forget. Do go ahead and teach your dog the yard boundaries, though. He needs to know where they are. Just don't assume that will stop him from "forgetting" the rules at a critical moment.

What to Do

With Fido on-leash, approach the boundary line of the yard. When you and your dog get near the line, tell him "Stay in the YARD!" Continue walking up to the line, but stop before crossing over it. If Fido stops with you, praise him "Good Stay-in-the-YARD!" If he keeps going, pull him back sharply as he steps over the line and, in a voice that sounds like you think something terrible and dangerous is happening, say "Fido! Stay-in-the-YARD!!!" Then act very relieved that he's okay as you pet and praise him.

Now, try it again. Approach the boundary, tell your dog to Stay-in-the-YARD, and stop just before stepping over the line. Praise or correct your dog, depending upon whether he stays with you or crosses the line. Repeat these training steps again and again. When Fido has chosen correctly THREE TIMES IN A ROW to stay within the boundary limits you've set, move on to the next side of the yard. Do this on all sides of the property or yard.

Some dogs are quicker to understand boundary rules than others. If your dog seems to be having trouble remembering where the line is, you might try stretching a length of string along the border at first to give him a visual clue and help him get the right idea.

Boundary training is NOT sufficiently secure as the sole means of keeping Fido safe while you're away. It IS, however, very useful when you're WITH your dog. Once he understands the concept of "Stay-in-the-Yard" your dog will be able (with a little help from you) to respect that command in places away from the home territory also. For example, while you're visiting friends whose yard is not fenced, Fido will be able to learn the borders of their yard and not venture into the neighbor's garden while you're there to remind him. At home or away, boundary training requires your vigilance and consistent enforcement.

...Which brings us to the subject of some more secure ways of keeping your dog home.

FENCES

A good fence is the safest and surest means to keep Fido in or out of an area. There are many types of fences, some are better than others for keeping a dog home. When thinking about building a fence, consider the nature of your dog. Dogs may try to jump, climb, dig, pry, gnaw, or shred their way out of confinement if motivated to do so. The fence must be able to withstand a dog's escape attempts, AND the dog must be trained to respect the fence. You may have decided to hire a professional fence builder, or perhaps you're thinking about installing the fence yourself. Either way is fine, but plan your fence carefully because you'll probably not be eager to change it once it's in place.

Locating the Fence

Whether the property is large or small, the best location for your dog's yard is as close as possible to your house. It's kindest and most sensible to arrange Fido's fenced area to be entered through one of the doors of your home. You'll be able to let him in and out conveniently that way, even when you're in your pajamas, and Fido will feel like he's still included in the family. The fence for your dog's yard could be the fence for your yard. That would be the BEST situation.

Free-Standing Kennel Runs

Many people erect free-standing kennel runs for their dogs. These folks go to this expense hoping to provide a safe outdoor exercise area for a well-loved puppy while the family is away. Unfortunately, after Little Fido has a few too many potty accidents in the house, he may find himself spending quite a bit of time alone in his outdoor kennel.

These kennel runs are usually set up twenty feet or more from the back door. This makes it inconvenient for the pup's owners to let him in and out of the house and may cause them to leave the dog in the pen for long periods of time, even when the family is home. This arrangement isolates Fido and often leads to such unpleasant habits as territory aggression or continuous barking.

Kennel runs are usually too small for a growing pup or an adult dog to exercise freely. The space is often further cramped by the addition of a doghouse. Add to this the everpresent problem of "whose turn it is" to clean up the dogpoop... and the poor dog has hardly any room to move. The penned dog generally takes on a bad oder and over-exuberant greeting habits. When he spends much time alone in a pen like this, Fido becomes less attractive to his human family. This may result in the dog's permanent relegation to the cramped and isolated kennel run. This cruel situation can develop when well-meaning people do not understand the needs of a dog.

It's kindest to build a fence around your yard which allows your dog access to and from your home. He'll be much happier and have fewer behavior problems.

Types of Fences

Some people balk at the thought of a fence because they assume it will be expensive or unsightly. Neither needs to be the case if you plan ahead and select the right materials for your particular situation. A fence could be costly, but there are lower priced materials available as well. A fence could be unsightly, but a few rose bushes or some wildflower seed can easily fix that. (By the way, rose bushes really like dog poop.)

Be sure the fence material is appropriate to contain your dog. Field wire is not secure for Toy breeds, for example, but it's fine for medium to large dogs. Likewise, a cute little wooden fence backed with wire mesh might hold a tiny dog but not be secure for anything larger. There are many materials to choose from when building a fence. The important thing is to be sure it's the right fence for your dog.

Chain-Link. This is the type of interlocking wire fence material commonly used around tennis courts and school yards. This fencing is fairly costly but very strong and durable. Chain-link makes a good dog fence if the bottom is reinforced and anchored to the ground. Most people who choose this type of fence for their yards have it installed by professionals.

Wire-Mesh. Welded or woven wire mesh is an excellent choice for do-it-yourself dog fencing. This type of fence material is available in a variety of wire gauges and mesh sizes. It's easy to put up and take down, it's relatively inexpensive, and it's durable. Many dog owners are able to install their own wire mesh fence in an afternoon.

Unlike chain-link fences, which require heavy posts set in concrete, wire-mesh can be strung on much lighter supports. Steel "T-Posts," which are easily pounded into the ground, can be used to support a very serviceable fence. The posts can even be pulled up and moved quite easily later on if you desire. This type of fence ideal for renters or folks who expect to relocate.

Solid Fencing. A solid fence would be good if your yard has a view of some activity that excites your dog to bark. Fido may carry on noisily if he sees parades of people jogging by or has a view of where the neighbor ties his dog.

You can help prevent this frustration-barking by placing a visual barrier between Fido and the scene that excites him. The barrier could be as elaborate as you'd want to make it, with wooden stockade fencing and thick flowering hedges, or as simple as a tarp strung between trees. It just needs to block the dog's view.

Collar-Activated Electronic Fences

What about the "invisible-type" fences? The "fence" itself is just a wire buried shallowly in the ground. The dog wears a special battery-powered collar. A device on the collar sounds a reminder tone when Fido gets too close to the "fence" and delivers a shock if he crosses over the line. This type of fence will work to keep a dog in if he's trained properly and if the collar battery is fully charged.

The dog must be trained to respect the warning tone and the limits of his "fenced" area. The training is similar to that described for boundary training earlier in this chapter.

The electronic fence is effective to keep a dog home but it will not prevent other animals from coming into his yard to fight with him or eat his food. There's another drawback to this type of fence, the dog must be wearing the special collar for the fence to work. Many dogs figure this out quickly after a few slip-ups occur.

Really, a tangible fence is the safest way to keep your dog home and content. Whenever possible, put in a "real" fence around your house and yard if you want the best for your dog. In situations where a visible fence is impossible for some reason, the electronic fence is the next best thing.

The Gate

Any fence is only as good as its gate! A gate must be easy for a person to open, but NOT for a dog. The gate must also close securely and, preferably, automatically. If a gate is difficult to operate it's more likely to be left ajar, permitting Fido to easily slip away.

Make your gate a good one with strong hinges and sturdy support posts. Be sure to allow no dangerous gaps along the sides or underneath. Even an opening too small to permit escape may still trap and injure a dog's paw. The gate latch should open smoothly and close solidly. Pay special attention to your gates, they're important!

How to Prevent Escapes

Some dogs are veritable geniuses when it comes to escaping from fenced yards. They've usually become so proficient because their owners unintentionally provided a step-by-step education. The fence you use for a puppy must not be flimsy or makeshift. If he escapes just once he'll KNOW it's POSSIBLE. Then he'll <u>always</u> try to find a way to do it again. As you patch each little squeeze-through and raise the height of the fence one board at a time, Little Fido will put in just a little more effort each time to succeed. Each time he thwarts the increasingly difficult barrier, he'll become more confident of his ability to escape ANY enclosure. It's MUCH better to build an adequate fence to start with.

Teach Little Fido that when you put him in his yard he'll have to stay there for a reasonable period of time and then you'll come to let him back into the house. Follow the same basic directions as for crate training to teach your dog to accept confinement in the yard. It's wise to crate-train and yard train your dog right away, to help him learn to accept normal limitations of all kinds. Secure fences and early confinement training with the dog crate will help prevent the Houdini Syndrome. It's important to keep that dangerous habit from becoming established in your dog.

If your dog is an un-neutered male he'll be driven by his hormones to try to escape every time a local female dog comes in heat. If Fido's genes are not required in a carefully planned breeding program, why not have him neutered? He'll stay home better and be far less frustrated. It will save you both a lot of stress.

One way to help prevent escape attempts is to give your dog a routine to look forward to. Fifteen or twenty minutes each day of obedience lesson time and at least another twenty minutes spent playing educational games will use your dog's energy in a positive and creative way. These activity periods with your dog should be spaced throughout the day if possible. He won't have much fun, and neither will you, if you put them all together; that would be too tiring. These efforts will give your dog interesting things to do with you each day. Fido will feel he has a job and an important place in your pack, which may eliminate his need to escape in search of other adventure.

A Few "Tricks" With Fences

If your dog is already a champion pole-vaulter or a tunneler you have a tricky problem to solve. It will be necessary to teach Fido that fences are to be respected and not escaped. He already has a different notion, so you'll need a good fence. You'll also need some "tricks" that will give your dog the impression there's more to fences than he thought.

Digging under the fence is a common escape method. A remedy that often works is to fill any new hole along the fence line with rocks and dogpoop. Top off the filled hole with a few inches of clean soil. Your dog may go to that spot again and start to dig, then stop in amazement and disgust. Most dogs will not dig in holes that have been filled with their own feces.

Jumping out or climbing over the fence is the second-most popular escape means. The majority of dogs who climb or jump out of their yards choose only one or two sections of the fence as escape routes. If you increase the height of just those particular sections it may not be necessary to raise the entire fence. Be sure to raise the height sufficiently the first time to make it IMPOSSIBLE to escape. Don't just make it more challenging or you'll be training an "Olympic" jumper!

Electric Stock-wire Fence

If Fido continues to find a way out of the fence even after you've followed the above suggestions, you'll need "stronger medicine" to stop his dangerous escape behavior. A tactic that works extremely well is to put up a strand of electric stock-wire fence a few inches above the regular fence. This delivers a surprise that reforms most climbers and jumpers. A strand about six to twelve inches above the ground also keeps dogs from digging out.

The shock from this fence is not harmful but it's certainly unpleasant. Some styles are now made with a lighter zap, specifically for dogs. It only takes a couple of experiences to give Fido a GOOD SUPERSTITION. He will stop thinking that fences are to escape.

Teach your dog to respect the magic zap-wire before he has a chance to somehow defeat it. You can do this by making the new wire attractive to your dog's curiosity. **Do the following steps out of your dog's sight.** Smear some cheese or liverwurst on strips of aluminum foil, then twist these yummy smelly strips onto the new electric fence wire. (Did I mention to do this step before plugging in the fence?) Each side of the yard should have one or two of the "baited" foil strips, (Now go turn the fence on.)

When you let Fido out into the yard he'll smell the delicious aroma of liverwurst and will rush to explore the source. ZAP! Fido jumps back. "What the hey?" he wonders. The shock is surprising and quite unpleasant, but not harmful. (A little "bite" from this fence is certainly less potent than a deadly "bite" from a car's bumper!) He ponders this new development. Soon the little escape artist's curiosity overcomes him again, he just has to try it one more time. ZAP! He yips and jumps back. Now he wonders about the whole fence... is it ALL this way? Only a very adventurous dog would check further. Most dogs quickly give up touching the fence.

Leave the foil twisties on the wire for a few days, then tear off all but the "knots." Leave those in place for the rest of the week, then take them off too. Most dogs learn within a few days to avoid any contact with the fence. In fact this method works so well that after the first week it may not even be necessary to keep it plugged in!

Farm and pet supply stores and catalogs sell the power units and all equipment necessary to install an electric fence.   Check your local ordinances about electric fences before installation.

TIE-OUTS AND CHAINS

Chains and tie-outs are a very poor substitute for a well-fenced yard. However, in the "real world" sometimes the only means available to keep a dog from straying is a tie-out. Hopefully it will only be used as a temporary solution, perhaps while visiting friends or camping. Cables, ropes and chains have many serious drawbacks.

If you MUST tie your dog instead of fencing him you'll need to consider some safety issues. A tied-up dog is vulnerable to attack and harassment by other animals. He may become overly aggressive, especially if teased by passersby. A tie-out or chain can become a twisted mess and a potentially lethal hazard for the tangled dog.

But, just in case you <u>must</u> tie your dog instead of fencing...

A tie-out must be strong enough to hold your dog's running-weight, as must the collar and whatever the tie-out is fastened to.

Slip collars are very dangerous for tying a dog. Don't use them for that! Have your dog wear a strong and smooth buckle-type collar instead. (If you ever have no choice but to tie a dog with a slip collar, be sure to switch the collar to "safety" as described in this book.)

Overhead Trolley Tie-Outs

These can give a dog a fairly big exercise area if there's nothing he can get the line snagged around. The end posts holding the overhead wire are often the worst tanglers. This can be fixed by putting a knot or other obstruction in the overhead wire at a distance from each supporting post. That will solve the tangling problem, as the tie-cable will not run all the way to the posts and won't tangle around them. It also reduces the exercise area.

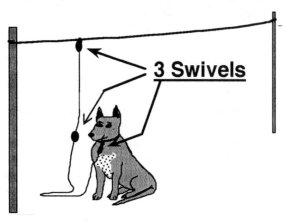

3 Swivels

The tie-cable should have three tangle-prevention swivels: one on the clip that attaches to the dog's collar, another at the top where the cable attaches to the overhead wire. The third swivel should be at the level of the dog's shoulders, on the tie-cable that hangs from the overhead wire. (Check the illus-

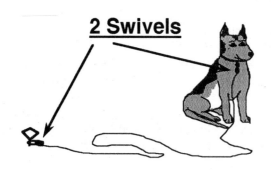

2 Swivels

tration for proper placement.) These swivels are very important for your dog's safety. Check frequently and keep them oiled so they'll work properly.

Chains and Ropes
Chains and rope tie-outs should have two swivels, one at each end. Fasten your dog's chain or rope to your porch so he'll be able to come up and stand by the door. That will make it easier for you to let him in and out. If you have to walk all the way out to the muddy backyard to bring Fido in, you may be tempted to leave him out there longer than you should.

Some dogs learn how to break chains to escape. One way to solve this problem is to fasten a strong inner tube (from a big truck tire) to the chain and to whatever the chain is attached. The rubber yields a little as the dog jumps or lunges at his end of the chain. That little bit of "give" will make chains last much longer. By the way, a dog who behaves that way is probably frustrated and under-exercised. Spend more time with him or recruit someone else to.

Never tie or chain your dog to anything that couldn't withstand his most intense efforts to escape. If he breaks a tie-out once, he'll discover that it's possible and will try to do it again. He may keep trying harder as you make it progressively more difficult for him.

THE YARD

The best dog yard is also a people yard. Your dog will be most well-adjusted if he's "part of your family." To make this a pleasant arrangement there is some work to be done. Your dog must be taught appropriate yard manners and you'll need to keep an eye on him for awhile.

Yard Sanitation
It's important to keep your dog's poop picked up regularly. The proper tool makes this rather yucky job much less nasty. Do yourself a favor and purchase a long-handled poop scooping tool made especially for that purpose. Poop scoops, digesting enzymes and containment devices are all available through pet supply sources. The enzymes hasten decomposition of dogmess and will improve sanitation in your dog's potty area.

When you scoop the yard, pay attention to what Fido's poop looks like. You can tell a lot about a dog's health by the consistency and color of his stool. If you notice peculiar changes in your dog's stool (especially if it's runny or has a worse-than-usual smell) take a sample to your veterinarian to be checked. She may find nothing significant, but if there IS something eroding Fido's health, medical treatment should be started immediately. The early health warnings an alert dog owner notices can greatly improve a dog's chances for a quick and complete recovery.

The Hole Truth... Dogs Dig

This fact may have been adequately demonstrated to you by Fido himself. Digging occurs for a number of reasons. Dogs often dig where they smell "buried treasure" in the ground, like mouse-trails or manure-fertilizer. Many dogs will dig a nice cool hole to lie in when summer sizzles. Some also dig "caves" for shelter from winter winds. Some dogs excavate for exercise or to relieve frustration. I even met a dog who dug where he heard a funny noise... which turned out to be a leak in the under ground irrigation system. His digging stopped when the leak was fixed.

Good Hole/Bad Hole

If your dog has been mining up your yard there are a few things you can do to solve the problem. First of all, pick one spot in the yard where it will be okay for your dog to dig a hole. The spot should NOT be right by the fence, for obvious reasons. Start a hole using a shovel and encourage your dog to explore it. Tell him it's a "Good Hole." The smell of freshly turned earth may be enough to entice Fido to start digging there. If not, take one of his toys and partially bury it in the new hole; that should give him the idea. Praise him for digging in the "Good Hole."

Next, go around to all the old holes the dog has already dug and fill them most of the way with dirt, Take your poop scoop around and clean the whole yard. Dump piles of Fido's poop into all the old holes, then fill them up the rest of the way with more dirt. If your dog attempts to re-dig one of his old "Bad Holes" he'll get a yucky surprise! Most dogs will not dig in a hole that has their own poop in it.

Whenever your dog digs a new hole, TAKE him to it. DON'T call him to the crime scene, that's treachery. He wouldn't want to come the next time you called, either. Point to the hole and announce "This is

a BAD HOLE!!! Did YOU dig this BAD HOLE???? BAD HOLE!!!"
Then hit the hole! Remember, hit the <u>hole</u>, NOT the dog.

When your dramatic monologue is finished, pause for a moment, then go over to the approved "Good Hole." Call Fido in a friendly voice. Tell him this is his "Good Hole" and playfully encourage him to dig there. Praise him for any interest he shows in the "Good Hole." Don't expect too much at first. He may think you hate <u>all</u> holes. (Maybe he's right.)

Then go fill in his latest "bad hole" with dirt and dogpoop. It may take several repetitions of this lesson for it to sink in, but it works well with most dogs.

Boredom and Bad Habits

Digging and other bad habits are often caused by boredom, loneliness and insufficient exercise. Obedience training with Fido on a regular basis is a good activity. It will reduce or eliminate a surprising variety of unpleasant doggy behaviors. Regular exercise and social contact with you and the rest of the family will help your dog form better habits as well.

Let the Dog In

It's important to a dog to know he's part of a group. Dogs do not do well emotionally living in isolation. They're cooperative and sociable creatures who really should be welcome to live with us in our homes.

Some folks have different ideas about dogs. They may have been taught, or just decided, that dogs must always stay outside. "After all... they're <u>animals</u>." These people have come to believe that a dog's place is <u>not</u> in the home. Dogs (and people who really know dogs) disagree strongly with that misguided point of view.

I've probably heard about every excuse people use to justify making their dogs live outside. The same dog owners often complain about certain misbehaviors that can be predictably traced to their dog's isolation and loneliness.

A dog belongs with the family. To argue otherwise is to deny two great truths about the affection and loyalty of dogs: They <u>love</u> us, and, They <u>need</u> us.

Here, debunked, are the main excuses people give to justify denying their dogs a rightful place in the home.

Poor Excuse #1: *"He smells bad and sheds hair all over the house."* ... Have these people ever thought about bathing and brushing their dog?

Poor Excuse #2: *"He has bad manners."* ... We must <u>teach</u> dogs to have good, reliable manners. It takes effort, of course, just as it does to teach good manners to children. We'd never expect a baby or toddler to automatically know how to act politely. How could a dog learn proper manners without being taught? It's our responsibility to educate our youngsters (human and canine). The work is well worth it; the rewards are enormous.

Poor Excuse #3: *"Our house just isn't big enough to have the dog inside."* ... Oh boy, now that must be a REALLY tiny place! When any of our dogs are in the way, we simply step over them or politely tell them to move. That seems to work just fine.

Poor Excuse #4: *"We got him as a hunting dog, so he needs to live outdoors."* ... There are so many lovely Labs, Goldens, Springers, etc. who are relegated to the backyard or a lonely kennel run. These poor dogs spend their lives alone and frustrated, waiting for the annual three or four weekend jaunts to the field with their "master." Never have I heard from one of these "masters" that they themselves find it necessary to live outdoors all year in preparation for their sporadic sport.

Poor Excuse #5: *"Someone in the family is allergic to dogs."* ... (Actually, I'm slightly allergic to dogs myself, but the red eyes and itchy nose are well worth it for the wonderful love we share!) There <u>are</u> treatments for allergies; ask the doctor. Frequent doggy baths and combings by a professional groomer or a non-allergic family member can help quite a bit. The dog will feel much more comfortable as well. Failing these possibilities, it would be kinder to the dog to find him a home with healthier people than to force him to live a lonely life out in the yard.

Poor Excuse #6: *"We want him as a watchdog."* ...Purchase an electronic security system for outside your home; they are readily available, quite reliable, and rather less expensive than food and health care for a dog. Plus, the electronic system won't get lonely out there all by itself. Besides, if Fido is in your home <u>with</u> you, you'll be much safer from "badguys" than if the dog was kenneled out back.

Poor Excuse # 7: *"It's too warm for him inside; he prefers to live outdoors."* ... If someone actually believes this is so, they need a doggie door so Fido can come in and out at will. Most dogs like to spend some time inside and some time outside. A dog door to a fenced yard is the obvious solution to this problem.

There are other Poor Excuses, too, and they're all debunk-able. Dogs have been bred for thousands of years to be our helpers and companions. They are social animals who crave human company. Why get a dog and then deny such an important innate need as companionship? To do so is cruel. It is also unnecessary. There is always a solution if a person is first willing to admit that there is a problem. There IS a problem! Too many dogs are going bonkers in solitary confinement out back, while their longed-for human families ignore or even punish their cries for companionship.

Let the dog in!

AWAY FROM HOME

As Your dog learns how to please you, he'll become a better companion. You'll be proud to take him places with you.

Be sure the places you plan to take Fido are dog-friendly. Check your local ordinances for the rules about leashes and licenses. Find out if there are any specially designated areas for off-leash dog exercise. It would also be helpful to know in advance about areas where dogs are <u>not</u> permitted. Some public places are strictly off-limits for canines except working assistance dogs. Respect the local laws. You and your dog will be setting a good and proud example for others.

Fido's Fan Club

If your dog has good manners, he'll be welcome many places with you. In fact, he may develop a "fan club" of admirers who look forward to his visits. Many people truly enjoy socializing with a polite and obedient dog.

Some Necessary Equipment

When you and Fido are away from home there's some equipment you should remember to take along. You won't always need everything on Fido's "must pack" list, but when you DO, you'll be very glad to have it. "Be Prepared" is a good traveling motto for dog owners.

Collar

First of all, be sure Fido is wearing a collar when he's out and about. If he'll be off-leash in the Great Outdoors, running through meadow and thicket, he should wear a buckle-type collar or his training collar switched to **safety**. (See "Collars & Leashes.") A branch or piece of old fencewire could snag a choke collar and fatally entrap a romping dog. Be sure your dog's collar is safe before you turn him loose, even in your own yard at home.

I.D. Tags
Be sure your dog wears an up-to-date I.D. tag attached to his collar. Your phone number should be clearly written on the tag. If your dog doesn't have a personal I.D. tag but wears a license or rabies tag, inscribe your phone number on the back of one of those. (If the tag is aluminum, you can write on it with a sharp nail.) I.D. tags with the owner's phone number should be worn by all dogs, even those who are tattooed or identified by microchip implants. Readable I.D. tags have saved many lost dogs and their worried owners from permanent separation.

Leash
Always take a leash with you! Whether you and Fido plan a day on the town or a tour of the countryside, never go anywhere without a leash. Even if you don't think you'll need one where you're planning to go, TAKE ONE ANYHOW! You could run into unexpected variables and a leash might be just the tool you'll need to avert disaster. Keep it in your pocket or wear it as an extra "belt" when not needed on the dog. That way you'll always have it handy.

Clean Drinking Water
If you plan to be out with your dog for more than a couple of hours your dog will certainly need a drink of water. Take care of that need! Lack of water can cause great discomfort and some serious health problems for dogs. This is as true in winter as it is in summer. Carry a bottle of water from home and offer some to your dog at reasonable intervals. When you feel thirsty he probably will too.

A clean plastic bag works well as a makeshift on-the-trail waterbowl for Fido. Just roll the top down almost all the way and set the bag on the ground. It will hold water like a portable clean drinking puddle for your dog. After he's quenched his thirst, shake out the extra drops and refold the bag for later use.

Don't count on natural water sources for Fido to slake his thirst. Not all water you'll find along the trail is good to drink. Dogs can become ill from microbes and parasites found in clean-looking streams, just as we could. Giardia is one of those microscopic nasties... and our dogs can share that "bug" with us, too.

The "natural" water found around "civilization" can be much worse. Even though your dog might be willing and eager to drink from convenient mud puddles in town, there can be horrible toxins lurking in that water! Antifreeze is a frightening example of one of the suprise ingredients in some puddle-water. It even has a sweet taste that appeals to animals... and it can KILL a dog.

So, carry a canteen of clean drinking water from home instead. You and Fido will both get thirsty, so be sure to take enough.

"Porta-Poop" Tool

Although it's certainly natural, dog-doo is not nice stuff. It stinks, it's nasty to look at, it draws flies, carries disease and parasites... and NOBODY likes stepping in it! A responsible dog owner would NEVER knowingly leave dog feces lying about where other folks might be bothered by it. Many communities have found it necessary to enact special dogmess clean-up ordinances to force dog owners to do what we all should have done all along... PICK UP OUR OWN DOG'S POOP!

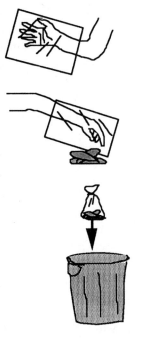

There are several disposable poop scooping devices commercially available. You might prefer a less fancy method. A plastic bag makes a dandy porta-poop tool. One or two can be kept folded in your pocket for clean-up detail. They take up little space and weigh practically nothing. No fancy gadgets are required, just a plastic bag.

Poop pickup using the bag method is simple. Just put your hand inside the baggie and grab up the "pile" from the ground. Then turn the bag inside out, so the poop's inside. Tie up the top of the bag, and throw the whole thing into a proper waste receptacle. That's it. Not a very aesthetic procedure, but it gets the job done. Several spare bags can be kept in a pocket, ready for instant use.

Now... Is everything ready? Great!... Then, OFF WE GO!

SAFETY AND MANNERS AWAY FROM HOME

Dogs like to go with us to exciting places, do interesting things, meet new friends and visit old buddies. If a dog's manners are good he will be welcome many places.

Good manners go along with safety for our dogs. If Fido can walk on leash, come when called, sit, lie down, and stay on command, his good manners will help keep him safer when traveling.

It's up to us to teach our dogs. It's our job to be aware and protect them from harm. Advance preparation for traveling, plus an understanding of the dog's way of thinking, is a good combination for safer outings.

In The Car

Most dogs love to ride in the family car. Your dog can be trained to be quiet and well-mannered when he rides with you. Some dogs get so excited they leap around and bark in the car. That makes a journey quite unpleasant and even dangerous.

It's very important for your dog to learn how to behave properly and safely in a moving vehicle. If your dog is rowdy in the car, you should teach him some car manners and practice "travel drill" before you take him out on a "real" drive.

Car Travel Do's & Don'ts...

◆   ALWAYS make Fido WAIT to enter or leave your vehicle untill you give him the release command. A dog should never be allowed to leap into or out of a car without permission. He could be badly hurt, lost, or even stolen as a result of that bad habit.

◆   NEVER allow your dog to ride unrestrained in the front seat. He could cause the driver to lose control of the car. A friend of our family and his dog both lost their lives suddenly when the dog leaped across his master's lap to say "Hi!" to a puppy by the side of the road. That man and his dog had ridden together in the front seat, without mishap, for years before that day. It only takes one mistake!

Your dog will be better off in the back seat in case of sudden stops also. It's even safer to transport him in his dog crate. There are also safety car seatbelts for dogs available through pet supply outlets.

◆   NEVER let your dog ride loose in the back of an open truck. It's quite hazardous, even though dogs enjoy feeling the wind in their hair. Many areas now have laws that forbid carrying a dog unrestrained in the cargo area of an open truck. If you don't have a sturdy canopy or camper on your truck, use a dog crate to contain Fido. Be sure to fasten the crate securely to the truck bed, or a sudden stop or swerve could send the crate and the dog flying.

If ever you must tie a dog in the back of a truck, be very careful. It's essential to prevent him from leaning out over either side. A sharp turn can unbalance a dog. If he's tied with too long a line he could be thrown off the truck and be dragged or hanged. Cross-tying is the safest way to tie a dog in the back of a truck. One line from either side keeps the dog centered in the truck, unable to jump or slip off accidentally.

◆   NEVER leave your dog unattended in your car on a hot day. A parked car, even one with the window rolled down a little, can reach a lethal temperature surprisingly fast. Parking in the shade is risky too, because as the day progresses your shady patch will move. You could return to your car to find the shade gone and your poor dog in desperate straits.

If you doubt how terribly hot a car can get in the summer time try it yourself. Leave your <u>dog</u> home when you try this! Park the car in the sun, then roll up the windows and sit there for awhile. You may be astonished at how quickly it becomes unbearable. A DOG WILL DIE IF HIS BODY TEMPERATURE GOES TOO HIGH! Even dogs lucky enough to survive heat illness may suffer permanent brain damage. This can happen with the car windows partially open and a bowl of water locked in the car with him. This is very serious. Protect your buddy! He counts on you to keep him safe. Do Fido a favor and leave him home in your shady fenced back yard on hot days.

AT THE PARK

When at the park with your dog be sensitive to the other people who are there or who will come later. Many communities have found it necessary to close their public parks to all dogs because of the careless, rude, and arrogant behavior of a FEW irresponsible dog owners. Even towns which still allow dogs to share the parks with people have severely limited the areas in which pets are permitted. Leash-laws and poop ordinances are springing up everywhere and anti-dog sentiment is on the rise. To avoid enactment of further limitations we dog owners must demonstrate good manners to prove there is no need for more restrictive dog laws.

Meeting Children

Children are sometimes wary around dogs. At other times they may rush right up to hug and kiss them. Even if your dog is friendly and well-mannered you may need to control him. Parents who want their children to pet your dog will, we hope, seek your permission first. Ask the parent if the child is experienced with dogs. If your dog likes children and is obedience trained, the child fairly calm and the parent willing, you could let them meet. Put Fido on a SIT-STAY for the introductions. Place your hand on his chest to remind him to stay seated. Be sure he doesn't jump up on the children. If you've been doing your obedience homework with your dog he'll probably make lots of nice new friends this way.

Joggers & Other Magnets

Joggers, bicyclists, skaters, horseback riders, dogs and other animals are particularly magnetic. Practice ABOUT-TURNS as your dog tries to spring off after these interesting distractions. Your sudden turns will refocus your dog's attention and help him remember to mind his own business.

People Who Dislike Dogs

Some people fear dogs for one reason of another. Some people are severely allergic to dogs. Some people, as hard as it is to imagine, just plain don't like dogs. Logic tells us to keep our dogs away from folks who don't appreciate them. Be considerate. If your dog is on a leash and both he and you are polite, nobody will have any reason to feel upset.

Picnic Areas

It's fun to command a dog to do unusual tricks, like hopping up onto elevated surfaces. In public places, we should remember to use common sense about what tricks we ask our dogs to do. We human packleaders are the ones responsible for our dogs' manners in public, however, the dogs are often the ones blamed.

Keep your dog OFF THE PICNIC TABLES! It's unsanitary and very rude to allow a "hairy beast" with dirty paws to lounge on top of an eating table. This behavior is (hopefully!) not encouraged or permitted at home. It's astonishing how many people actually <u>invite</u> their dogs up onto the picnic tables when they're at a park. Perhaps those insensitive dog owners forget, in the midst of their fun, that other people plan to use those picnic tables for food.

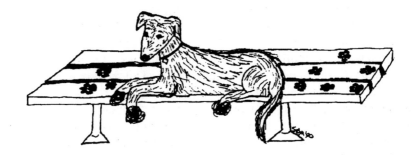

When Fido's pawprints are discovered on the picnic table at the park, they may be mistakenly attributed to the DOG'S lack of good manners rather than his OWNER'S.

Along this same line of thinking...

◆   Keep dogs out of children's public wading pools and other areas where animals are obviously not appropriate.

◆   Keep Fido on a leash except when in designated off-lead areas.

◆   Always scoop your dog's poop and dispose of it appropriately.

◆   Give EVERYONE ELSE the right-of-way.

It's up to us, as responsible dog owners, to set a good example for the rest of the pack. We can encourage others by our behavior. Perhaps if we do we won't wake up one day to find ourselves and our furry buddies locked out of all the parks. Let's work together to make a responsible change in the way dogs and dog owners are perceived.

IN THE COUNTRY

Going off to "The Country" with your dog is relaxing and invigorating. It may mean freedom from many rules and restraints, however, it does NOT mean freedom from responsibility. There are wonderful rural and wild places to roam and explore with your dog, but keep in mind that most of them belong to somebody. Private property is the country REALLY IS PRIVATE PROPERTY. Be respectful of the rights of others. If you wish to cross private property, ask permission first. Also, keep your dog on leash, even if he's the most obedient dog in the world... it <u>looks</u> more like you'll keep him with you that way.

Livestock and Wildlife

Many fairly remote places are populated with grazing cattle. Even nice friendly dogs can get into MAJOR TROUBLE with cows. Farmers and ranchers don't appreciate a dog who seems too "curious" about livestock. In many locales a dog seen chasing farm animals may legally be destroyed.

Another activity which can get Fido (and you) into serious legal problems is chasing wildlife. Most places it's illegal for dogs to chase (or even APPEAR to be chasing) deer, elk, and other enticing critters. A witness to a chase can, in most areas, LEGALLY shoot the dog. Although it's quite natural for a dog to chase wild creatures it is, in most cases, against the law. Keep a leash on your dog when you're likely to encounter wildlife.

Hiking and Camping

Dogs are permitted on certain hiking trails only if kept on leash. Some trails are not open to hikers with dogs at all. The same sort of restrictions apply at many beaches and campgrounds. Check the rules <u>before</u> you go, if you're planning to take your dog with you on vacation.

Other Pleasures

One other "country" thing... most dogs like to roll in the yuckiest mess they can find when they take a trip to the woods or the seashore. If you can keep Fido in sight, you may be able to call him back just before he does the ritual nose-dive-and-slide into a fresh cow-pie or not-so-fresh "whatsit" he's found.

If he does manage to apply his perfume before you can stop him, there's something you can do to make him a little less smelly on the ride home. Scrub a few handfuls of fresh moist dirt into the stinky stuff on his coat and let it dry. Repeat if necessary. Dirt will remove more of the stench than water. I don't know WHY fresh soil works so well to take the "organic" perfumes off a dog's coat, but it does. (As you may guess, I've had occasion to use this method.)

♦   ALWAYS keep your dog with you when you trek with him to the countryside. Don't let him get into trouble by running wild. The natural beauty of the "Great Outdoors" is so much more fun shared with a well-behaved canine companion.

WHEN YOU JUST CAN'T TAKE FIDO ALONG

Sometimes we must go places we cannot take our dogs. This is normal on a day to day basis if we go to work or school. Our dogs can adapt comfortably to waiting for us with most normal routines. If we must be gone longer than a day, though, we'll need to make some special arrangements for Fido.

Home Alone?
Unless you'll be gone only for the day... and in some cases, overnight, it's not a good practice to leave your dog home alone. Even if you set out plenty of food and water for him, things could go wrong. Some other animal may eat up the food, the water may get spilled, or an unexpected storm could put the unattended dog in a life-threatening situation.

Dogs also worry quite a bit when their pack doesn't return at the end of the day. Some wait nervously, hoping someone will be back at any moment. Others may bark at every sound or try to escape and go looking for the rest of the pack. If the master doesn't return at night... and then not the next day either, some dogs do desperate things.

Many events that don't bother a dog when his person is home become disturbing or frightening when the packleader is absent. Sudden storms, unexpected visitors, even ordinary delivery persons and passersby take on a worrisome new dimension when a dog is left to handle the home front on his own.

Caretakers & Critter-Sitters
A friend or relative who knows your dog might be persuaded to house-and-dog sit if you are VERY LUCKY. Often that's not available and other options must be explored.

A good caretaker who would stay at your home with your dog while you're away is a rare find. More frequently found are pet sitters who will visit your home once or twice each day to care for your dog. This can be a very useful service for dog owners who must be away for extra-long or late work days. It can also be a low stress and comfortable way for your dog to stay home while you travel or vacation.

Ask a doggy friend or your groomer or veterinarian for a referral to a reliable pet sitter in your area. The sitter should be experienced and bonded. Good references are a must. And your <u>dog</u> must like her.

Be sure the sitter meets Fido <u>before</u> the day of your departure. Fido should KNOW and LIKE the person who will be dropping by the homeplace during your absence. Show the sitter how obedient your dog is; give her a list of the command words Fido knows. (Maybe you'll want to give her a copy of this book, also!) Have the new sitter take your dog for a short walk and give him a tidbit of special food. If the sitter does this in your presence, your dog will know you approve. That way when she comes to take care of him while you're gone, it will seem okay to Fido.

Provide the sitter with clear and complete <u>written</u> information about caring for your dog or dogs. Leave a contact number for yourself, your veterinarian's name and number of course, and who else to call in case of various emergencies. Feeding info should include where the dog food is kept, which bowl to feed which dog out of and <u>where</u> each dog eats. Special diets, feeding routines, watering information and rules about treats should also be written. Then there are all the miscellaneous details, such as who has a spare key in case it's needed and what to do if your return is unexpectedly delayed. You may be able to add more to this list. Write it all down, make several copies and give one to your pet sitter.

Although many dogs do quite well at home with a couple of daily visits from a friendly sitter, others are not so adaptable. Dogs who need tending more than twice a day may be better off at a kennel or boarded with the veterinarian.

Boarding Kennels

Some boarding facilities are great... like summer camps or vacation resorts for dogs. Others are more like prisons. Thoroughly check any kennel you're thinking about for your dog... long before your planned departure date.

Ask to see the facilities where your dog will stay. It's reasonable for kennel owners to object to someone just popping in off the street and demanding to inspect the place. Ask if they hold "open-house" times when you'd be welcome to tour the kennel. If they just flat refuse to let you see where your beloved dog would be kept, look elsewhere for boarding.

Ask about kennel routine. How many times a day are the dogs fed? Will they feed your dog his regular brand if you provide it? If not, what brand do they feed? Can Fido have his favorite toy in the kennel with him? Will he get a walk or exercise session each day? The more you know about how your dog will be cared for, the less anxious you'll feel about leaving him.

Popular boarding kennels may require reservations be made months in advance, especially for holiday seasons. Some kennels require a non-refundable deposit. Most will wisely insist upon proof of current vaccinations. Make all your boarding kennel arrangements long before your planned absence.

If you've never boarded your dog before and you'll be going away for more than a few days, it may be a good idea to try a "practice run." Make arrangements to board your dog just overnight at the kennel. That way his worry-time will be short. When you return the next morning to pick him up, he'll realize the separation was only temporary. This should be done as matter-of-factly as you can manage. No teary good-byes or apologies... that would worry your dog more. Make his first kennel experience short and low stress. When you leave him for the real thing he'll already believe that you WILL indeed return.

OUR WONDERFUL DOG-FRIENDS

Now that you've read this book and applied what you've learned, your dog is probably much more enjoyable to be around. I hope so, because that's the real reason for training him! It's WONDERFUL to have a dog who can "go everywhere" with you. You and your gentle well-mannered companion will undoubtedly make quite a few friends. You'll share exciting adventures together and become a real team. You will be your dog's leader and friend. He will be a happy dog.

Some Special Activities With Dogs

You and your trained dog can become involved in a number of fun and fulfilling activities together. Once basic level training has been completed, you may want to start some specialized education. There are many directions to explore with advanced training.

You could get involved in showing your dog in competition obedience or conformation. Agility training is an exciting sport to engage in with your dog, as is Tracking. Pet Therapy volunteer work at nursing homes and hospitals is another activity you and your well-mannered dog could enjoy while bringing love and smiles to others.

There are so many ways you and your trained and socialized dog can spend quality time together. Explore the options and find some new "hobbies" you and your furry companion can enjoy together. You'll surely meet many wonderful new friends who love dogs too!

Training Our Way To A Better World

Responsible, loving dog ownership, not ever-stricter laws, is a way to solve the "dog problems" the headlines shout about. If ll the public sees are ill-mannered obnoxious and dangerous dogs the laws will continue to tighten. Responsible dog owners don't deserve that!

Let's work together for greater acceptance of well-behaved dogs in public. Our trained and happy dogs will set a new example, create a new standard of expectation. If everyone who loves dogs would train them to be gentle and polite, we and our canine companions will be welcome many more places. I think that would make the world a bit finer place for everyone. It's certainly worth working towards that goal! Enjoy your journey along that path. Happy Tails!!!

DOGS LOVE TO PLEASE... WE TEACH THEM HOW!

Index